PRAISE FOR *RETAI* AND DIGITAL BANK

'This book is a comprehensive and readable summary of retail and digital banking in the UK. The structure guides the reader towards an understanding of the dramatic history and changes in the sector, and benefits from reflections and learnings from the most recent financial crisis. All of the concepts are clearly articulated and underpinned with useful summaries, exercises and pointers to further reading.' **John Needham, former President of The Chartered Banker Institute**

'This book takes you on a journey that is both thought-provoking and challenges many of the misconceptions about change in banking. It is a must-read for practitioners and highly recommended for everyone wishing for an understanding of the retail banking sector and its role in the economy.' **Malcolm Pettigrew, Senior Lecturer and Subject Group Leader, Financial Services, The Business School, Edinburgh Napier University**

'This book is a well-written and comprehensive reflection on the history and evolution of an ever-changing and agile industry, which has always been faced with a challenge and constant need to adapt. It provides a perspective on more recent drivers to change and sets expectations for the future.' **David Bowerman, former Vice Chairman, Citizens Bank**

'There are many books about digital banking but very few from the perspective of the banks themselves. Every bank across the world is taking up the digital challenge and this book is essential for those struggling to understand the subject as well as those in a position to shape strategic responses.' **Brian Brodie, Chief Executive Officer, Freedom Finance**

OTHER BOOKS AVAILABLE IN THE CHARTERED BANKER SERIES

Commercial Lending: Principles and practice
Relationship Management in Banking: Principles and practice
Culture, Conduct and Ethics in Banking: Principles and practice
(forthcoming)

Chartered **Banker**

RETAIL AND DIGITAL BANKING

PRINCIPLES AND PRACTICE

JOHN HENDERSON

First published in Great Britain and the United States in 2019 by Kogan Page Limited

2nd Floor, 45 Gee Street	c/o Martin P Hill Consulting	4737/23 Ansari Road
London EC1V 3RS	122 W 27th St, 10th Floor	Daryaganj
United Kingdom	New York NY 10001	New Delhi 110002
www.koganpage.com	USA	India

ISBN   978 0 7494 8271 8
E-ISBN   978 0 7494 8272 5

British Library Cataloguing-in-Publication Data

A CIP record for this book is available from the British Library.

Library of Congress Cataloging-in-Publication Data

Names: Henderson, John, 1968- author.
Title: Retail and digital banking : principles and practice / John Henderson.
Description: London ; New York : Kogan Page, [2019] | Includes
   bibliographical references.
Identifiers: LCCN 2018036801 (print) | LCCN 2018039693 (ebook) | ISBN
   9780749482725 (ebook) | ISBN 9780749482718 (pbk.)
Subjects: LCSH: Banks and banking. | Internet banking.
Classification: LCC HG1601 (ebook) | LCC HG1601 .H46 2019 (print) | DDC
   332.1–dc23

Typeset by Integra Software Services, Pondicherry
Print production managed by Jellyfish
Printed and bound by CPI Group (UK) Ltd, Croydon, CR0 4YY

*For Alison – you are the inspiration and energy for everything
that is wonderful in my life.
To my boys – Scott, Ben and Mark, you fill me with fun, love and
joy. Stay happy and make others happy too.
All my love, as always.
To my mum and dad for always believing in me.
To the many colleagues and friends who have been by my side
during 30 years of working in the banking industry, especially the
'Cambridge Bar' crew – you know who you are.*

CONTENTS

ABOUT THE AUTHOR

John Henderson is married with three sons. He is passionate about long-distance cycling, Scouting in his local community, football coaching at Edinburgh City and supporting his beloved Heart of Midlothian Football Club.

John has worked in retail banking for 32 years, having spent the first half of his career in various retail banking roles and working in different channels with Bank of Scotland, before joining fledging supermarket bank, Sainsbury's Bank. John then headed the multi-channel customer experience team for Bank of Scotland before moving to Royal Bank of Scotland in 2002 to manage branch design and distribution for RBS and NatWest. Latterly John has managed offshoring of back-office operations and he now looks after global operations capacity management systems and forecasting for RBS.

John has two MBAs, his first from Edinburgh University and his second from the Chartered Banker Institute. John is a Fellow of the Chartered Banker Institute.

LIST OF ABBREVIATIONS

ACD	Automatic Call Distributor
AER	Annual Equivalent Rate
AFBD	Association of Futures Brokers and Dealers
API	Application Programming Interface
ATM	Automated Teller Machine
BBA	British Bankers Association
BCBS	Basel Committee on Banking Supervision
BSB	Banking Standards Board
C&CCC	Cheque & Credit Clearing Company
CASS	Current Account Switching Service
CCA	Consumer Credit Act
CCBS	Campaign for Community Banking Services
CEO	Chief Executive Officer
CMA	Competition and Markets Authority
COO	Chief Operating Officer
DPA	Data Protection Act
ECB	European Central Bank
EU	European Union
FCA	Financial Conduct Authority
FDIC	Federal Deposit Insurance Corporation
FIMBRA	Financial Intermediaries, Managers and Brokers Regulatory Authority
FPC	Financial Policy Committee
FSA	Financial Services Authority
GDP	Gross Domestic Production
GDPR	General Data Protection Regulation
GSIB	Globally Systemically Important Bank

ICB	Independent Commission on Banking
IMRO	Investment Management Regulatory Organization
JV	Joint Venture
LAUTRO	Life Assurance and Unit Trust Regulatory Organization
LOLR	Lender of Last Resort
LSE	London Stock Exchange
MPC	Monetary Policy Committee
NIM	Net Interest Margin
NINJA	No Income No Job or Assets
OFT	Office of Fair Trading
PEP	Personal Equity Plan
PIN	Personal Identification Number
PPI	Payment Protection Insurance
PRA	Prudential Regulatory Authority
PSD	Payment Services Directive
RDR	Retail Distribution Review
RFTS	Ring-Fencing Transfer Scheme
RWA	Risk-Weighted Assets
SIB	Securities and Investment Board
SIFI	Systemically Important Financial Institutions
TARP	Troubled Asset Relief Program
TESSA	Tax Exempt Special Savings Account
TSA	The Securities Association

ACKNOWLEDGEMENTS

Thanks to the Chartered Banker Institute for giving me the opportunity to write this book. Whilst challenging, it has been a pleasure and a privilege to write it.

Thanks to Kogan Page for publishing my work. I would like to thank Melody Dawes my Commissioning Editor for having faith and belief in me and for her unwavering encouragement and support throughout this journey. Thank you to Katherine Hartle my Development Editor for having incredible patience and understanding, for providing rewrites, edits and advice, as well as moral support at every stage of the commission. I could not have done this without you.

I would also like to thank my reviewer, who read my early versions (and reread subsequent iterations) and provided me with advice and direction to ensure the book aligned with the objectives of the Chartered Banker Institute.

Finally, thanks to my family and friends who have given me the freedom to complete this book.

Sola Virtus Nobilitat.

Introduction

Retail banking is and has been a fascinating and agile industry, which has been intertwined with our culture and day-to-day living for almost 3,000 years. Having adapted and changed over the centuries in response to the dynamic environment within which we live, the financial sector has always been full of ups and downs, twists and turns.

It occurs to me that retail banking is very much like riding a bike in the Alps or the Pyrenees, with the mountains not only acting as the metaphor for the trials and tribulations we have faced, but also for the emotional peaks and troughs that we have gone through during the journey. It starts by slowly meandering through the plateaux, cruising along, with the sun on our backs, everything appearing rather straightforward with not much to worry about and then, slowly and surely, the mountain comes into view. The organization slowly grinds its way up the foothills, occasionally taking a momentary breather to regroup, re-energize and ensure it is still on the correct road. Navigating the bumps in the road we go again, steadily making our way up the growth and profitability incline. This is not a sprint; this is long distance, this is long haul and it will take time. This is endurance and only the strong will achieve it; a few will fall by the wayside as we go. One revolutionary stroke at a time. Lots of effort, immense concentration combined with a relentless focus and desire to achieve the ultimate goal. A huge investment of energy and resources eventually sees us arrive at the peak, our goal achieved. This generates a huge feeling of self-accomplishment. We can bask in the glory of our achievement thus far. We can indulge in some celebrations. But that's it. We have hit the summit. What happens next?

Brace yourself, hold on with both hands – really tightly. As we go over the top, some people grimace and scream as the first sharp drop or shock impacts upon the cycle and we are catapulted into the first hairpin bend. Sweaty palms as you try to get a better grip and maintain control. For a gut-wrenching few seconds, it feels like we are freewheeling out of control.

Do the brakes work? Where is the exit route? Are we prepared for the next switchback? Am I safe? Is my helmet on securely to protect me from any impending impact? What to do about being on the cusp of being totally out of control when the precipice is in such close proximity? Scared to look over the edge for the fear of what lies beyond. Weightlessness, a passenger, clenched teeth. Almost in free fall, but you need to sit there and take it – deal with it. You can't just get off. How to survive, how to navigate the rapid downhill cycle safely? Remain focused – adjust to the conditions, feather the brakes – but don't overdo it. An over-reaction could be equally if not more devastating. Maintain control as best you can. Keep controlled forward momentum. Others zip past looking equally as scared, some with tears in their eyes. I'm in this with everyone else and they don't seem to know exactly what the right thing to do is either. For some, this isn't even their first time experiencing this, yet they look just as scared as the first-timers. When will this stop? When will we reach the plateau once again?

Then the sector consolidates. Time gives the opportunity to reassess and for a reappraisal of the situation. What have we learnt? How do we deal with the next phase? How do we prepare better for the future shocks and unforeseen events? We need to feel the reassurance of the road beneath us and we need to trust in our own ability to get back on track. All we know for certain is that the cycle is not yet over, more mountains need to be climbed, and more unforeseen shocks will come. We don't know when, we don't know for how long, and perhaps more worryingly of all, we don't know how steep and tight it will be and if we will get to our destination safely. For a while at least, the pace slows and we can allow ourselves to momentarily relax to gather our senses, take a deep breath, let pulses return to normal levels and hearts return to the safe confines of the chest cavities. The elation of surviving the first descent is almost simultaneously met with hysteria. Some people laughing, some people crying, some people unbelievingly rubbing their eyes; mostly people are simply stunned – speechless and in awe of what has just happened.

The exhilaration of the thrill-seekers' growing within the financial marketplace combined with the creative innovation of new products and the seemingly never-ending upward spiral of success leads to an air of anticipation and unbridled joy – and then we reach the tipping point again. As we tentatively creep ever closer to the edge, everything comes into view. It becomes clear, just what a perilous situation has been created and we wish we had never got into it. The risk and reward bubble is about to burst. And now we must come back down and we all know that the descent will take far less time than the ascent we have worked so hard to achieve. The down turn starts and very quickly the shocks and switchbacks are upon us. Rapidly and almost unexpectedly (but you knew it would happen at some point) the tragedy and drama of financial crises hit us and just when we think everything is levelling off and once again normality can return, there is at least one more last surprise.

On an emotional level, the lows can fill you with fear and dread and make you feel sick to the pit of your stomach, yet the highs are intense, immense and invigorating. This high-powered, adrenalin-driven business creates financial sector junkies. One thing is certain – everyone got on the ride, perhaps for various reasons, but nonetheless we all got on. We have all been part of the cycle and it has been one amazing journey and a hell of a trip. For some, they never want to get involved with the retail banking cycle ever again – it was all too much for them – but for many addicts they want to get back on and do it all again, time and time again – seeking new mountains and new challenges. It's how you deal with the highs and lows, how you manage the addiction, that will determine the future evolution of retail banking. This book will take you on the journey to date and present a view of the road that as yet has still to be laid.

The fact you have picked up this book and started to read it means you have an interest in the topic. You may well be relatively new to the banking and finance sector; perhaps you are about to embark upon a programme of formal study or you may be a seasoned long-time financier who simply wants to reflect over the trials and tribulations of the recent decades. Either way, I hope you find the retail and digital banking journey both an enjoyable and an informative read. I have endeavoured to draw upon as many practical examples as possible to embellish the story and to bring a richness to the theories that often surround the subject matter.

This book will take you on a journey, starting right at the very beginning, with the genesis of money itself. We will learn how technology and innovation throughout the ages have been the catalyst for step changes in the banking sector and how retail banking continually needs to adapt to the emerging technologies and needs of society both today and in the future. We will investigate the rise and fall of various retail banking distribution channels, culminating with a perspective on both multi-channel and omni-channel operating models. We will reflect over financial crises, the lessons that can be learnt from these experiences and what implications and limitations post-crisis interventions have upon retail banks. We will discuss the pros and cons of regulation and deregulation and what the impact has upon both retail banks and customers. We will then delve further into various other elements of the environment such as the political climate, emerging technology and social trends that influence and will set the future direction of retail banking.

Retail banking is about the decisions and actions we take. How we assess and manage risk, how we embrace technology, how we lend prudently, how we grow sensibly, how we respond to customer need, how we respect shareholder investment and how we act – with integrity and honesty. It is not about rhetoric and taking short-cuts. It is not about making the fast buck or gambling. It's not about sailing close to the wind and thinking what is the maximum I can get away with here? It is not about simply conforming to regulation and policy. We need to break the culture of doing the minimum to conform and transition to a place whereby we intrinsically do what is right. We must resist the temptation to be drawn towards the bright lights of short-term successes. This drives the wrong behaviours and inevitably leads to an even steeper decline.

It is about doing the right thing all of the time – in good times and bad. It's about ethics. It's about social responsibility. It's about adding value – true value. It is not enough to say what we are going to do. We have to do it.

Deregulation and the subsequent removal of barriers to entry leads to the creation of a more competitive environment, whilst conversely an increase in regulation leads to consolidation and tightening of the competitive environment. Mergers, acquisitions, joint ventures and strategic alliances have arisen to create global banking giants during the boom times, yet post-crises we witness rapid consolidation leading to bank closures and drastic loss of jobs. The highs and lows of retail banking have ramifications on all other parts of the economy too. Policies introduced to resolve one set of problems invariably serve to create the next generation of dilemmas.

All stakeholders have a part to play. Governments, central banks, the retail banks themselves, bank staff, customers, shareholders, the media and society at large all have a vested interest in retail banking. The success or otherwise of retail banking has a bearing on all our lives.

01

The birth and development of retail banking

INTRODUCTION

Whilst traditional banking has been in existence for just over 300 years in the UK, the story of money and banking occurred much further back in time. To enable us to understand what is currently happening within retail banking, it is important to reflect upon what has happened in the past and how those events have laid the foundations for the organizations that we know today.

LEARNING OBJECTIVES

By the end of this chapter you will be able to:

- reflect upon how the barter system works and evaluate how the digital age can provide an enhanced platform for 21st-century bartering and trade;
- analyse how early commoditized trading established the principles for currency exchange rates and future trade deals that we know today;
- appraise the role played by Industrial Revolutions and the impact of evolving technologies on UK banks;
- assimilate the implications of Overend Gurney on the Bank of England and how the principles apply to banks such as yours today.

The last 3,000 years...

For us to understand retail banking, we should firstly understand why and how money evolved, as there are many fundamental principles of banking that originated in the creation of money itself. This step back in time helps us understand and contextualize the reasons why banks materialized and how they have adapted and changed to meet customers' needs over time. These principles are as relevant today as they were almost 3,000 years ago. Money and banking are inextricably linked. To understand banking we must first understand money. The need for money in one form or another has been in existence for almost 3,000 years.

In the days long before banks and money, the **barter** system was used, where a direct exchange of specific goods or services would take place by agreeing to trade a specific product or service for another specific product or service. Arrangements for an exchange took time and the deals were not always perfect. It is not easy to find two parties who specifically want to exchange what each other has. Placing an agreed value on one commodity versus another was a complicated business. How do you determine the value of producing handmade tools against the skill of being able to kill a wild animal or to purchase food? How did the participating parties get together to discuss and agree the components of the exchange? This is where negotiation and a common understanding of the trade deal had to be established at the outset. Specific details as to how many flint axes would equal the slaying of a beast and the timing of the delivery of the product exchange all had to be agreed, but communication and practical execution of the respective exchanges often proved to be chaotic and troublesome.

> **Barter** The agreed exchange of one commodity or service for another commodity or service.

Further volatility arose when the over- or under-supply of commodities would have a direct impact on the value of the exchange and so came the birth of basic economics, where Supply v Demand = Price. Hence if you possessed sole access to the raw materials and had the unique skills to make flint axes, then you could command a high price of exchange (as well as a competitive advantage if you could protect your raw materials and skills) if demand for your product outweighed supply. The value of flint axes would, however, come under threat when other suppliers gained access to similar raw materials and copied the design – combined supply would increase, therefore value of exchange would fall. The creation of low-cost alternative products, or new technologies such as the bow and arrow would mean that potential buyers of flint axes could switch to alternative products and the demand (and the value of the commodity) for flint axes would decline rapidly.

ACTIVITY 1.1
Understanding bartering and the modern-day equivalents

- What are the pros and cons of bartering? How do the principles of bartering apply to modern-day trading?

- Is there a place in the digital age for bartering of goods and services? What mobile apps exist to facilitate the modern-day bartering process? How successful do you think mobile apps will be in creating a forum that will enable bartering and trade?

- Does bartering still have a place in the fabric of society in the 21st century? If so, why? What groups of society do you think are most likely to adopt bartering as a way of acquiring goods and services?

Over time, basic commoditized trading began, where a recognized value of exchange was attached to everyday items, albeit there was a degree of fluctuation that was determined by supply and demand economics. If a flint-tipped spear was expected to be worth three sheaves of crops, then communities and individuals would have an idea of the price or **rate of exchange** and the items themselves became a **medium of exchange**. In the world of economics, if everything else remained constant, then one flint-tipped spear would always equal three sheaves, the rate of exchange being one flint-tipped spear = three sheaves (similar to £1 = \$1.25 or one barrel of oil costs \$50 today). This brings another challenge: if the spear owner or maker doesn't need or can't consume three sheaves of crops, then the deal cannot happen, unless he can sell on the excess crops that he does not need.

> **Rate of exchange**   The ratio of one product or service against another product or service.
>
> **Medium of exchange**   The physical commodity that has a perceived value.

We also know that we do not live in a constant world where nothing ever changes. Just as today, external environmental factors will have a significant bearing on the value of the exchange. If, in the past, the crops failed and subsequent supply dropped, but demand remained the same, then the value of crops would rise against the value of flint-tipped spears. One flint-tipped spear might now be worth two sheaves, as the value of the crops has increased. Rate of exchange has moved from 1:3 to 1:2. This principle of exchange is exactly the same today, whether in the currency markets, eg pound sterling vs US dollar, or in the future commodities markets for oil, gold or securitized mortgages. Prices fluctuate as a result of demand and supply that is under-pinned with anticipated speculation in the movement of the future markets that leads to the price being determined. Therein lies the exchange risk – that the predicted future value may or may not actually transpire.

It is believed to be around 1,000 BC that the Chinese developed tokens that represented physical commodities, negating the need for the actual transfer of products and services; the tokens represented the value of such tradable items. Circular pieces of bronze were stamped with the image of the product and so the first tokens of exchange came into being. The first true coins in Europe emerged in around 600 BC, in a kingdom in Ancient Greece known as Lydia (Whipps, 2007). The coins featured the head of a lion and were made of electrum, which was an alloy metal made of gold and silver.

Further evolution of coins took place for almost 2,000 years with development of coin denominations and more formal minting of the currency. Whilst the creation of paper-based bank notes had been developed by the Chinese around 500 BC, it would not be until around 1,400 AD that Europe would see the introduction of the first **merchant banks** and bank notes (History World, nd).

> **Merchant banks**   Historically merchant banks were created to support the trade of commodities. The first merchant banks were established in Italy in the Middle Ages. Today merchant banks provide a wide range of complex financial services to organizations and companies (rather than personal individuals and distinct from retail banking). Services include the provision of business loans, supporting foreign trade and underwriting.

The earliest form of merchant banks initially emerged in Italy. Over the following decades the merchant banks grew in the trading ports of France and Spain to meet the needs of the shipping trade. Initial services included deposit taking, redeeming the value of early-form bank notes and provision of advances and loans against the future delivery of commodities such as grain crops.

The evolution of **promissory notes** entitled the bearer to redeem the paper-based note for its face value either on demand or within a timescale that was annotated to the original document. The introduction of promissory notes led to the increase of early continental trade, avoiding the need for the physical shipment of large amounts of physical coins to purchase goods, thus eliminating the associated risk of piracy.

> **Promissory note** Written, signed unconditional, and unsecured promise by one party to another that commits the maker to pay a specified sum on demand, or on a fixed or determinable date.

Banking in the UK did not exist until the late 17th century (British Banking History Society, 2010). The first real banking entrepreneurs were the goldsmiths. Initially seen by wealthy individuals as a safe and trusted place to keep treasured gold safe, their place in banking became immortalized after the reigning King, Charles I, irrevocably damaged the brand of Royal Mint as being the most secure place, by seizing the gold that was held in the Tower of London. The London-based goldsmiths took advantage of the situation and capitalized on the error of the King's ways. They started to create side line banks, separate from their goldsmith businesses, that paid interest on gold deposited with them as well as providing receipts for the gold they received. The receipts themselves generated a secondary market whereby the original holder could then hand on the receipt to another party. This became virtual money. Wealthy private individuals used the trusted services of the goldsmith banks from the mid to late 17th century. One of the most famous was Coutts & Company, which was founded in 1692 and is still in business today as part of the Royal Bank of Scotland Group.

The last 300 years...

The Bank of England was founded by Royal Charter in 1694 to finance the defence spending of the English government as they entered war with France (Intriguing History, 2018). In Scotland, Bank of Scotland was formed one year later in 1695 with the specific objective of supporting the Scottish business sector and was explicitly intended not to lend money to the government (Rampant Scotland Directory, nd).

As international trade expanded from central Europe to the UK, Merchant banking eventually arrived in London in the late 18th century. The first two London-based merchant banks were established by the Rothschild and Baring families. Merchant banks rapidly grew in other major UK cities as trade expanded in the UK. The rise of the Industrial Revolution led to unprecedented developments in telegraph communications and transportation along with new technologies such as the steam engine and the spinning jenny, which acted as a catalyst for mass production and powered machinery which in turn revolutionized the production of iron, coal and textiles in the UK. This led to many more local or country banks emerging to support the growth of business. In similar ways to the rise of goldsmiths in London, industrialists became bankers, aiding their own industries by accepting deposits as well as making payments. Many industrialized merchants, be they in mining or steel, diversified into banking, creating tokens for wages and paying interest on deposits. One such bank was the Miner's Bank of Truro. It was established in 1759 to serve the needs of the mining community and continued to serve the needs of the local Cornish community for more than a century before a series of acquisitions ultimately led to the bank becoming part of Barclay & Co Ltd in 1905 (Barclays Bank Ltd in 1917).

For all the ingenuity and entrepreneurship in establishing country banks to meet the demand of local businesses and communities, there was still a need for links to be made with the ever-powerful financial centre in London. London was the centre for paying Crown revenue and it was the investment centre for the country as a whole. Further, all trading instruments such as **Bills of Exchange** were drawn on London, so in the interest of trade, payments and financial settlement, London was the hub for all banking activity.

Bill of Exchange A written, unconditional order signed by one party addressed to another, to pay a certain sum, either immediately or on a fixed date for payment of goods and/or services received.

Bailey's British Directory outlines the rapid growth in UK banking outside London in the late 18th century (British Banking History Society, 2010):

- 1784 – 119 banks outside London;
- 1797 – 230 banks outside London;
- 1804 – 470 banks outside London;
- 1809 – 800 banks outside London.

After a period of rapid growth, the impact of the Napoleonic war caused great financial uncertainty and many banks failed during the early part of the 19th century leading to major consolidation of the banks across the UK.

One of the first multi-branch-based banks to emerge from the post-Napoleonic era was National Provincial Bank, established in 1833; the bank remained in existence until 1970 when it merged with Westminster Bank to create National Westminster Bank. National Provincial Bank was unique in so far as it focused upon a large number of smaller accounts rather than a small number of large accounts. The bank, like many others, embarked on a rapid, sometimes opportunistic and haphazard programme of expansion in England and Wales focusing its operations outside a 65-mile radius of London, so that it could issue its own bank notes (RBS Heritage, 2017). After opening their first branch in Gloucester in 1833, the bank had almost 200 branches by the beginning of the 20th century.

The first piece of significant legislation emerged in 1844 in the form of the Bank Charter Act. The Act was necessary to restore confidence in the banking sector after many of the small privately owned banks had failed. Up until this point all banks could issue their own bank notes. An integral part of the Act decreed that only the Bank of England could produce and issue new bank notes and if a bank was taken over, then they would have to give up their rights to produce their own bank notes (National Archives, nd). As smaller banks were taken over and their ability to produce their own bank notes diminished, this led to the Bank of England having absolute control of the supply of money. The creation and dominance of the UK central bank had been established. Nowadays, only three Scottish banks (Bank of Scotland, The Royal Bank of Scotland and Clydesdale Bank) and four Northern Irish banks (Bank of Ireland, AIB Group, Northern Bank Limited and Ulster Bank Limited) can and still do produce their own sterling bank notes.

A financial crisis towards the latter part of the 19th century led to the Bank of England adopting the role of **lender of last resort** and being brought in to question the **moral hazard** between central banks and the organizations they served. The then editor of *The Economist*, Walter Bagehot, wrote in the book *Lombard Street: A description of the money market* (1873) how he believed central banks should perform the role of lender of last resort and specifically how the central banks should consider the economy as a whole, rather than over the bank's own interests, to ensure funding of other solvent but temporarily **illiquid** banks. The principles of Bagehot's writings have become enshrined following the case of Overend Gurney and they are as relevant today as they were 150 years ago.

Lender of last resort   To protect and ensure the stability of a specific bank or the banking and financial system at large, usually via central bank intervention (eg Bank of England) to ensure the affected bank(s) have sufficient liquidity to meet their day-to-day obligations. The lender of last resort will also guarantee/protect customer deposits, thus preventing 'run-on-the-bank' deposits.

Moral hazard   Encouraged to take additional risk through the perception of a safety net being in place.

Illiquid   Owned assets or possessions that are not easily converted into cash.

CASE STUDY
Overend Gurney

Overend Gurney had been the largest discount house in the City of London, but had changed its business model and had moved into riskier lending markets that it was less familiar with; it finally ran into trouble in 1866, but the insolvency problem had been brewing for several years beforehand. In 1865 the partners were fully aware of their losses and that Overend Gurney was close to collapse. They considered their options to raise capital and even the potential sale of the business. The decision was taken to convert the organization into a limited liability company. Overend Gurney were not completely transparent in the provision of all the facts in the short prospectus that was issued; there was no reference to the known bad assets. Whilst investors may have been impressed by the existing partners guaranteeing any losses on the asset value being transferred to the new company, few, if any, were aware of the time limit condition that was attached. New directors failed to perform due diligence upon the business – no accountants were invited to review the organization's financial position at the time of the capital request. A re-emphasis upon their traditional market of bill brokering rather than lending gave customers confidence that Overend Gurney were on the right track, but it was all a smoke screen. There was, however, a further challenge in that many of the partners in Overend Gurney were also partners in Norwich Bank. If Overend Gurney failed and the partners' assets were seized, then this would undermine the stability of Norwich Bank. The smoke screen continued to create the illusion that all was well. Whilst the partners knew they could not separate the profit-making bill-brokering business out from the loss-making lending business within Overend Gurney, they could create a new partnership (which would exclude the partners that were liable for Overend Gurney) for Norwich Bank that would protect it from the impending losses from Overend Gurney. The new partnership for Norwich Bank was established on 23 April 1866.

Two weeks later events contrived to push Overend Gurney to the brink. Against a backdrop of economic and political instability matters came to a head and a **run on the bank** ensued. The partners approached the Bank of England for assistance on 9 May 1866. The partners' request was rejected on the basis of insolvency and on 10 May 1866 they suspended payments. The systemic impact was seismic – On Black Friday, 11 May 1866, depositors queued up outside branches and suffocated banking halls of all financial institutions to withdraw their money. Nowhere, it appeared, was a safe place to hold money.

Run on the bank   Usually predicated by concerns or rumours about a bank or financial institution's solvency, bank runs happen when large numbers of customers hurriedly withdraw their deposits. Scenes of mobbed banking halls and queues around the block are probably confined to the pages of history books now, as the digital and mobile age means customers can move their money far more easily and more quickly without the need to visit their branch to take physical cash out. Irrespective of the era, a run can and will undoubtedly happen. Arguably, a modern-day run would be even more devastating due to the ease with which customers can gain access to their money and the speed with which they can transfer it elsewhere – unless of course the affected bank's mobile and digital banking applications don't crash under the strain. Inevitably bank runs cause widespread consumer panic and confusion and could lead to other financial institutions suffering a similar fate.

Bank of England had to act and act fast. The first step was to suspend the Bank of England Act in Parliament so that Bank of England could inject liquidity into the market without having the actual gold reserves to back the bank notes it had printed. The action restored confidence in the monetary systems and whilst a few businesses did fail as a direct consequence of the panic, stability resumed.

Overend Gurney shareholders tried and failed to raise an action of fraud against the partners for the issue of the limited liability company prospectus and they were all liable for an additional £25 per share payment. Norwich Bank was unaffected by the demise of Overend Gurney.

In reviewing the demise of Overend Gurney and the actions taken by the Bank of England the directors summarized that it had executed its duty – it had an obligation to support the banking community, albeit it did not support Overend Gurney itself, it did support the firms that were directly affected. Bagehot inferred from these comments that the Bank of England would do exactly the same again if a similar set of circumstances emerged. This reaction concerned the Bank of England's directors. They were still running a private company, so had accountability to pay dividends. The thought of having to bail out all banks that failed was a major concern to them. Further, the thought of small banks having the comfort of lender of last resort support could lead to a moral hazard, whereby firms could be risk-taking and carry on with adventurous profiteering, safe in the knowledge that if the worst was to happen, then the Bank of England would step in to bail them out.

In 1873, Bagehot published *Lombard Street*, which set out the principles of lender of last resort. The main points were: a) loans can be provided, but only at very high interest rates so the appreciation of the advance was real and banks that did not really need the funding would be deterred; b) loans would be provided against (what would be seen in normal times to be) good securities; and c) advanced notification that the affected bank would continue to lend, thus avoiding customer panic.

To summarize, in the case of Overend Gurney, its primary business was bill brokering – not banking. It was proficient at bill brokering, but reckless with lending. Whilst its lending ineptitude led to the failure, Overend Gurney itself was not deemed 'too big to fail' – whilst there were indeed systemic impacts, they were relatively small. The swift actions of the Bank of England stemmed customer panic and quickly returned confidence to the financial market. The foundations of central banking had been rewritten and Bagehot's principles remain as valid today as they did at the end of the 19th century.

Questions

1 Financial crises are not new. Identify some key triggers and/or events that appear to have been part of the underlying cause of historic bank failures and can you identify any modern-day similarities with more recent devastating events within the financial sector?

2 Apply the key lessons of the failure of Overend Gurney to the financial sector as it exists today. What observations and similarities can you identify that would cause potential concern?

3 Due diligence is a fundamental component of managing risk and informing the decision-making process. How does due diligence apply to your role and that of the financial institution you work with today?

4 Why is speed of central bank intervention and clarity of decision making essential during the early stages of a financial crisis? What would the adverse impact be of delayed and indecisive central bank intervention upon banks, the financial sector and wider society?

5 Identify and compare a recent financial institution failure of your choice, which demonstrates that the lessons from Overend Gurney may still not have been fully learnt.

Chapter summary

Within this chapter we have covered:

- The emergence of the social necessity of bartering, trade and exchange.
- The evolutionary creation of coinage and bank notes and the emergence of early banks.
- As industry grew and trade markets became increasingly global, the emergence and prominence of merchant banks set the tone for the organizations we know today as retail banks.
- Bank failures and banking crises are not new, yet the lessons learnt almost 200 years ago seem to have largely gone unnoticed.

Objective check

1 How does the barter system work? What are its limitations and how did it lead to the ultimate evolution of money? How can the digital age provide an enhanced platform for 21st-century bartering and trade?

2 How did early commoditized trading establish the principles for currency exchange rates and future trade deals that we know today?

3 How have Industrial Revolutions and evolving technologies impacted upon UK banks?

4 What were the implications of Overend Gurney on the Bank of England? How do the principles apply to your own bank?

Further reading

Bank of England (nd) Timeline [online] https://www.bankofengland.co.uk/about/history [Accessed 29 May 2017]

Bank of England (nd) Scottish and Northern Ireland banknotes [online] www.bankofengland.co.uk/banknotes/Pages/about/scottish_northernireland.aspx [Accessed 29 May 2017]

Bank of England (2016) The demise of Overend Gurney, 5 July [online] www.bankofengland.co.uk/publications/Documents/quarterlybulletin/2016/q2/2pre.pdf [Accessed 31 May 2017]

History.com (nd) Industrial Revolution [online] www.history.com/topics/indusrial-revolution [Accessed 29 May 2017]

References

British Banking History Society (2010) A history of English clearing banks [online] https://www.banking-history.co.uk/history.html [Accessed 30 May 2017]

History World (nd) History of banking [online] http://www.historyworld.net/wrldhis/PlainTextHistories.asp?groupid=2451&HistoryID=ac19&gtrack=pthc [Accessed 30 May 2017]

Intriguing History (2018) Bank of England history and timeline, 24 April [online] http://www.intriguing-history.com/bank-of-england-history/ [Accessed 28 May 2018]

National Archives (nd) Bank Charter Act 1884 [online] https://www.legislation.gov.uk/ukpga/1844/32/pdfs/ukpga_18440032_en.pdf [Accessed 29 May 2017]

Rampant Scotland Directory (nd) History of Scottish banks and bank notes [online] http://www.rampantscotland.com/SCM/story.htm [Accessed 28 May 2018]

RBS Heritage (2017) National Provincial Bank Ltd [online] https://www.rbs.com/heritage/companies/national-provincial-bank-ltd.html [Accessed 30 May 2017]

Whipps, H (2007) The profound history of coins, *Livescience*, 16 November [online] https://www.livescience.com/2058-profound-history-coins.html [Accessed 30 May 2017]

02

The growth of retail banking and its place in the economy

INTRODUCTION

This chapter focuses upon the most recent events of the last 100 years or so, including the emergence of credit unions, building societies and savings banks and the role they have played and will play within the financial sector. We will also consider how and why the number of financial institutions grew throughout the 1900s and then subsequently consolidated again in the 2000s.

LEARNING OBJECTIVES

At the end of this chapter you will be able to:

- articulate how and why credit unions, building societies and savings banks have emerged and evolved and what role they play in modern-day banking in the UK;
- outline the functions, activities and services provided by retail banks and the opportunities this represents in the digital age;
- apply the pros and cons of previous bank mergers to the opportunities that will materialize in the 21st century;
- rationalize why financial institutions went through a period of aggressive consolidation in the late 1900s/early 2000s and evaluate what implications this may have in the financial sector in the future.

At the start of the 20th century, only a few retail commercial banks were in existence, and they effectively controlled the majority of retail banking activity in the country. To all intents and purposes, an oligopoly existed between Barclays, Lloyds, Midland, National Provincial and Westminster (otherwise known as the Big 5). However, the retail banks were not the only providers of financial services during this time. Other emerging organizations were playing their part in the provision of social finance in the form of credit unions, building societies and savings banks, and by the 1960s the Big 5 were becoming concerned about the potential threat from the growing number of these businesses in the UK.

The role of credit unions

Credit unions are formed by individuals who have a common bond (for example, they might be part of the local community, work in the same industry or be part of the same trade union, club or religious group) coming together as a co-operative group, to save their money so that their combined resources can then be used to make loans to fellow credit union members. Unlike traditional banks, credit unions have no shareholders and therefore do not need to generate profit – their sole aim is to serve the needs of their members. Credit unions have played and continue to play a vital role in the local economies of countries around the world, in particular through the provision of financial services to some of the most vulnerable communities in society.

Why people become members of credit unions:

- to help themselves by saving on a regular basis;
- it is social responsibility to support and help other members and the community;
- to generate an alternative source of credit for the benefit of members at a fair and reasonable rate of interest;
- to maximize community financial resources and to support the need of individuals.

> **Credit union**   A group of people with a common bond, who save together and lend to each other at a reasonable rate of interest.

The evolution of credit unions

Franz Hermann Schulze-Delitzsch established the first credit unions in the 1850s in Germany to give those (in the first case mill workers) lacking access to financial services the opportunity to borrow from the savings pooled by themselves and their fellow members (World Council of Credit Unions, 2018). The first rural credit union was established a decade later by Friedrich Raiffeisen in southern Germany in 1849. The primary objective was to provide groups of individuals who share a common bond access to financial services. This remains the underlying principle today.

In the early 20th century, the credit union concept expanded to North America. At the end of the 19th century and in to the start of the 20th century, Alphonse Desjardins became aware of a worrying situation whereby individuals were being exploited by loan sharks (more than 100 years on, arguably the same modern-day equivalents still exist today) and he was motivated to develop the credit union concept for his local Quebec community that would enable working-class families to have access to credit at fair and reasonable rates of interest. Desjardins then progressed to help a group in Manchester, New Hampshire, to create St Mary's Cooperative Credit Association. This would be the first formal credit union in the United States and it opened its doors in 1908. As a result of the combined efforts of Edward Filene, a merchant and philanthropist, and Pierre Jay, a Massachusetts banking commissioner, the first piece of US legislation for credit unions was created – the Massachusetts Credit Union Act became law on 15 April 1909 (MSIC, 2006).

By 1934, US President Franklin D Roosevelt signed the Federal Credit Union Act into law, creating a national system to charter and to thereafter supervise federal credit unions. The Credit Union National Association (CUNA) was formed.

Twenty years later, CUNA's World Extension Department came into being, with its purpose to attack usury, one of the greatest abuses in developing countries. The department's vision was to provide a simple, effective, yet potent weapon to improve people's economic situations on a global scale.

Undoubtedly the ethical stance and the community-centric approach taken by credit unions means that they hold the moral high ground within the financial services sector. Further, if credit unions do not hold the deposits, then they cannot lend out the advances – this means they have no need to seek funding or support from the wholesale money market. Whilst arguably this may restrict credit unions from growing their balance sheets, that is not ultimately their aim. They are there to serve the needs of their customers and will do so within the limits of their operating model. They do not have shareholders that demand year-on-year profits and expect dividends. Socially they can be trusted. Whilst many people rely on credit unions week in week out for their day-to-day financial needs, it is in times of trouble and strife where you see particular spikes in credit union usage. It stands to reason that when trust in other financial services providers has been lost, customers look for organizations that they can rely on. Such surges in credit union use are seen particularly after wars and financial crises.

Credit unions in the UK

The UK has long had a tradition of forming co-operative alliances to create self-help organizations, charities and trusts. The credit union is a further extension of this kind of coming together to do the right thing for people who share a common bond; therefore, it is unsurprising that credit unions have enjoyed a long history and that they continue to grow, particularly during sustained periods of recessions and hardship.

In the UK today, there are approximately 700 credit unions, with at least one new credit union registering every month (London Mutual Credit Union, 2018). For the past decade people in the UK have achieved a better way of life through their participation in their credit unions. Today, thousands of members enjoy the benefits of credit unions by saving together and being able to borrow at a reasonable rate of interest when the need arises. The credit union movement is strictly non-sectarian and non-political. The Association of British Credit Unions Limited (ABCUL) is the representative body for credit unions and provides a wide range of support services for all affiliated credit unions.

Whilst in the US credit unions are used by 46 per cent of consumers, in the UK just 2 per cent of the adult population are members of a credit union (Milligan, 2014). Even though credit unions in the UK provide good value on loans, they have failed to make a breakthrough impact in the UK financial system. The main reason for the low take-up in the UK can be attributed to the fact the UK credit unions fail to attract sufficient deposits of scale. This is primarily due to the lack of clarity as to the rate of return people will receive for their investment. Even with changes in legislation, UK credit unions do not advise their savers as to what rate of return they will receive at the outset. Only when the financial year is concluded and a dividend agreed, do depositing customers know what return they will receive.

REGULATION

For updates on Prudential Regulatory Authority's regulation of credit unions, check here: https://www.bankofengland.co.uk/prudential-regulation/supervision/credit-unions

Without growth in the organic deposit base, credit unions cannot make further advances as they can only lend against the deposits they hold. They cannot acquire funding from external money markets, and therefore credit union growth in the UK is suppressed. Credit unions still perform a vital role in the provision of financial services in the UK, but it is a particular niche social market that they serve and is a segment of retail banking that has largely gone unchallenged by the traditional retail banks.

ACTIVITY 2.1

- What could be done to encourage more people in the UK to consider credit unions as a viable, positive alternative to more broadly used financial institutions?
- Could credit unions attract customers from wider areas of the social spectrum? How could this be achieved?

The role of building societies

Originating in England in the late 18th century, the **building society** was owned by its mutual members with the intention that all members would ultimately own their own home. The earliest societies were established by a limited number of people, usually no more than 20, who provided funding (in the form of savings) and the labour needed to build their own homes; the society remained in existence until all its members had their own home. Thereafter the society would be wound up and terminated having achieved its objective (The Building Societies Association, 2017).

The role of the modern-day building society focuses upon helping people acquire homes through pooling customers' savings and then using the deposits to provide home loans. This differs slightly from the role of credit unions, where their focus is more upon thrift and using customers' savings to provide socially responsible unsecured lending. Neither institution has shareholders; they are owned by their members. The only real differentiating factor between a credit union and a building society is the need for credit union members to formally apply for membership and to be part of a common bond (this can be done either through employment, where they live or through a social group such as a religious organization). Building societies do not require the common bond, yet there are some instances where the common bond does apply to building societies' activities:

- Carlisle-based Cumberland Building Society is classified as a building society, yet its current accounts are only available to individuals living within its branch operating area (The Cumberland, 2018).
- Reliance Bank, originally known and founded in 1890 as the Salvation Army Bank, utilize some of their profits to 'further the Salvation Army's evangelical and charitable work' (Jones, 2013).

Building societies are formed as mutual organizations. The mutual is not a public company and accordingly it has no shareholders or the need to pay dividends. Customers are members and they alone have a right to a share of the building society's profits.

> **Building society**   The modern-day term relates to a member-owned, mutual-oriented financial institution that provides a broad range of services similar to that of a retail bank, but without having accountability to shareholders as it is not a public company.

The evolution of building societies

The first known building society was formed in 1775 and is recorded as Richard Ketley's, at the Golden Cross Inn, Birmingham. By 1860 over 750 societies were in existence in London and 2,000 in the provinces as local communities combined their financial savings to enable the funding and growth of new homes. In the early 19th century, societies evolved to attract people who had money to invest, but who did not necessarily want a house.

Such people could help the society provide housing for its other members and depositors were recompensed with the payment of interest. This was a fundamental shift in the original building society operating model and formed the framework for the financial institution we know as building societies today, which pay interest to those people that make savings, with the amalgamated funds being used to lend to other members to build or buy their own homes.

The first building societies were first certified under the Friendly Societies Acts of 1829 and 1834. The Building Societies Act 1836 extended to them the Friendly Society regulations as far as they were applicable, and under the 1874 Act they became corporate bodies possessing full legal powers corresponding to those of a limited company (The National Archives, nd).

The numbers of building societies continued to increase throughout the 19th century so that by the beginning of the 20th century the number peaked at 3,650 societies. As the societies began to achieve their original goal with all members now having their own home, the number of societies began to fall.

During the war years the numbers of building societies fell to less than 1,000. At the same time the role and importance of building societies grew rapidly as they were an important mechanism to support Lloyd George's vision of building 'homes fit for heroes' mainly in the owner-occupied sector. The number of owner-occupied houses in Britain soared from around 750,000 in the early 1920s to more than 3,250,000 by 1938 (Gardiner, 2010). What proliferated this extraordinary period of growth was that home loans were increasingly easy to obtain. Savers were looking for a safe alternative location for their money following the financial crash of 1929 and they flooded the building societies with money. Eager to capitalize, the cash-endowed building societies sought out new mortgage customers with attractive all-in packages, calculating that a regular wage of around £4 a week was just adequate security for a mortgage. In addition, the building societies relaxed their requirement for a deposit from 25 per cent of the purchase price to 10 or even 5 per cent and extended repayment periods from 15 years to 30. This proved to be an extremely attractive proposition to social groups that would previously never have been able to consider private home ownership. Many low-paid workers became starry-eyed at the proposition of owning their very own home, freeing them up from poor areas of deprivation, and they were duped by the marketing, entering into long-term financial agreements that they were ill-prepared to deal with should they fall upon hard times. Even the home-building companies of the day were getting in on the act to make it even simpler for people on low incomes to get onto the housing ladder. Builders set up a pool of advance money to make it easier for low-income families to come up with a deposit of less than 5 per cent of the purchase price.

When the inevitable happened and low-income families struggled to meet their financial obligations for whatever reason, the building societies acted ruthlessly and indiscriminately and home repossessions soared.

ACTIVITY 2.2

- When considering the UK mortgage home-buying marketplace of the 1930s, what similarities can you draw with the underlying causes of the global financial crisis of 2008?

- What lessons should have been learnt from the 1930s' home-buying experience that could have established the principles for future mortgage lending?

- Identify key warning signs that may indicate that the lending market is spiralling out of control.

In 1937 a legal case was brought by Elie and Jim Borders against Bradford Third Equitable, where the couple ceased to make their mortgage repayments, as they disputed the legality of collateral security and claimed that societies should be responsible for ensuring that the condition of property to be mortgaged was suitable for lending purposes. Whilst the courts found in favour of the building societies, the unscrupulous practices of both the lenders and of the building trade led to the 1939 Building Societies Act which forced building societies to take the residential property as security against the home loan advance, thus protecting the lender should the customer be unable to repay their advance and attached strict controls over the builders' pool system that made it no longer effective.

Building societies underwent a further major legislative overhaul when the Building Societies Act of 1986 replaced the more than 100-year-old 1874 legislation and gave wider powers to Building Societies in terms of housing and personal banking services.

Further refinements took place in 1997 and then again in the year 2000 when building societies came under the broader powers of the Financial Services and Marketing Act 2000 (The Building Societies Association, 2017).

REGULATION

For updates on building society regulation, check here:
https://www.fca.org.uk/firms/banks-building-societies-credit-unions

Demutualization of building societies from the late 1980s–2000

In a devastating 10-year period towards the end of the 20th century, 10 traditional UK building societies had either been taken over by a traditional retail bank or had converted their status from mutual building society to become publicly owned by shareholders, becoming retail banks in their own right. Below is a list of the 10 building societies that became banks (BuildingSociety.com, nd):

- Abbey National: converted to plc in 1989;
- Cheltenham and Gloucester: taken over in 1994 by Lloyds Bank plc;
- National & Provincial Building Society: taken over in 1995 by Abbey National plc;
- Alliance & Leicester: converted to plc in 1997;
- Bristol and West: taken over in 1997 by the Bank of Ireland;
- Halifax: converted to plc in 1997;
- Northern Rock: converted to plc in 1997;
- The Woolwich: converted to plc in 1997;
- Birmingham Midshires: taken over in 1999 by Halifax plc;
- Bradford & Bingley: converted to plc in 2000.

And now, at the time of writing in 2018, whilst some of the above brand names still have a place on the high street (eg Halifax and Bank of Scotland) they have been consumed by parent financial institutions such as Lloyds Banking Group and many others have disappeared entirely from the UK financial services landscape.

The role of savings banks

Savings banks, or more fully, trustee savings banks, are uniquely different to credit unions and building societies. Like credit unions and building societies, savings banks do not have shareholders as they too are not publicly owned institutions. Unlike building societies and credit unions, however, the members do not have voting rights or the power to influence the organization hierarchy in respect of goals and direction; rather, savings banks are controlled by volunteer directors or trustees emanating from the aristocracy, landed gentry and clergy.

> **Savings bank**   Non-publicly owned financial institutions that do not have shareholders and whose members do not have voting rights or the power to influence the organization directors or trustees.

The evolution of savings banks

The first known trustee-based savings bank, known as Ruthwell Parish Bank, was formed by Reverend Henry Duncan in the Scottish rural community of Ruthwell in Dumfriesshire in 1810. The objective was to help serve the financial needs of the poorest local parishioners in the community, and enable customers to look after themselves in case of ill health or unemployment and to prepare for old age. Savings banks aimed to engender and provide a prudent, sensible and thrifty approach to personal finance for members of society whose banking needs were not supported by the established commercial banks.

During this time, the traditional banks were still experiencing turmoil, with bank collapses being commonplace and customers of savings banks being equally anxious about the safety of their money. To create trust in savings banks, the Savings Bank (England) Act 1817 required funds to be invested in government bonds or deposited at the Bank of England to protect savings banks from any associated traditional bank failures. The Act allowed the funds of English and Welsh savings banks to be deposited with the government, in an account at the Bank of England. The account was administered by the Commissioners for the Reduction of the National Debt. In return, the banks received an attractive rate of interest, part of which was passed on to depositors. This led to a rapid period of expansion for savings banks. By 1817, over 80 savings banks had been set up in Scotland, England and Wales, and by 1818, over 465 savings banks had opened across the UK (World Savings Banking Institute, nd).

Yet even as far back as the middle of the 19th century, savings banks were not immune to the threat of new competitors caused by the creation of new legislation and the fraudulent acts of rogue dealers. In 1861 the Post Office Savings Bank Act was passed, which led to the rapid rise of more than 2,500 Post Office Savings Banks. Many of the new Post Office banks were in direct competition with existing savings banks and within 10 years, more than 200 savings banks had closed.

In 1886, the savings bank industry's very foundations came under scrutiny when it transpired that the actuary at Cardiff Savings Bank had embezzled £30,000 (equating to 15 per cent of total deposits). The events, fallout and public outcry of the fraud at Cardiff Savings Bank led to the whole savings bank movement coming under review. Whilst up until this stage all savings banks were being run locally and independently, it was apparent that greater cooperation between savings banks was required. In 1887, the Trustee Savings Bank Association was established with the aims of protecting the interests of depositors and increasing cooperation among savings banks.

ACTIVITY 2.3

What modern-day equivalent practical examples can you cite that demonstrate that the lessons of what happened to the savings banks in the mid-1800s have not really been learnt? The lessons can be seen as:

- How well-intended legislation can cause a lasting and detrimental impact upon existing players in the financial services marketplace.
- How the erroneous actions of one person can have a devastating impact on the financial sector at large.

During the period of the First World War, savings banks continued to grow, fuelled by the government's encouragement for UK residents to save more money to support the war. Savings banks played a crucial role by acting as agents for the sale of government stocks, including war savings certificates and defence bonds, which proved to be popular with customers as investment products.

In 1947 an innovative scheme of mutual assistance was formed to encourage the richer savings banks to support the growth of new banks, by providing funding to new banks that wanted to expand further. A further 59 new banks were formed as a direct result of this initiative.

Over the next couple of decades, savings banks continued to expand their branch network and merge with each other. By the beginning of the 1970s the number of savings banks fell to 73.

In 1971 the Page Committee was created by the government, with the objective of reviewing how savings banks worked in practice. As a direct result of the Page report findings, The Trustee Savings Bank Act of 1976 was passed, which permitted savings banks to offer a similar range of services as the traditional banks. The Act also consolidated the number of savings banks from 73 to 20 and created a new regional structure which was overseen by the new TSB Central Board. The new Board took over the regulatory and supervisory powers previously held by the National Debt Commissioners and Inspection Committee (TSB Group, nd).

The consolidation of the savings bank did not stop there. As the savings banks capitalized upon the ability to promote new products and services, there was a need to restructure to maintain control of the rapid growth. In 1983 the remaining 16 savings banks merged together to form four larger regional groupings: TSB England & Wales, TSB Scotland, TSB Northern Ireland and TSB Channel Islands.

In 1985, a further iteration of the Trustee Savings Bank Act permitted the group to restructure further to amalgamate the four regional businesses into a single organization known as TSB Group plc, which would become a public company on the London Stock Exchange in 1986. At this time, Airdrie Savings Bank chose not to join the single entity, and instead remained the only independent savings bank in the UK until the 182-year-old institution announced its closure in 2017 (Fraser, 2017). In becoming a public company, TSB Group plc had to become and behave like one of the established big banks. The new bank was now accountable to shareholders and had to immediately focus on profitability in order to return dividends to their investors. TSB Group plc could now gain access to the inter-bank money markets to acquire finance and funding to drive growth. Operating in the public market sector carries potential risks and TSB Group plc was now vulnerable to market pressures; in 1995, TSB Group plc merged with Lloyds Bank to form Lloyds TSB Group.

Following the financial crisis of 2008, the European Commission ruled in 2009 that the enlarged Lloyds TSB Group (that now included Halifax and Bank of Scotland post the 2008 financial crisis) had to divest part of its business to become a smaller bank and to enable greater competition in the UK banking sector. This led to the TSB brand returning to the high street in 2013 when more than 630 Lloyds TSB branches were brought together to form the new bank.

The role of retail banks

Throughout time the reasons for being a bank have not fundamentally changed and the way banks make money has not really changed either. The way in which the activities are performed has, however, changed radically over time. The banking system in the UK performs three main activities:

1 Payments – banks exist to help customers store, receive, make and settle financial obligations. Banks aid the transmission of money from one place/person/business to another.

2 Intermediation – providing a safe and secure place for customers depositing money, whilst simultaneously providing advances, loans and mortgages to customers; customers being personal, businesses or, at central bank level, government. Customers who deposit money with banks are creditors, as the bank owes them money, whilst customers who borrow money from banks are debtors, as they owe the bank money. The bank is therefore the intermediary between the two groups.

Depending on the notice period or **liquidity** of the assets and liabilities, banks will charge a compensatory interest rate. The difference between the deposit and lending interest rates is where banks make their intermediation profits. It is at this point where banks differ in their pricing strategy. Some banks prefer to adopt a risk-averse strategy, hence tighter interest rate margins, so potentially fewer customers or lower market share versus an alternative strategy which might be at a higher margin, attracting more customer and product sales but at greater risk of bad debts.

> **Liquidity**   The ability of an individual or a business to meet their immediate and/or short-term obligations through the holding of sufficient cash and/or assets that can be quickly converted to cover their indebtedness. Current (short-term) assets should equal or exceed current (short-term) liabilities.

3 Transferral of risk – banks have developed a wide variety of services to help customers to protect themselves from adverse market movements. These include simple on-demand deposit accounts to provide immediate resolution to short-term liquidity issues should funding be a problem, all the way through to more complex risk-spreading products such as securitization services.

Clearing banks provided a generic range of basic personal banking services. In the 1960s customers' funds were 60 per cent held in non-interest-paying current accounts with immediate access and 35 per cent held on deposit in interest-bearing time deposits. The clearing banks had to make use of the customer deposits, so the other side of the equation shows 35 per cent held in cash and government-based treasurer bills (very liquid and very secure), 28 per cent in gilt-edged securities (again government-based, but related to war debt) and only 30 per cent being used to fund lending activities (Davies *et al*, 2010).

> **Clearing bank**   Refers to a group of banks that had an organized arrangement to clear customer cheques and settle claims between them. All clearing banks were large financial institutions and they all provided a broad range of services to various customer segments.

The evolution of modern-day retail banks in the 21st century

The benefits for the merged financial institution are twofold. First the joint banks created greater balance sheet strength to enable more lending to take place and thus drive more income, whilst simultaneously on the other side of the equation, substantial costs could be taken out of the combined organization through staff reductions, closure of overlapping branches and elimination of duplicated services in support functions.

During the last half of the 20th century and the first decade of the 2000s, there was a major period of consolidation and rationalization within the retail banking sector in the UK. Of the 32 banks and building societies that were in existence in 1960, 26 were absorbed into just six major organizations by 2010 (Barclays, HSBC, Lloyds, RBS, Santander and Nationwide).

The number of building societies fell from its peak of 700 institutions in 1960, to only 52 by 2010 (Davies *et al*, 2010). By the end of the 20th century many of the large UK banks had become major global financial institutions; however, the financial crisis of 2008 led to retrenchment of the banks, with many consolidating their businesses into their traditional core markets. The financial crisis also led to the actual reduction in the number of banks in the UK when many of the failing banks were taken over. The reduction in the number of banks led to a concentration of market share, as highlighted by the Competition and Markets Authority in July 2014: the largest four banks accounted for 77 per cent of the UK personal current account market and 85 per cent of small and medium-sized enterprise accounts (CMA, 2014). Observations from the review identified that the marketplace had effectively become stagnant, with minimal fluctuations in market share amongst the main players. There appears to be a very high degree of consumer apathy, perhaps due to the lack of product differentiation and perceived complications with switching bank accounts. Either way, customers seem to be making do with their existing bank as they can't see a compelling alternative that would serve as a stimulus for moving.

With the number of banks and financial institutions reducing, whilst simultaneously growing their balance sheets through acquisitions and mergers, the new enlarged players actively sought new non-interest-earning sources of income, moving away from their traditional intermediary form of interest earnings for deposits and advances. This led to the super-sized banks participating on the global stage, participating in more complex international market trading in securities, funds and derivatives. This form of activity now accounts for 60 per cent of banks' earnings (Davies *et al*, 2010).

By 2010, as the traditional retail banking participants became more concentrated, the Bank of England embarked upon a range of initiatives to encourage new players by lowering the capital required by barriers of entry and simplified the process for obtaining a banking licence, with the result being that 15 new banks have been granted a licence, but perhaps even more could be done to reduce the barriers to entry for the new players.

Chapter 5 is dedicated to the emergence of new financial institutions and the part they play in the UK banking marketplace, including supermarket banks, new brand banks such as Virgin, and the fintechs.

Chapter summary

Within this chapter we have covered:

- Credit unions provide an invaluable service to meet the financial needs of lower-income individuals in the UK, yet the proposition is not widely adopted when compared to credit unions in the United States.

- Building societies have provided a vital role in the private home-ownership market for centuries; however, the number of building societies today has drastically reduced, primarily due to a process of mass demutualization towards the end of the 20th century that was predicated by a change in legislation.

- Savings banks grew rapidly in the 19th and 20th centuries to serve the local needs of many rural communities throughout the UK. Over time, savings banks became consolidated and ultimately disappeared when TSB Group plc was acquired by Lloyds Bank in 1995.

- The experiences of credit unions, building societies and savings banks should have helped shape the banking sector of today, yet similar mistakes of the past are still occurring.

- The fundamental roles of retail banks are to enable customers to make payments, to provide an intermediary service between depositors and lenders, and to help customers manage risk.

- Merged and enlarged financial institutions benefit from greater balance sheet strength to enable more lending and the ability to generate substantial cost synergies.

- The financial crisis of 2008 led to even more consolidation, with the largest four banks accounting for 77 per cent of the UK personal current account market and 85 per cent of SME accounts.

- Bank of England have simplified the process for obtaining a banking licence and reduced the capital threshold in an attempt to attract new competitive, innovative financial institutions.

Objective check

1 How and why did credit unions, building societies and savings banks emerge? Elaborate upon what, if any role they play in modern-day banking in the UK.

2 What are the key functions and activities provided by the large retail banks?

3 What are the pros and cons of bank mergers and acquisitions?

4 Financial institutions went through a rapid period of rationalization in the late 1900s/early 2000s – explain why.

Further reading

BuildingSociety.com (2012) List of current UK building societies [online] http://www.buildingsociety.com/current.shtml [Accessed 21 January 2018]

PwC (nd) Who are you calling a 'challenger'? How competition is improving customer choice and driving innovation in the UK banking market [online] www.pwc.co.uk/challenger-banks [Accessed 1 June 2017]

Reliance Bank [online] http://www.reliancebankltd.com/About/Reliancebank.asp [Accessed 21 January 2018]

Woodruff, M (2014) Here's why you're better off using a credit union rather than a big bank, *Business Insider*, 30 January [online] http://uk.businessinsider.com/should-you-use-credit-unions-or-big-banks-2014-1?r=US&IR=T [Accessed 21 January 2018]

References

Building Societies Association (2017) The history of building societies, 18 April [online] https://www.bsa.org.uk/information/consumer-factsheets/general/the-history-of-building-societies [Accessed 21 January 2018]

BuildingSociety.com (nd) Past Building Societies [online] http://www.buildingsociety.com/past.shtml [Accessed 21 January 2018]

CMA (Competition and Markets Authority) (2014) Personal current accounts and small business banking not working well for customers, Gov.UK [online] www.gov.uk/government/news/personal-current-accounts-and-small-business-banking-not-working-well-for-customers [Accessed 23 July 2018]

The Cumberland (Building Society Home Page) [online] https://www.cumberland.co.uk/current-accounts [Accessed 21 January 2018]

Davies, R *et al* (2010) Evolution of the UK banking system, *Bank of England Quarterly Bulletin 2010 Q4* [online] www.bankofengland.co.uk/publications/Documents/quarterly bulletin/qb100407.pdf [Accessed 1 June 2017]

Fraser, D (2017) Airdrie Savings Bank to close its doors, *BBC News*, 18 January [online] http://www.bbc.co.uk/news/uk-scotland-scotland-business-38669275 [Accessed 3 February 2018]

Gardiner, J (2010) How Britain built Arcadia: The growth of the suburbs in the thirties brought a better life to millions, *Daily Mail*, 29 January [online] http://www.dailymail.co.uk/femail/article-1247156/How-Britain-built-Arcadia-The-growth-suburbs-Thirties-brought-better-life-millions.html [Accessed 3 February 2018]

Jones, R (2013) Ethical alternatives to the Co-operative Bank, *The Guardian*, 23 August [online] https://www.theguardian.com/money/2013/oct/23/ethical-alternatives-co-operative-bank [Accessed 21 January 2018]

London Mutual Credit Union (2018) About us [online] http://www.creditunion.co.uk/about-us/ [Accessed 21 January 2018]

Milligan, B (2014) Why are credit unions not very popular? *BBC News*, 13 June [online] http://www.bbc.co.uk/news/business-27804947 [Accessed 21 January 2018]

MSIC (2006) The Credit Union Movement [online] https://www.msic.org/the-credit-union-movement [Accessed 21 January 2018]

National Archives (nd) Records relating to the regulation of building societies [online] http://discovery.nationalarchives.gov.uk/details/r/C1185 [Accessed 3 February 2018]

TSB Group (nd) 1810–1895, The early years, Lloyds Banking Group [online] http://www.lloydsbankinggroup.com/our-group/our-heritage/our-history/tsb/tsb-group/ [Accessed 3 February 2018]

World Council of Credit Unions (2018) Our History [online] http://www.woccu.org/about/history [Accessed 21 January 2018]

World Savings Banking Institute (nd) Trustee Savings Banks in the UK 1810–1995 [online] https://www.wsbi-esbg.org/About-us/History/Pages/HistoryUK.aspx [Accessed 2 February 2018]

03

Problems and opportunities caused by financial crises

INTRODUCTION

In this chapter we will look at recent financial crises that have happened in the UK and the United States. We will explore the problems that triggered the crises, how the events unfolded, the actions that were taken and the opportunities and lessons that have been learnt from the experiences. We will also look at the actions that have been taken to prevent similar events happening again in the future.

LEARNING OBJECTIVES

At the end of this chapter you will be able to:

- articulate how and why financial crises happen and what the resultant impact is upon both banks and customers;
- explain the role central banks play when a financial crisis occurs;
- identify preventative measures that have been introduced to protect customers against the aftermath of bank failures;
- elaborate upon the changes made to banking regulations following the financial crises in 2008;
- identify the best practices banks should adopt to protect themselves against future financial crises.

What is a financial crisis?

Since banking began, there has always been the spectre of an impending crisis occurring within the sector. Throughout time, there have been challenges and problems within the financial marketplace. Whether in small communities or as part of global business, the banking industry seldom has had periods of complete tranquillity when all aspects of business are in perfect harmony.

When financial crises happen, they often come as a bolt from the blue, causing panic and turmoil in the industry and beyond. This is because the systemic impact of financial crises is seldom initially known and the ramifications of a bank failure are not always isolated within the sector itself; rather it has knock-on effects on other areas of business as well as affecting people at an individual level. When a crisis strikes, speed of resolution to contain the panic is vital to restore confidence and stability in the financial sector and to prevent contagion from spreading.

Before delving into the depths of financial crises, it is worth reflecting on the complexity of the challenge faced by participants within the banking sector. All financial institutions aim to strike the sweet spot between satisfying customers who want the best return possible on their deposits and charging those who borrow money the lowest possible rates whilst still being able to make a profit margin that will satisfy shareholders. Yet this is only one part of the equation; we still have to overlay added complexity due to the competitive nature of the financial marketplace. This includes being able to design products to obtain market share, meeting regulatory obligations and being able to respond favourably to the external changing aspects of technology and social requirements. Bearing all of this in mind, we start to understand the complexity and almost impossible task of achieving a sustainable balance in banking.

Banks typically face three main areas of risk – **credit risk, liquidity risk** and **interest rate risk**.

Credit risk When credit card balances, loans, overdrafts and mortgages fail to be repaid and may need to be written off as bad debts.

Liquidity risk Where the need for a bank to pay short-term debt obligations cannot be met due to lack of readily available cash or short-term liquidity that can be converted to cash.

Interest rate risk Occurs when a bank has to pay more money out on its deposits than it receives on its loans.

Another area of risk to the bank is the valuation they place upon asset values. Should a bank overstate the value of their mortgage book, for example, and there was a sharp reduction in the property values, then this could lead to a perilous situation where the advances they have provided exceed the value of the property that is owned. This is a classic situation of negative capital or **insolvency**.

Insolvency   Occurs when a person or company has an inability to meet their financial obligations when they are due.

Some crises may be isolated to an individual bank which may result in a run on the bank (as highlighted in the Overend Gurney Case Study in Chapter 1). As you will remember, this is when a single institution gets into difficulties and depositors and investors desperately attempt to withdraw their funds, leaving the bank in a position where it has insufficient cash or liquidity to fund its immediate loan repayments. Unless the cause of the bank failure can be attributed and isolated to a unique and specific set of circumstances, such as the internal fraud that led to losses of £827m, ending Barings Bank in February 1995, or the internal corruption that led to the demise of Bank of Credit and Commerce International in July 1991, then invariably broader environmental conditions may well lead to further runs on multiple banks, wider panic and **systemic** crises.

Systemic   Refers to the knock-on effects of an event that impact upon the interconnected parts of the financial system and beyond into other aspects of society.

Should a bank suffer the indignity of a run happening to them, this will inevitably lead to an imbalance between being able to hand all on-demand depositors' balances back to them and having the ability to meet short-term obligations to settle outstanding loan repayments that it is due to make. If the bank has insufficient readily available capital to both repay its on-demand deposit requirements and meet its short-term loan repayments, it becomes illiquid.

It is important to be very clear on the difference between insolvency and illiquidity. It is entirely feasible for a bank to be solvent, but to suffer from liquidity-related issues. They simply have liquidity cash flow problems. In other words, they have a mismatch between what they owe short-term and what they can realize short-term. Illiquidity or management of liquidity is, however, a vital component of all banks' treasury functions to ensure they are never caught short and they can always fund their short-term demands. The temptation to seek better investment returns through committing funds for longer periods can lead to a mismatch between assets and liabilities, which in turn could jeopardize a bank's ability to meet its obligations when they fall due.

The role of a central bank

The role of a central bank is brought into sharp focus when a financial crisis occurs. They have powers that far exceed those of normal banks and they have the ability to protect not only banks, but the wider economy, from shocks that may have originated far from the home country. There are three types of immediate liquidity shortage that central banks can help resolve in order to keep the system operating. But before addressing them, at a macro-level, the central bank has, in the past, had the obligation of being lender of last resort (as referenced in Chapter 1 and within the Overend Gurney Case Study). This grandiose title enables the central bank (as we will see in the section below on the financial crisis of 2008) to intervene, or at least take steps to help prevent financial instability from affecting an individual bank or the collective financial marketplace itself, thus preventing systemic failure or further contagion effects. Even just taking the decisive step of notifying its intent to become involved in resolving an issue can restore confidence in the marketplace.

Central bank liquidity

This form of liquidity relates to financial institutions having a lack of a specific type of capital reserve which may lead to their inability to meet their immediate repayment obligations. Essentially there is a mismatch between the liquidity patterns of what they hold and what they owe. The cause of such events derives either from mismanagement of the liquidity position or from a technology faux pas. Typically, there is no real underlying issue of insolvency, rather this is a short-term position that can be readily resolved with swift support from the central bank.

Funding liquidity

This is a much more severe challenge and requires support from the central bank for a longer period of time. A shortage of funding liquidity inevitably leads to insolvency concerns and the implicit subsequent worries that other banks will have in dealing with the affected institution. Invariably the central bank needs to provide sufficient comfort so that the troubled bank can rebuild, reorganize and re-enter the marketplace. The central bank will only intervene if it believes that failure to do so would cause systemic failure to the wider banking system. If the financial institution is systemically engaged, then intervention and support is likely; if not, then the affected financial institution may well be allowed to fail.

Market liquidity

This is the worst of both the previous scenarios – a combination of both systemic funding and market liquidity. When markets become scared, they experience runs in the same way as individual financial institutions do. As consumers defect from a market, the underlying asset values drop, hence the revaluation of assets leads to an effective negative equity position. Should assets need to be realized then the material value will be less than the previously anticipated accounting value that had been apportioned to them. The dot.com crash in the early 2000s is a perfect example of a market that was overhyped and overpriced. When reality struck, it was too late:

> At its peak the Nasdaq, the US technology index, closed at 5048.62 – more than double its value just 14 months before. That Friday night, the young investors who had won millions in funding at networking events and were pumping much of that cash into marketing probably felt little reason to worry. The net was the future, and they were part of it. However, it was all downhill from there. By October 2002, the sector had plunged to 1114.11, a total loss of 78 per cent against its peak only two years earlier (Alden, 2005).

Deposit protection insurance

In 1933, as a direct result of the greatest financial crisis of the 20th century (known as the Great Depression) the US Federal Deposit Insurance Corporation (FDIC) emerged. Against the backdrop of a virtually complete meltdown in financial services in the United States, this US government policy was designed to reinstate confidence and reassure the public that their money would be safe in US financial institutions, should the worst ever happen. The UK resisted introducing deposit insurance until 1979 and then it only did so as a result of a European Directive (Lilico, 2014). Up until 2007, only the first £2,000 of deposits in UK financial institutions were fully insured. Deposit insurance, whilst on the face of it a positive initiative to protect customers, gives rise to what is known as moral hazard for banks (as discussed in Chapter 1). The dilemma is that banks could take a riskier approach to their management of customer deposits, safe in the knowledge that if the worst was to happen, at least the customers' money would be guaranteed (in part at least) by the government.

Arguably the moral hazard could also be extended by customers, in that they could take a riskier approach in search of the banks paying higher interest (irrespective of their stability) and invest £2,000 in each of these institutions, again safe in the knowledge that they would get their money back, even if the bank should fail. This is a classic example of where a policy or regulation which is intended for good reasons, to address a specific requirement, finds itself driving a completely different set of behaviours to those of its original objectives. A second key point is that deposit insurance does not actually resolve the underlying reason as to why bank runs happen. The existing schemes merely provide guarantees that deposits will be repaid at a later date. Whilst designed with the intention of giving customers reassurance in times of crisis, it does not and will not prevent future runs on banks. The existence of deposit insurance will not stop customers clamouring to get their money out of a troubled financial institution. Bank runs represent the immediate concern of customers being able to have access to their cash to purchase goods and services. Deposit insurance in its current form fails to mitigate that very real concern that customers have. At the time of writing, the level of deposit insurance, with effect from 1 January 2017, is £85,000 (Financial Services Compensation Scheme, nd).

ACTIVITY 3.1

Moral hazard is arguably a human condition that arises through the provision of insurance – taking risks, safe in the knowledge that should the worst happen then some form of protection will recover the situation:

- What examples of moral hazard have you experienced both within and outside the financial sector?
- How should banks counter the temptation to take unnecessary risks when they believe they are safe to do so?
- Did moral hazard have a part to play in the financial crisis of 2008?

It is, however, fair to say that as banking has become more globalized and increasingly complex, the scale and the number of the crises have increased too. Laeven and Valencia (2012) report that 147 systemic banking crises happened between 1970 and 2011. The more recent crises all have a familiar feel to them – built on foundations of excess and euphoria, inappropriate supervision, accounting errors or oversight (or both), growth mentality and an underpinning blasé belief that all is well and that nothing can go wrong. Often built on a boom and the good times, the emergence of a financial crisis of one description or another inevitably occurs to bring all around us crashing down. This is inevitably followed by a supervisory review which can lead to some degree of regulatory reform.

When will the next financial crisis happen?

If only we could know for sure. What is certain is there will be another one. As we stabilize and work our way out of the last banking crisis, we should do so with open eyes as the next one is likely to be lurking around the corner. It is during the rebuilding phase that the dangers lie. As new regulations bed in, creativity starts; during periods of stability, innovation commences; as growth happens, risks are taken – the next financial crisis will already be forming and we haven't really recovered from the last one yet. Trends would indicate that financial crises happen once every decade, if not more frequently (Pollock, 2015).

Are we ready for another financial crisis?

The short answer is no.

At the time of writing (almost a decade on), many banks are still recovering and are continuing to rebuild their way out of the last financial crisis of 2008. Whilst banks' respective regulatory enforced capital positions are undoubtedly more resilient than they were 10 years ago (see Financial Policy Committee Stress Testing section later in this chapter), few would feel confident should another financial crisis happen in the 2010s. Crises are not easy to predict – commentators also failed to identify that technology companies were overpriced before the dot.com crash in the early 2000s (Alden, 2005). More glaringly perhaps was the International Monetary Conference speech made by Ben Bernanke, Chairman of the Federal Reserve System on 5 June 2007, when he rebuffed any suggestions that the collapse of the US **subprime** mortgage business would lead to wider systemic failure, even though the trends at the time were indicating a downturn in the sub-prime and near-prime housing sector. Bernanke stated that, 'at this point, the troubles in the sub-prime sector seem unlikely to seriously spill over to the broader economy or the financial system' (Bernanke, 2007). How wrong he was. The reality is, the next banking crisis might just happen soon. There are sufficient indicators present today that would point to that being entirely feasible and what is worrying is the lack of defence strategies at central banks' disposal to combat any downturn in the sector.

Sub-prime   Infers the provision of loans and credit facilities to customers who are unlikely to have sufficient means to meet their obligations should they come under any additional pressures. Some customers may already have a poor credit rating and/or history.

Where could the crisis originate from?

The largest growth area in recent times has been China; however, the tightening of available credit is causing a slowdown in the Chinese economy. If credit tightens further, then there may well be a systemic impact from the Chinese market. Other emerging markets such as Brazil and India are also sensitive to the availability of credit and the importance of international trade. As markets tighten and retrench the growth in emerging markets could slow down dramatically. In the United States, Donald Trump became the 45th President on 20 January 2017. His aspiration is very much for 'Made in America', and the reinvigoration of home-grown industries. Whilst this may be good for the United States' local domestic industries, it will have a bearing on the demand for imports from other countries. This may well result in a contraction of need for the United States to have as many global partners – including banks.

How prepared is the UK to respond to a new financial crisis?

The traditional defence mechanism has been to drop interest rates to make lending and mortgage payments less stressful for UK citizens and to enable them to have more disposable income for day-to-day living. The reality has been that since the last banking crisis of 2008, interest rates have been extremely low in the UK. Between 5 March 2009 and 4 August 2016 interest rates were held constant at 0.5 per cent – then, for almost a year the rates were further reduced to 0.25 per cent, before returning to 0.5 per cent on 2 November 2017 (Bank of England, nd). The Bank of England has not had the opportunity to recoup all their reserves since providing substantial bailouts following the crisis of 2008. Whilst Lloyds Banking Group has returned to full private ownership and managed to dispose of its TSB brand branch network, RBS has yet to commence its state ownership share repayment programme. Even with the modest recent increase of interest rates in November 2017, should another financial crisis hit the UK financial banking system, the Bank of England is not in a position to use interest rates as a relief mechanism and with monetary policy already at its limit, the only option available to the Bank of England would be to inject more money into the banking system.

What impact would a second crisis have on UK society?

As I write, the UK is still coming to terms with the fallout from the 2008 banking crisis. Recent political events such as Brexit are also causing uncertainty and instability. Whilst the UK government has offered an initial £44bn as the basis of a 'divorce payment' to the European Union, the final figure may be much higher (BBC News, 2017). The financial cost to the government and the country as a whole of leaving the European Union is still largely unknown. The immediate concern would be that another recession would cause businesses to retrench further, causing a further reduction in UK jobs.

Financial crisis of 2008

Background

The financial crisis of 2008 had its origins as far back as the late 1970s at a time when **deregulation** happened in the US and UK financial markets. Prior to this, restrictions, particularly in the United States, were in place to prevent banks from operating outside local state boundaries, let alone outside their own country. Further, there were tight controls over cash and capital rations and more specifically the extent of depositors' balances that could then be loaned out to customers. Deregulation of controls was intended to encourage trade across geographic boundaries and through a wider range of activities. With relaxation of local control came increased access to global money markets and with this came the creation of globally operating **systematically important financial institutions** (SIFIs), though not all SIFIs operate globally – some SIFIs only have systemic impact in the local, domestic market. Global SIFIs (also known as G-SIBs in the Basel Accords – see Chapter 9) are extremely large, complex, cross-border organizations that arose as a direct result of deregulation. The very nature of such organizations means that governments and central banks have to protect them rather than risk the worldwide impact of failure upon the financial system. With reliance no longer based solely upon a bank's ability to source funding from customer deposits, so commenced a rapid period of change, as banks borrowed money from other banks to fuel their growth aspirations. In turn, this led to the mass availability of consumer credit – particularly loans and mortgages.

> **Deregulation**   The reduction or removal of government powers, usually intended to stimulate competition within the marketplace of the industry.
>
> **Systematically important financial institutions**   Financial organizations whose failure or collapse would pose a major risk to an economy; accordingly, SIFIs are subject to increased regulation and control to ensure their safety and security.

By the early 1980s, the feelgood factor was all around us as sustained property values continued to grow year after year and the ease with which people could buy homes and indeed additional homes, such as buy-to-let, only served to stimulate the home buyer market further. As competition intensified banks became increasingly aggressive in the offers they were making to customers, offering enticing salary multipliers of up to six or seven times a customer's income (traditionally three times had been the maximum norm) and offering advances in excess of the property value were not uncommon either. Offers of 110 per cent of the value of the property, combined with innovative short-term introductory offers of discounted rates for the first 12–24 months became market norms for mortgage products as banks sought to retain and grow their market share in the increasingly competitive marketplace.

Taking this to its extreme, a new (sub-prime) mortgage customer segment was evolving in the US mortgage market; known as NINJAs, the acronym stands for customers with No Income, No Job or Assets. No one really thought or indeed cared about the consequences of properties losing value or what would happen to a customer's ability to repay once the short-term incentive period disappeared. Affordability wouldn't be a problem, they would simply remortgage – wouldn't they? Property values were always going up, and everything was rosy in the garden. Wasn't it?

ACTIVITY 3.2

History tends to repeat itself within the financial services sector:

- How did the home-buying feelgood factor of the 1980s compare to the post-war housing boom of the building societies in the 1930s that we discussed in Chapter 2? Identify the similarities between the two scenarios.

- What principles should we adopt to protect our industry from boom and bust home loan lending in the future?

- Would you describe sub-prime lending as a moral hazard? Explain your reasoning.

Whilst everyone knew the good times could not last forever, banks carried on making hay whilst the sun was shining and at this moment in time it was shining very brightly indeed. But prices were slowly creeping up elsewhere, fuel was costing more, food was costing more and in the United States health-care was costing more too. Disposable income was slowly being squeezed. Meanwhile back in the banking sector, the massive growth in banks' mortgage books gave rise to the new creation of a financial instrument that was to play a major part in the forthcoming banking crisis. Perhaps some banks had become worried about their exposure to the mortgage sector, perhaps others just wanted to get some capital on to their accounts for alternative expansion plans; either way the creation of mortgage-backed **securitization** (sometimes also referred to as collateralized debt obligations or CDOs) was born – and this was a major trigger event that would lead to the ultimate calamity that happened in 2008. Mortgage-backed securitization is essentially the pooling together of a collection of mortgage loans that had, say, a total value of £100m, that are then sold on to another bank for £90m. This gives the selling bank a paper loss of £10m but £90m of cash, and the receiving bank £100m of mortgages for only £90m – a paper gain of £10m.

But they took the mortgages on at face value, with no real idea as to the underlying quality of the respective mortgages that were included in the securitized package. With hindsight, it didn't help investors that independent credit rating agencies such as Moody's and Standard & Poor's provided AAA ratings to many of the banks offering mortgage-backed securitized packages, hence they felt more assured as to the quality of the underlying assets being sold. All that really mattered at the time was the efficient accountancy of the numbers on the respective banks' balance sheets. Banks, such as Northern Rock, continued down this path for many years to come, but all would change in the summer of 2007.

> **Securitization**   The process of packaging together a group of loans or mortgages of a similar nature, with the intention of selling them on as a marketable commodity to raise finance from investors.

The first event that happened was within the financial sector – oil prices rose sharply, triggering global concerns of a recession, and this was quickly followed up by rising unemployment in the less affluent areas of the United States. As unemployment rose in these poorer areas, so increased the number of defaults on lower-end mortgages; here the quality of the housing was low, as was the credit rating of the individuals who had taken out the mortgage loans at the peak of the good times.

So now we are on the precipice – as banks became aware of the emerging situation in the United States, they started to reflect and consider their own underlying mortgage book quality and the associated robustness of their lending practices. Furthermore, and perhaps more scarily, what skeletons would they find lurking in the mortgage-backed securitized packages they had bought many years before from institutions whose practical mortgage lending criteria they had little or no knowledge of? Banks had no idea as to the true extent of the time bomb they were sitting on, but they knew it was ticking… The immediate action was for banks to no longer trust one another. Effectively the shutters came up and everyone retrenched into their own institutions, frantically trying to get a better understanding of their own respective situations.

The ability to borrow money in the short term from one another dried up. The ability to obtain cash, short-term liquidity, from other banks had gone and this instantly placed pressure upon banks to meet their immediate obligations to repay short-term loans. Everyone was looking around at each other with cautionary eyes; trust had evaporated. Suspicion all around. Wondering who would flinch first. No one really knowing who had exposure to what, and if they did lend their excess deposits short-term, would they get it back? The previous deregulation that had encouraged so much cross-boundary and inter-bank funding and led to the credit boom had come to a grinding and almost immediate halt. Now was the time. Now someone was going to fail. But who would be first and just how far would this go…?

The event (August 2007–08)

9 August 2007 will forever be etched in the memory, but it wasn't events in the United States or the UK that caused the final bell to toll, it was events in France. Global credit concerns were ignited by the French bank BNP Paribas when it suspended three of its major investment funds that had exposure to the troubled US sub-prime market. The *New York Times* reported BNP Paribas as saying, 'The complete evaporation of liquidity in certain market segments of the US securitization market has made it impossible to value certain assets fairly regardless of their quality or credit rating' (New York Times, 2007). Almost instantly, share prices fell as banks stopped lending to one another and the European Central Bank (ECB) had to inject €94bn (US $130bn; £65bn) of liquidity into the European banking system.

The demise of Northern Rock

Four days later, Northern Rock would be the first bank to break cover in the UK. Adam Applegarth, CEO of Northern Rock at the time said, 'The world stopped on August 9. It's been astonishing, gobsmacking. Look across the full range of financial products, across the full geography of the world, the entire system has frozen' (The Telegraph, 2007). Empowered by the ability to generate money from the sale of securitized mortgages on the wholesale market rather than from customer deposits, Northern Rock had created a self-fulfilling model that generated incredible growth, writing mortgages faster than anyone else; almost as quickly they packaged them up and sold them as securitized bundles on the wholesale market. In January 2007, Northern Rock raised £6.1bn that way; a second securitization in May brought the first-half total to £10.7bn and made Northern Rock the top securitizer among British banks. This perpetuated the situation still further – the more mortgages they could write, the more securitization they could do and the more money they could make; on and on it could go. The mortgage-centric profit-generating machine could seemingly only get bigger and better. Their model captured huge market share in the lucrative mortgage market and subsequently huge profits followed. Almost all city commentators endorsed the approach and competitors were envious of the Rock's performance, but they were about to come unstuck as they relied on the short-term funding for their day-to-day liquidity position. The 'Credit Crunch' had arrived. As soon as the availability of money market funding ceased, it was the end for Northern Rock.

ACTIVITY 3.3

Prior to the financial crisis of 2008, Northern Rock was actively pursuing a relentless programme of securitization of mortgages:

- Would you consider Northern Rock's actions as a moral hazard?
- Explain how the financial crisis of 2008 had an instantaneous and devastating impact upon Northern Rock.

Northern Rock notified the FSA about its liquidity problem on 13 August 2007, thereafter recovery discussions with Bank of England and the FSA commenced. By 16 August 2007, a unilateral decision was for Northern Rock to be put up for sale for purchase by a stronger bank – there would be no taxpayer money-backed bailout at this stage. Ill-fated attempts to try to offload the bank to Lloyds left the government with no choice and on 13 September 2007 agreement was reached that the Bank of England would act as lender of last resort and provide emergency lending to Northern Rock – formal announcement came one day later on 14 September 2007. As speculation swirled and swelled, queues developed outside branches, and The Bank of England stepped in to provide £13bn of immediate financial support to prevent the first major run on a bank in the UK for 140 years. But far from calming matters, the general public were becoming increasingly concerned. Savers and investors were particularly worried as the existing deposit protection scheme only guaranteed the first £2,000 of money on deposit and only 90 per cent of the next £30,000. This meant that an individual's savings with the bank would only be capped to the extent of £31,700 should the bank collapse entirely. Customers panicked and flooded banking halls to get their hard-earned money out of the bank before everyone else. The panic only abated three days later when the government publicly guaranteed 100 per cent safety of all deposits in Northern Rock.

On 19 September, the Bank of England made another U-turn. Previously the bank had refused to pump money into the liquidity market, sensing instead that they would let the failed bank feel the pain. But that day it announced that it would inject funds to help free up the bunged-up three-month money market that had effectively paralysed the UK financial community. Further, it would take steps to relax the basis upon which it would provide liquidity by allowing more risky assets such as mortgages to be used as collateral – this was a major reversal of the position initially adopted by the UK central bank.

By 1 October 2007 the government relaunched the deposit protection insurance scheme to assure customers that 100 per cent of deposits up to £35,000 would be guaranteed. This action itself, whilst intended to quell the immediate concerns of Northern Rock depositors, also led to depositors seeking high-rate deposit accounts with less reputable financial institutions, safe in the knowledge that the Bank of England would protect them if anything went wrong. For the next few months conversations were held with the government and potential buyers of the stricken bank. Potential suitors included a Virgin-led consortium and an in-house Northern Rock management buy-out team proposal.

ACTIVITY 3.4

Following the collapse of Northern Rock, the Bank of England intervened to try to stabilize the financial market. For the three distinct actions below, which if any would you think would give rise to a moral hazard?

- Injection of cash into the liquidity market.
- Allowing mortgages to be used as security for short-term liquidity.
- 100 per cent protection, up to £35,000 via deposit protection insurance.

On 17 February 2008, the Chancellor announced that neither proposal provided sufficient value to the UK taxpayer and accordingly Northern Rock would be nationalized as a temporary measure – in reality, it would take a further four years before that would actually happen. Shares in Northern

Rock were suspended when the market opened on 18 February 2008. In the aftermath, The Financial Services Authority accepted that more could have been done through supervision oversight to prevent the collapse from happening. The Bank of England also came under severe criticism for being tardy in their initial response to the impending crisis, particularly in relation to injecting liquidity into the short-term money markets – many commentators believe that Northern Rock may well have managed to survive if this decisive action had been taken much earlier.

Figure 3.1 Timeline of events for Northern Rock

13 August 2007
- Northern Rock notifies the FSA about its liquidity problem

16 August 2007
- Northern Rock is put up for sale

13 September 2007
- Bank of England agrees to act as lender of last resort for Northern Rock

19 September 2007
- Bank of England agrees to inject funds into the money market

1 October 2007
- UK government relaunches the deposit protection insurance scheme

17 February 2008
- Chancellor announces that Northern Rock will be nationalized

18 February 2008
- Shares in Northern Rock are suspended

Timeline of events March–October 2008

Speculation about who would be next dominated conversations in the City and beyond. Below is a timeline of events as they unfolded over the next few months.

14 March 2008. The next bank to fail was Bear Sterns in the United States. A longstanding investment bank, only a year earlier it was valued at US $18bn. It was eventually rescued by JP Morgan and the US government.

7 September 2008. US mortgage-providing giants Fannie Mae and Freddie Mac had to be rescued by the US government. Speaking about the financial bailout, US Treasury Secretary Henry Paulson stated, 'Fannie Mae and Freddie Mac are so large and interwoven in our financial system that a failure of either of them would create great turmoil in financial markets here and around the globe' (Mathaison, 2008). As the US housing prices began to fall, people who had taken 100 per cent mortgages were now facing negative equity situations. From a bank perspective, this meant that if a customer defaulted and was unable to keep up repayments, even by selling the house, the bank would not be able to recoup the value of the advance that had originally been made. What was known as secure lending was now no longer secure. The writing was on the wall.

16 September 2008. The biggest bank failure to date was the humiliating demise of Lehman Brothers – the 158-year-old, Wall Street-based, global banking institution, was heavily exposed to the sub-prime mortgage market. It collapsed and failed with liabilities of $600bn. Significantly this time, no rescue package was forthcoming from the US government. One of the oldest, biggest and arguably the best in the United States, it had been allowed to fail. At the same time Merrill Lynch agreed to be taken over by Bank of America for $50bn. This raised the panic level exponentially – no one trusted anyone else any more. No one would lend to anyone else. Businesses held on to their cash. Bizarrely the government ended up having to spend more on subsequent intervention than they would have had to spend on saving Lehman Brothers in the first place. Protection from the central bank was no longer a guarantee of stability. The safety net had been removed.

Back in the UK, speculation was rife. Since the failure of Northern Rock, rumours circulated like vultures over a dying wildebeest in the middle of the Savannah. The City could sense further impending bloodshed and it was about to fall.

17 September 2008 was another tumultuous day – the UK's largest mortgage lender HBOS was rescued by Lloyds TSB after the Prime Minister stepped in to wave any competition law concerns aside. The £12bn deal to take over Britain's biggest mortgage lender created a banking giant which now held close to one-third of the UK's savings and mortgage market. The deal followed a run on HBOS shares – and that was after a rights issue on 21 July 2008, which saw only 8 per cent of HBOS investors agree to take up the new shares offered in its £4bn rights issue, because they were priced higher than existing shares were trading on the stock market. HBOS still achieved the £4bn it wanted, as the unsold new shares were purchased by the issue's underwriters. The deal was struck swiftly to prevent any further run on HBOS from arising. But that wasn't quite the end of the story...

29 September 2008. Bradford & Bingley became nationalized, with the UK government taking over the bank's £50bn in mortgages and loans. The savings business was sold to Santander.

30 September 2008. Ireland's government promised to underwrite the whole of the Irish banking system; however, this turned out to be a pledge they could not fulfil. Two years later at the end of November 2010, European ministers agreed an €85bn bailout package.

3 October 2008. The US House of Representatives passed a $700bn (£394bn) government plan to rescue the US financial sector. On the same day, the Financial Services Authority announced further enhancements of the deposit protection scheme, increasing the guaranteed protection limit to £50,000 should a bank fail.

The week of **5 October 2008** saw the share prices and value of the UK's largest banks plummet. On 8 October, the UK government was ready to announce its contingency measures – a £50bn bank bailout along with a further £200bn in short-term lending support. The Bank of England united with all other European Banks to cut interest rates further.

Yet the markets still plunged.

13 October 2008. The UK banking sector is under sustained pressure. The Bank of England bails out RBS, Lloyds TSB and HBOS initially to the tune of £37bn. A complete failure in the UK banking system is narrowly averted. Just.

But the problems were not over for RBS. Earlier in April 2008, the bank announced a plan to raise money from existing shareholders via a £12bn rights issue, following an announcement of a £5.9bn credit crunch write down, which had been further exacerbated by the ill-fated acquisition of ABN AMRO only one year earlier. In August 2008 and for the first time in 40 years, RBS posted pre-tax losses of an eye-watering £691m. By November 2008 the UK government had increased its stake in RBS to 58 per cent for £15bn. Only three months later the government was back to support RBS yet again.

14 October 2008. Back in the United States, the government unveiled a similar package to the UK and invested $250bn in several banks in an effort to restore confidence in the sector.

24 October 2008. According to the Office for National Statistics, the UK was now on the brink of recession. The economy shrank for the first time in 16 years between July and September, as economic growth fell by 0.5 per cent.

The other UK banks were affected too – but they avoided the indignity of having to receive government aid. Barclays did not seek UK government help; instead they sought solace and support from a £4.5bn share issue to bolster their balance sheet. On 24 June 2008, the Qatar Investment Authority, the state-owned investment arm of the Gulf state, invested £1.7bn in Barclays, giving them a 7.7 per cent share in the business.

By comparison, HSBC had a relatively good financial crisis. Though not needing a UK government bailout, HSBC did need to go to the market to raise £12.85bn in capital through a rights issue in early 2009. Having earlier departed from its normally prudent approach to growth, the behemoth banking group had hastily acquired an Illinois, US sub-prime consumer lending business as it desperately sought to follow the rest and gain a foothold in the lucrative US sub-prime mortgage market. Household International was acquired in late 2002 for $14.8bn. Moody's credit rating agency maintained HSBC's A1 credit rating, but highlighted at the time that the acquisition of Household International was a 'material diversification' from its traditional retail and commercial business. It didn't take long for the bank to realize that the underlying assets were perhaps more dubious in terms of quality and the decision was taken to wind down the newly acquired business. After the financial crisis five years later, the troubled sub-prime lender was effectively worthless.

Banks all across Europe were taking similar actions to those of the UK to save their banks, with Iceland and Greece effectively losing their financial sector completely.

In the United States, a total of 25 banks failed during 2008.

Impact upon banks

Governments have increased their levels of borrowing to bail out banks and to protect the financial system, thus they have had to embark upon a programme of austerity to reduce spending and curtail further borrowing for other investment projects. Whilst many individuals and businesses have seen their personal wealth eroded and their businesses fold, they themselves were not bailed out and nor did they benefit directly from the bailouts given to the banks. Understandably there has been much public reticence towards the banks, as they were perceived to be the instigators of the crisis in the first place, driven by greed and the need to deliver ever larger profits; yet paradoxically perhaps, they were the very businesses that received support from the government. On a moral level, that simply appears to be wrong. Even after the substantial government backed bailouts, banks were loath to use the capital investment to kick-start the economy and aid the very businesses that needed it.

The systemic impact of the 2008 financial crises has led to a lack of bank lending since the credit crunch, which in turn has led to a lack of investment and therefore reduced consumer spending. Credit facilities were withdrawn and not replaced. Mortgages in the UK are more difficult to acquire and are more expensive, albeit at the time of writing, interest rates remain very low.

Due to stringent parameters around provision of mortgages, the demand for houses has slumped and property values have fallen.

In the immediate aftermath and as part of the European Commission competition conditions of UK government provision of financial aid, both Lloyds Banking Group and Royal Bank of Scotland had to divest part of their banking businesses. The story thereafter has been radically different for the two organizations; we'll now go on to consider how.

Lloyds Banking Group

- Initial government investment: £17bn – subsequently rose to £20bn.

- Percentage of LBG owned by UK government post-crisis: 43 per cent.

- Outline of European Commission divestment programme: 632 branches would be transferred to a new business. The new business would be formed from some Lloyds TSB branches in England and Wales, all branches of Lloyds TSB Scotland plc and Cheltenham & Gloucester plc, and would operate under the rejuvenated brand of TSB Bank plc.

- Sale-back of shares: Completed on 17 May 2017. Lloyds returns to private ownership.Upon completion, the sale returned £21.2bn to the taxpayer, £894m more than the initial investment, including over £400m in dividends (Murden, 2017).

- Percentage of the bank owned by the government as at end of 2017: 0 per cent.

- Divestment strategy update: Chapter 2 outlined the growth of various Trustee Savings Banks – the collection of banks designed to serve the industrious poor – and how the TSB brand was reincarnated on 9 September 2013. Whilst the intended sale of the divested bank to the Co-op fell through, the business was floated successfully as a separate entity in 2014.

Royal Bank of Scotland Group (data from RBS, 2018)

- Initial government investment: £20bn – subsequently rose to £45bn.

- Percentage of RBS Group owned by UK government post-crisis: 60 per cent, subsequently rose to 84 per cent.

- Outline of the European Commission divestment programme: to divest five businesses, including the creation and selling on of 'Williams & Glyn' bank consisting of 307 bank branches in the UK, including the RBS branches in England and Wales, and NatWest branches in Scotland.

- Sale-back of shares as at end of 2017: 5 per cent of shares had been sold.

- Percentage of the bank owned by the government as at end of 2017: 73 per cent government owned.

- Divestment strategy update: Royal Bank of Scotland managed to divest four out of the five businesses including Sempra in 2010, Worldpay in 2013, Direct Line in 2014 and Citizens Bank in the United States in 2015. RBS has, however, scrapped an eight-year effort to create Williams & Glyn (Financial Times, 2016). An alternative strategy has been proposed and has been agreed by the European Commission, predominantly focusing upon better choice for SME customers. The alternative remedy package is equivalent to the original objective to meet RBS State Aid requirements. The overall purpose is to increase competition in the SME banking market. The revised package focuses on two remedies: a £350m Incentivized Switching Scheme and a £425m Capability and Innovation Fund. Both elements have yet to materialize and are due to be implemented by the end of half 1, 2018 (RBS, 2017).

ACTIVITY 3.5

The impact of the financial crisis 2008 had a devastating impact upon the UK banking sector:

- Compare and contrast the post-crisis recovery of Lloyds Banking Group and Royal Bank of Scotland Group.

- What impact did the crisis have on other financial institutions such as building societies and credit unions?

- Describe the customers' perception of banks following the financial crisis of 2008.

Impact beyond banks

The previously buoyant construction and housing market dried up. In the United States, the crippled car manufacturing industry sought a bailout from the US government. Whilst some political commentators felt that the US car manufacturing business should be allowed to fail, the swift intervention of the George W Bush administration believed the right thing to do was to support it. Bailout packages of $80bn were quickly put in place in 2009 for General Motors and Chrysler. The Troubled Asset Relief Program (TARP) has now concluded, and the automotive industry is no longer financially supported by the US government, with all stock holding returned to private ownership. Whilst it estimated that the total loss on the bailout was around $13.7bn, including $11.8bn relating to the General Motors investment, this arrangement was never about turning a profit. It was more to do with saving the industry, saving jobs and protecting the further systemic impacts that would have arisen should the bailout not have happened. It is estimated that the intervention not only saved 1.5 million US jobs, but preserved $105bn in personal and social insurance tax collections.

The outcome

Increased capital and liquidity requirements

Following a period of deregulation in the 1980s, the capital positions of the banks were extremely low and the financial sector was in a vulnerable situation. The Basel Committee on Banking Supervision (BSBS) was formed to review the stability of banks' capital and liquidity positions. Upon review, BSBS provide recommendations for future regulation and banking laws. The most recent version or Accord builds upon the previous frameworks. Basel III was introduced in 2011 to bolster the capital requirements that banks need to hold to protect themselves against future banking crises and it specifically targets and addresses the problems that arose as part of the financial crisis of 2008, particularly around the tightening of what is deemed as eligible capital. Key changes to Basel II are:

- Common equity is adjusted to now exclude assets that cannot be liquidated, eg goodwill. The increase of **risk-weighted assets** (RWA) increased from 2 per cent under Basel II to 4.5 per cent under Basel III.

- Tier 1 (which includes common equity and retained earnings) increased from a collective minimum of 4 per cent RWA under Basel II to a minimum of 6 per cent RWA under Basel III.

- Tier 2 (which includes Tier 1 plus supplementary capital such as revaluation reserves) increased from a collective minimum of 6 per cent RWA under Basel II to a minimum of 8 per cent RWA under Basel III.
- Introduction of three additional capital buffers that add a further 2.5–7.5 per cent of RWA to the capital a bank requires to hold subject to respective conditions. The following section explains each of the new buffer requirements in more detail.

> **Risk-weighted assets** Where a bank's assets are adjusted or weighted in accordance with a risk profile aligned to the capital requirement or capital adequacy ratio for a financial institution.

Conservation buffer

The conservation buffer is an additional mandatory 2.5 per cent of RWA capital requirement that helps banks retain additional capital during the good times, so that it builds up additional reserves for when the bad times return and it protects the bank as a going concern. When a bank's capital ratio falls below 7 per cent, banks will not be permitted to make discretionary payment of bonuses and dividends.

Countercyclical buffer

The countercyclical buffer is a flexible, additional capital buffer that can be adjusted by local countries to help build up capital reserves in times of less stress to help protect against future shocks that the banking system may encounter. The range can be 0–2.5 per cent of RWA and can be drawn down during periods of difficulty. In the UK the Financial Policy Committee has decided to increase the UK countercyclical capital buffer rate from 0 to 0.5 per cent of risk-weighted assets.

Globally systemically important financial institutions buffer (capital surcharge)

The globally systemically important financial institutions buffer (otherwise known as the GSIFI or G-SIB Buffer) applies an additional extent of capital reserves beyond that of all the other buffers mentioned above. It is designed to help protect the largest of global banks. Annually in November, all banks are reviewed and the largest banks will then become liable for the additional buffer in January 14 months later.

In light of the banking crisis of 2008 when some large banks, such as Lehman Brothers, were allowed to fail, yet others were saved (being considered as too big to fail and therefore received lender of last resort support from the central bank), we are led to consider how we determine which banks and financial institutions should be deemed to be too big to fail in the future and by default, which ones would be allowed to fail. Further, the industry needs to take proactive steps to ensure that the lender of last resort role that central banks have previously provided becomes a thing of the past. This has two main repercussions. First, it instantly removes the moral hazard where banks that knew they were too big to fail could take a riskier approach to their banking practices, safe in the knowledge that the central bank would have intervened to save the bank should the worst have happened. Second, no longer will taxpayer money be used to bail out and support failed banks. This is important from both a social perspective and from a monetary policy perspective, as it means that the central bank can direct its resources to the people that need support, rather than having to use excessive resources to bail out the banks. Fundamentally it should be the respective banks' responsibility to hold sufficient cash reserves (capital) to be able to meet their 'too big to fail' status and associated obligations.

The Financial Stability Board presented its recommendations for how best to manage the 'too big to fail' problem to the G20 nations in November 2011.

Step 1: Identify which banks are globally and systemically important (G-SIBs). We discussed systematically important financial institutions (SIFIs) earlier in this chapter and whilst some SIFIs may have global impact (and accordingly could be more accurately classified as GSIFI or G-SIB) others may only have national significance and may not necessarily have a global impact, hence all G-SIBs will be GSIFIs, but not all SIFIs will be G-SIBs. The methodology used was developed originally by the Basel Committee on Banking Supervision and is based on 12 indicators that can be regrouped into five broad categories:

1 size;

2 interconnectedness;

3 substitutability;

4 complexity;

5 cross-jurisdictional activity.

Once each and every bank has been measured against the above criteria, it is possible to identify which are G-SIBs. The 2016 list of 30 G-SIBs was exactly the same as the original list that was completed a year earlier in 2015.

Step 2: G-SIBs by their very nature should be subject to greater, more intensive supervision of risk management, risk governance and internal controls. Frequent supervision should be further extended to assess the degree of interconnectivity that G-SIBs have with other banks and indeed with other G-SIBs so that the degree of potential systemic failure can be effectively and proactively managed.

Step 3: Additional capital buffer requirements are needed to protect the G-SIBs. The margin of buffer is directly correlated to the degree of 'too big to fail' as outlined in Step 1.

The Capital Surcharge does not apply for non-GSIFIs/G-SIBs.

To summarize the impact of Basel III, if we take Royal Bank of Scotland (RBS) as a working example, under Basel II, RBS would have had a minimum requirement to hold 6 per cent of RWA to cover Tier 1 and Tier 2 capital requirements. Under Basel III, however, RBS has to hold 8 per cent RWA for Tier 1 and Tier 2, plus 2.5 per cent RWA for Conservation Buffer, 0.5 per cent RWA Countercyclical Buffer, and a further 1 per cent RWA for being a SIFI. This makes a total of 12 per cent RWA under Basel III – twice that of the capital required under the original Basel II framework – and that is before considering the tightening of common equity to exclude previously acceptable items such as goodwill and deferred tax.

Quantitative easing

One of the main monetary policy tools government and central banks use to control growth is raising and lowering interest rates. Lower interest rates encourage people or companies to spend money, rather than save. However, as highlighted earlier in this chapter, interest rates in the UK have been consistently lower than 1 per cent since the banking crisis of 2008, so the Bank of England needed to adopt a different approach to monetary policy such as increasing the physical amount of money in the domestic financial system.

This is achieved when the central bank, the Bank of England, buys bonds from financial institutions with new electronic money it has created. This in turn reduces interest rates, which should stimulate people and businesses to borrow.

Following the financial crisis of 2008, both the Bank of England and the US Federal Reserve ran extensive programmes of **quantitative easing** as a way of kick-starting the UK and US economies.

Between 2008 and 2015, the US Federal Reserve in total bought bonds worth more than $3.7 trillion and the Bank of England created £375bn ($550bn) of new money between 2009 and 2012.

With continued financial uncertainty over rising inflation in Europe, ongoing liquidity concerns in the financial sector and the potential break-up of the Euro area to consider, the European Central Bank began a proactive programme of quantitative easing to meet the aim of achieving inflation rates below, but close to, 2 per cent. Monthly net purchases in public and private sector securities amount to about €60bn. The intervention started on 9 March 2015 and was originally intended to run until September 2016; however, that period was subsequently extended until the end of 2017.

As a direct consequence of the decision by the UK public to leave the European Union (Brexit) in the summer of 2016, the Bank of England took a preventative measure to buy £60bn of UK government bonds and £10bn of corporate bonds.

> **Quantitative easing** The process when central banks introduce new money into the monetary supply of an economy.

Stress testing

The Financial Policy Committee recommended in March 2013 that regular stress testing should be conducted to assess how well the UK banking system would respond to a future banking crisis. The main focus of the tests was to gauge how well the banking system's capital adequacy would bear up. The first stress test results were published in December 2014, with further stress tests being completed annually thereafter. In November 2016, the scenario used was a synchronized UK and global recession with associated shocks to financial market prices, and an independent stress of misconduct costs.

The test did not reveal capital inadequacies for four out of the seven participating banks, based on their balance sheets at the end of 2015 (HSBC, Lloyds Banking Group, Nationwide Building Society and Santander UK); however, three of the banks did have some issues to address. The below are taken directly from the Bank of England's 'Stress Testing the UK Banking System: 2016 results' report findings (Bank of England, 2016):

- The Royal Bank of Scotland Group (RBS) did not meet its **common equity Tier 1 (CET1)** capital or Tier 1 leverage rates before **additional Tier 1 (AT1)** conversion in this scenario. After AT1 conversion, it did not meet its CET1 systemic reference point or **Tier 1 leverage ratio rate**. Based on RBS's own assessment of its resilience identified during the stress-testing process, RBS has already updated its capital plan to incorporate further capital-strengthening actions and this revised plan has been accepted by the PRA Board. The PRA will continue to monitor RBS's progress against its revised capital plan.

- Barclays did not meet its CET1 systemic reference point before AT1 conversion in this scenario. In light of the steps that Barclays had already announced to strengthen its capital position, the PRA Board did not require Barclays to submit a revised capital plan. Whilst these steps are being executed, its AT1 capital provides some additional resilience to very severe shocks.

- Standard Chartered met all of its hurdle rates and systemic reference points in this scenario. However, it did not meet its Tier 1 minimum capital requirement (including Pillar 2A). In light of the steps that Standard Chartered is already taking to strengthen its capital position, including the AT1 it has issued during 2016, the PRA Board did not require Standard Chartered to submit a revised capital plan.

The more stringent 2017 stress test results were published by the Bank of England on 28 November 2017 and for the first time since 2014, the tests confirmed that no bank was identified as needing to strengthen its capital position. The report concluded that, 'the UK banking system is resilient to deep simultaneous recessions in the UK and global economies, large falls in asset prices and a separate stress of misconduct costs'.

The stress testing simulated an economic environment that was more severe than the 2008 banking crisis, with the scenario generating incurred bank losses of around £50bn in the first two years of the scenario. A decade ago, the impact of such a scenario would have decimated the common equity capital base of the UK banking system; however, with the introduction of additional capital buffers, banks now have a further layer of additional capital to protect themselves further (Bank of England, 2017).

Common Equity Tier 1 (CET1) The primary, high-quality component of Tier 1 capital that has the best potential loss-absorbing qualities and includes common share holdings held by a bank or other financial institution. CET1 is a capital metric that was introduced in 2014. It is anticipated that all banks should meet the minimum required CET1 ratio of 4.50 per cent by 2019.

Additional Tier 1 (AT1) A supplementary component of Tier 1 capital. AT1 comprises capital instruments that are continuous, in that there is no fixed maturity, and include items such as preference shares.

> **Tier 1 Leverage Ratio Rate** The relationship between a bank's Tier 1 capital (CE1 + AT1) and its total assets, though central banks will look at the specific relationship of CE1: Total Assets, before considering the extended use of AT1 to bolster the Tier 1 position. The Tier 1 leverage ratio is used by central monetary authorities to ensure the capital adequacy of banks.

The Prudential Regulatory Authority has a responsibility not only to carry out the stress tests, but to ensure the actions taken by the banks that failed the test are swiftly implemented. Chapter 9 covers regulation and legislation in more detail.

Deposit protection insurance guarantee

In March 2009, in the aftermath of the crisis, the EU raised the minimum level of deposit insurance to €50,000, which was subsequently reviewed and increased to €100,000 by the end of 2010, per depositor, per depositor bank. A further enhancement was the speed with which customers would be given access to their money, post-bank failure. Within 15 working days by January 2019, within 10 working days by 2021 and within 7 working days by 2024. These actions were taken by the EU to deliver a consistent Deposit Protection Scheme across the member states, as it was clear from the fallout of the financial crisis that member states had different levels of guarantees in place for their respective countries. This inconsistency across member states caused confusion and instability. This new arrangement provides all EU banks and customers with a much higher degree of protection and an improved understanding of when their money will be available should a crisis arise again.

Whilst intended to give greater reassurances and to mitigate potential runs, there are two potential problems with the Deposit Protection Insurance Guarantee scheme:

1 It is unlikely that the measures taken to date will actually prevent future bank runs from happening. The heart of the issue from a customer's perspective is having access to cash when a crisis strikes. This has not been addressed by the EU Directive.

2 Increasing the level of the Deposit Protection Insurance Guarantee only exacerbates the moral hazard for both banks and customers. From a bank's perspective, they can continue to adopt risky strategies with customer deposits, safe in the knowledge that the guarantee scheme will

look after the customer's deposit balances should the bank fail. From a customer's perspective, they can spread their bets (deliberate use of a gambling expression) across as many banks as they wish but to a much higher level with each of the respective institutions. They can also, of course, seek out the high interest-paying banks, perhaps those desperate to attract deposits for rapid growth reasons, without caring about the long-term security of the bank, so long as they are covered by the EU Deposit Protection Insurance Guarantee scheme.

Ring-fencing

Ring-fencing legislation was created specifically to protect the taxpayer from having to bail out a UK bank ever again and was one of several major reforms introduced by the UK government to address the lessons learnt from the 2008 financial crisis. Ring-fencing was recommended by the Independent Commission on Banking chaired by Sir John Vickers and became committed to law in 2013.

The premise is that very large banks should distinguish and legally separate their retail banking operations from other areas of their business, such as investment banking, with a view to protecting customers from unrelated risks that may arise in other parts of big banking institutions. Ring-fencing legislation does not impact small banks. Typical services include money transmission activities, including withdrawals and taking deposits.

Large UK banks that are considered within scope for ring-fencing before 1 January 2019 are financial organizations with a three-year average of more than £25bn 'core deposits'.

The UK government instructs all UK banks to ring-fence and separate their retail banking operations from investment and corporate banking activities by 1st January 2019.

> **Ring-fencing**   Refers to the process of separation of retail banking operations from the perceived riskier investment bank activities.

Ring-fencing from a customer's perspective

The impact of ring-fencing on customers should be minimal, as the large banks should be able to identify and carve out their retail-based operations from the rest of the parent organization with relative ease. There may be some operational issues that could affect customers, for example, bank account numbers and sorting codes may have to change subject to restructuring. If this is required, a legal process known as a Ring-fencing Transfer Scheme (RFTS) will enable the banks to transfer accounts from one part of the business to another (either in or out of the ring-fence) *without* the explicit consent of every customer. This can only happen after a successful application has been made through the UK courts.

In all cases, the bank will contact affected customers to provide advice and support through the change process.

Ring-fencing from the bank's perspective

For the large banks with a domestic focus, such as RBS and Lloyds Banking Group, ring-fencing should be straightforward, but for the large banks with a significant international presence such as HSBC and Barclays the separation process is going to be more complicated.

The costs associated with ring-fencing are substantial, with set-up costs estimated by the Treasury as being around £3bn, with annual costs thereafter of around £4bn… and the ramifications of the financial crisis of 2008 are still being felt today.

ACTIVITY 3.6

- How was the financial institution you work for affected by the financial crisis of 2008?

- What practical measures have you observed being implemented within your organization to redress the position post the events of 2008?

- In practical terms, how have customers responded to the changes that have been introduced over the last decade? In your opinion, how have social attitudes towards retail banks changed since the financial crisis of 2008?

- Ten years on from the financial crisis of 2008, with all the major banks still trading, to what extent do you think all the lessons have been learnt and sustainable measures and sufficient regulations put in place to prevent such events ever happening again?

- With many new entrants poised to enter the finance service marketplace, how vulnerable do you think the traditional retail banks are? Do you think they recovered sufficiently well from the financial crisis to fend off the threat of new competitors?

Chapter summary

- Financial crises are not new, nor are they over.

- Throughout the centuries, new policies and regulations have been introduced to respond to and rectify the errors of the past but rarely do they take the steps necessary to prevent future failures.

- Relaxation in regulation inevitably leads to even more risks being taken.

- Capital is the key to a bank's strength. Only lend what you've got. Resist the temptation to deliver beyond the demand of shareholders. Safety, security and stability first.

- When financial crises strike, central banks need to act swiftly and to take all-encompassing action to mitigate contagion.

- Post-crisis, as the financial marketplace recovers, evolves, grows and competition returns, the temptation to make rash decisions, take short-cuts or make illogical product offers that deliver exceptional market share are all clues that things are going wrong within the business.

- If financial crises happen every decade, then another one is due in 2018.

- Central banks have to take preventative action during the economic upturn. It is not acceptable to simply stand by and do nothing, for fear of upsetting the positive economic vibe. Intervention needs to be timely, decisive and robust during both good times and bad.

- Don't rely on what you don't own. Organic growth might take longer, but it is more reliable and sustainable.

Objective check

1 How do financial crises happen? What is the impact on banks and customers?

2 What role do central banks play when financial crises occur?

3 List the measures that have been introduced to protect customers against the aftermath of bank failures.

4 What changes were made to banking regulations following the financial crisis in 2008?

5 What are the best practices that banks should adopt to protect themselves against future financial crises?

Further reading

Anderson, S (2013) International financial review: A history of the past 40 years in financial crises, International Finance Review, September [online] http://www.ifre.com/a-history-of-the-past-40-years-in-financial-crises/21102949.fullarticle [Accessed 29 August 2017]

Aziz, J (2014) Why do financial crises happen? *The Week*, 29 May [online] http://theweek.com/articles/446527/why-financial-crises-happen [Accessed 29 August 2017]

Bank of England (2016) News Release – Financial Policy Committee statement from its policy meeting, 23 March [online] http://www.bankofengland.co.uk/publications/Pages/news/2016/032.aspx [Accessed 30 August 2017]

BBC News (2009) Timeline: Credit crunch to downturn, 7 August [online] http://news.bbc.co.uk/1/hi/business/7521250.stm [Accessed 25 August 2017]

BBC News (2008) US takes over key mortgage firms, 7 September [online] http://news.bbc.co.uk/1/hi/business/7602992.stm [Accessed 25 August 2017]

BBC News (2016) What is quantitative easing? 4 August [online] http://www.bbc.co.uk/news/business-15198789 [Accessed 30 August 2017]

BBC News (2017) Timeline: Northern Rock bank crisis, 5 August [online] http://news.bbc.co.uk/1/hi/business/7007076.stm [Accessed 24 August 2017]

Bing (2013) Crash course: The origins of the financial crisis [online] https://www.bing.com/search?q=economist.com%2Fnews%2Fschoolsbrief%2F21584534-effects-financial-crisis-are-still-being-felt-five-years-article&form=EDGEAR&qs=PF&cvid=8c86a4370ee04fa29837adbfe973be3b&cc=GB&setlang=en-GB&PC=HCTS [Accessed 24 August 2017]

BIS (2012) Bank International Settlements 82nd Annual Report, Section IV p64–83 [online] http://www.bis.org/publ/arpdf/ar2012e.pdf [Accessed 30 August 2017]

Claeys, G, Leandro, A and Mandra, A (2015) European Central Bank Quantitative Easing: The detailed manual, *Breugel*, March [online] http://bruegel.org/wp-content/uploads/imported/publications/pc_2015_02_110315.pdf [Accessed 30 August 2017]

Claeys, G and Leandro, A (2016) The European Central Bank's quantitative easing programme: Limits and risks, *Breugel*, 15 February [online] http://bruegel.org/2016/02/the-european-central-banks-quantitative-easing-programme-limits-and-risks/ [Accessed 30 August 2017]

Connon, H (2007) Why ninja mortgages could wreak havoc, *The Guardian*, 30 September [online] https://www.theguardian.com/business/2007/sep/30/5 [Accessed 29 August 2017]

Dunkley, E (2015) Global banks fret over UK ringfencing rules, *Financial Times*, 19 June [online] https://www.ft.com/content/a1ac7434-15c6-11e5-be54-00144feabdc0 [Accessed 30 August 2017]

The Economist (2007) Lessons of the fall, *Economist*, 18 October [online] http://www.economist.com/node/9988865 [Accessed 24 August 2017]

The Economist (2011) HSBC: Gulliver's Travels, 14 April [online] http://www.economist.com/node/18558236 [Accessed 25 August 2017]

Elliott, L (2014) The next crisis could be here soon, *The Guardian*, 20 January [online] https://www.theguardian.com/business/economocs-blog/2014/jan/20next-financial-crisis-could-be-here-soon [Accessed 24 August 2017]

European Central Bank (2017) Monetary policy: Asset purchase programme [online] https://www.ecb.europa.eu/mopo/implement/omt/html/index.en.html [Accessed 30 August 2017]

European Commission (2014) Memo: Deposit guarantee schemes – frequently asked questions, 15 April [online] http://europa.eu/rapid/press-release_MEMO-14-296_en.htm [Accessed 29 August 2017]

European Parliament (2017) Global systemically important banks in Europe, 3 May [online] http://www.europarl.europa.eu/RegData/etudes/BRIE/2016/574406/IPOL_BRI(2016)574406_EN.pdf [Accessed 29 August 2017]

Financial Conduct Authority (2016) Ring-fencing, 14 September [online] https://www.fca.org.uk/consumers/ring-fencing [Accessed 30 August 2017]

Global Issues (2013) Global financial crisis, 24 March [online] http://www.globalissues.org/article/768/global-financial-crisis#Acrisissosseveretherestsuffertoo [Accessed 25 August 2017]

Guardian (2011) RBS collapse: Timeline, 12 December [online] https://www.theguardian.com/business/2011/dec/12/rbs-collapse-timeline [Accessed 25 August 2017]

Kingsley, P (2012) Financial Crisis: Timeline, *The Guardian*, 7 August [online] https://www.the guardian.com/business/2012/aug/07credit-crunch-boom-bust-timeline [Accessed 24 August 2017]

Luyendijk, J (2015) How the banks ignored the lessons of the crash, *The Guardian*, 30 September [online] https://www.theguardian.com/business/2015/sep/30/how-the-banks-ignored-lessons-of-crash [Accessed 24 August 2017]

Reuters (2013) Auto bailout saved 1.5 million jobs, 9 December [online] https://www.reuters.com/article/autos-bailout-study-idUSL1N0JO0XU20131209 [Accessed 25 August 2017]

Slater, S and Neligan, M (2009) HSBC in £12.85 billion rights issue, Reuters, 3 March [online] http://uk.reuters.com/article/uk-hsbc-idUKTRE52100220090303 [Accessed 25 August 2017]

Tran, M (2002) HSBC takes slice of American Pie, *The Guardian*, 14 November [online] https://www.theguardian.com/business/2002/nov/14/money [Accessed 25 August 2017]

Treanor, J and Elliott, L (2008) Failure of financial heavyweights could have caused markets to implode, *The Guardian*, 9 September [online] https://www.theguardian.com/business/2008/sep/09/freddiemacandfanniemae.subprimecrisis2 [Accessed 24 August 2017]

Wallace, T (2017) Interest rates set to stay low for at least another two years, *The Telegraph*, 26 August [online] http://www.telegraph.co.uk/business/2017/08/26/interest-rates-set-stay-low-least-another-two-years/ [Accessed 29 August 2017]

Wintour, P (2016) UK voted for Brexit – but is there a way back? *The Guardian*, 29 June [online] https://www.theguardian.com/politics/2016/jun/29/uk-voted-for-brexit-but-is-there-a-way-back [Accessed 30 August 2017]

World Bank (nd) Banking crisis [online] http://www.worldbank.org/en/publications/gfdr/background/banking-crisis [Accessed 24 August 2017]

References

Alden, C (2005) Looking back on the crash, *The Guardian*, 10 March [online] https://www.theguardian.com/technology/2005/mar/10/newmedia.media [Accessed 30 August 2017]

Bank of England (2016) Stress testing the UK banking system: 2016 results [online] http://www.bankofengland.co.uk/financialstability/Documents/fpc/results301116.pdf [Accessed 30 August 2017]

Bank of England (nd) Statistical interactive database – official bank rate history [online] http://www.bankofengland.co.uk/boeapps/iadb/Repo.asp [Accessed 4 January 2018]

Bank of England (2017) Stress testing the UK banking system: 2017 results November 2017 [online] https://www.bankofengland.co.uk/-/media/boe/files/stress-testing/2017/stress-testing-the-uk-banking-system-2017-results.pdf?la=en&hash=ACE1E2FB544 82F5DC3412864C6907928B622044A [Accessed 23 July 2017]

BBC News (2017) Brexit: UK divorce bill offer worth up to 50bn euros, 29 November [online] http://www.bbc.co.uk/news/uk-politics-42161346 [Accessed 4 January 2018]

Bernanke, B (2007) The housing market and subprime lending, *Federal Reserve* [online] https://www.federalreserve.gov/newsevents/speech/Bernanke20070605a.htm [Accessed 30 August 2017]

Financial Services Compensation Scheme (nd) Deposit limits [online] https://www.fscs.org.uk/what-we-cover/compensation-limits/deposit-limits/ [Accessed 25 August 2017]

Financial Times (2016) RBS ditches Williams & Glyn spin-off after £1bn loss, 5 August [online] https://www.ft.com/content/d82643de-5ad3-11e6-9f70-badea1b336d4 [Accessed 5 January 2018]

Laeven, L and Valencia, F (2012) IMF Working Paper: Systemic banking crises database: an update, *IMF* [online] http://www.imf.org/external/pubs/ft/wp/2012/wp12163.pdf [Accessed 29 August 2017]

Lilico, A (2014) Why bank deposit insurance leads to more financial crises, *The Telegraph*, 8 October [online] http://www.telegraph.co.uk/finance/newsbysector/banksandfinance/11148323/Why-bank-deposit-insurance-leads-to-more-financial-crises.html [Accessed 24 August 2017]

Mathaison, N (2008) Three weeks that changed the world, *The Guardian*, 28 December [online] https://www.theguardian.com/business/2008/dec/28/markets-credit-crunch-banking-2008 [Accessed 25 August 2017]

Murden, T (2017) Taxpayer refunded as Lloyds back in private ownership, *Daily Business*, 17 May [online] https://dailybusinessgroup.co.uk/2017/05/taxpayer-refunded-as-lloyds-back-in-private-ownership/ [Accessed 5 January 2018]

New York Times (2007) BNP Paribas suspends funds because of subprime problems, 9 August [online] http://www.nytimes.com/2007/08/09/business/worldbusiness/09iht-09bnp.7054054.html [Accessed 24 August 2017]

Pollock, A (2015) Financial crises occur about once every decade, *Financial Times* [online] https://www.ft.com/content/5148cd1e-cf01-11e4-893d-00144feab7de [Accessed 30 August 2017]

RBS (2017) The alternative to Williams & Glyn… Five things to know [online] https://www.rbs.com/content/dam/rbs_com/rbs/Documents/News/2017/September/RBS-WG_ALTERNATIVE.pdf [Accessed 5 January 2018]

RBS (2018) Equity ownership statistics – government ownership [online] https://investors.rbs.com/share-data/equity-ownership-statistics.aspx [Accessed 8 January 2018]

The Telegraph (2007) Northern Rock: Why Northern Rock was doomed to fail, 16 September [online] http://www.telegraph.co.uk/finance/markets/2815859/Why-Northern-Rock-was-doomed-to-fail.html [Accessed 24 August 2017]

04

Preparing for external trends and influences to deliver high-quality income and cost-effective services

INTRODUCTION

All retail banks face the daily challenge of delicately and precisely balancing their operational activities in such a way as to deliver shareholder value, return profits and run their organizations efficiently. One of the key metrics used to assess retail bank efficiency is the cost-to-income ratio. This chapter will use the cost-to-income ratio as a mechanism to identify and discuss the ways in which retail banks choose to deploy various strategies to influence how they manage and control their costs and where banks derive their income and where they can make money in the future.

LEARNING OBJECTIVES

By the end of this chapter you will be able to:

- analyse the challenges that retail banks face;

- demonstrate how the cost-to-income ratio can be used to explain a retail bank's efficiency;
- identify and explain the strategic levers that can be pulled to influence both the cost and income components of the cost-to-income ratio;
- analyse how banks can make more income in the future;
- analyse the limitations of some of the strategies that are deployed by retail banks to influence the cost-to-income ratio;
- evaluate the speed with which banks can change to meet customer needs;
- evaluate the cost versus benefit proposition of banks updating their products and services.

The challenge that retail banks face: cost-to-income dichotomy

Cost-to-income ratios have become a standard performance measure, used by economists, accountants, investors and shareholders alike, to compare the efficiency of one bank against another.

> **Cost-to-income ratio** 'The cost-to-income ratio is a key financial measure, particularly important in valuing banks. It shows a company's costs in relation to its income. To get the ratio, divide the operating costs (administrative and fixed costs, such as salaries and property expenses, but not bad debts that have been written off) by operating income' (Money Week, 2013).

In its simplest form, the cost-to-income ratio states how much money a bank has spent (on administrative and fixed costs, including salaries) against how much income it has earned. Trends of reporting cost-to-income ratios can also highlight a) problems where a ratio increases, indicating that more costs and less income are being generated, as opposed to b) where the cost-to-income ratio is lowering, demonstrating an improving, more efficient position as costs reduce and income increases. Consider the two following scenarios.

Scenario 1

If Bank A has earned £20m, yet spends £15m, then the cost-to-income ratio is 15/20 = 75 per cent. Or in other words, for every £1 it earns, it spends 75p. If Bank B was able to deliver higher earnings (income) than Bank A of £30m and have a similar cost base as Bank A of £15m, then Bank B's cost-to-income ratio would be 15/30 = 50 per cent. In this case, for every £1 earned, only 50p is being spent. From this basic example, the summation would be that Bank B is being run more efficiently, as it is delivering significantly more income from its similar-sized cost base. The lower the cost-to-income ratio is, the more profitable the bank will be. Like-for-like comparisons within an accounting period can provide useful snapshots of respective banks' performance in the marketplace within which they operate.

Cost-to-income ratio trends are also very insightful. Looking at consecutive accounting periods and assessing a bank's cost-to-income ratio can shed light on a bank's performance.

Scenario 2

If Bank A has reported an increase (worsening) in their cost-to-income ratio, this means that the organization is spending more money at a higher and quicker rate than it is bringing in. Invariably one of two things will be happening: the slowing down, deterioration or loss of income revenue streams, or an increase in costs of running the business. Or worse still, income is slowing down and costs are rising. This is the worst-case scenario. A deteriorating cost-to-income ratio means more of every £1 earned is being spent on costs of running the organization and this is a trend that worries shareholders, investors and financial commentators.

If Bank B is seeing its cost-to-income ratio decreasing (improving) this means that it is running more efficiently. It will be achieving one of two things: it will either be maintaining its income streams but has managed to reduce its operating costs, or it will have managed to maintain its costs and growth income revenues at a better rate than its costs. In an ideal world, both facets of the ratio will be improving. Increasing earnings whilst simultaneously reducing costs is the panacea all businesses aspire to achieve, not just banks.

ACTIVITY 4.1

Cost-to-income ratios are powerful performance metrics for all retail banks:

- If a bank has a cost-to-income ratio of 75 per cent, how would you explain this in simple terms to your team?

- If subsequently the bank's cost-to-income ratio moves from 75 to 70 per cent, what may have caused this to happen? Is this an improved or worse position? Explain your reasoning.

- For a financial institution you know well, how has the cost-to-income ratio performed over the last three years? What are the underlying reasons for the changes in the ratio?

Retail banking strategies for managing operational cost

Whilst the main cost of running a retail bank is its headcount and subsequent salary wage bill, there are, however, many other activities that have a bearing on this side of the ratio. Typically, banks adopt a stringent prioritization process of choosing which costs and investment decisions the business should follow. Whilst the majority of costs are assigned to 'keeping the show on the road', priority will be given to reactive funding to ensure compliance and conformance with regulation. Other proactive decisions such as investment in new products and infrastructure will all be assessed upon their own merits, with the primary driver being respective projects' ability to generate a swift return on investment. Cost cutting is not always the best course of action in the long run – it can be seen as ruthless and result in severe reputational damage for the organization both internally and externally. Reducing roles within organizations can sometimes be seen as a last-step measure to create operational efficiency. Invariably headcount reductions are achieved through a variety of organizational redesign initiatives or through the adoption of new ways of working. This section will look at some of the options available to banks as they tackle the operational cost dimension of the ratio and will highlight some of the implications associated with deploying such tactics.

Centralization of UK back-office operations

In the late 1980s and early 1990s a new chapter in UK retail banking emerged. The centralization of labour-intensive and non-profit-generating tasks such as account opening, closing and maintenance (for example, changing addresses) became commonplace before the end of the 20th century. This is also true of centralized lending. The ease of moving work around was enhanced by the emergence of image and workflow technology that enabled traditional paperwork to be scanned, stored and moved as digital images. This meant that for the first time, traditional back-office work that was branch-centric could be moved electronically, in real time, from one processing location to another. The premise of this model required banks to identify common, highly repetitive processes and activities that were being duplicated in various multiple, disparate locations and then pool them together, to then centralize the work in a single location, or at least a significantly reduced number of locations. Process standardization best practice (one single way of doing things), combined with economies of scale, creates operational synergies. This means that the total amount of effort to deliver the work should be at far less cost than previously when the work was being sporadically managed. Teams should ultimately be able to deliver more output with fewer resources in the centralized model.

Processing team efficiencies

The first step in driving down proactive costs is looking to the processing teams themselves, the specific work they do and the efficiency with which the work is done. Centralization provides a greater opportunity to deliver improved consistency, greater quality and greater efficiency. Centralization benefits of 10 per cent should be readily achievable. Based on a hypothetical team of 1,200 processors, this would equate to savings of approximately 120 roles. If the average salary of a processor is £15,000, this could generate cost savings of £1,800,000.

Lean practitioners such as Boston Consultancy Group proport to be able to deliver even more benefits through a variety of customer-centric value-adding activities that can deliver in the region of 30 per cent cost saving through the deployment of Lean Advantage techniques. Again, based on a hypothetical team of 1,200 processors, this would equate to savings of approximately 360 roles. If the average salary of a processor is £15,000, this could generate cost savings of £5,400,000.

Spans and layers

Centralization of operations means that operational spans and layers can be adjusted to effect even further reduction in operational costs.

This can be achieved through both reducing the management layers (taking out superfluous layers of organizational structure) and increasing the number of direct reports each line manager has. The effect of doing this on large businesses can lead to significant cost savings. In addition, the physical space and resource costs saved in many [branch] locations will further help reduce and consolidate costs from around the organization.

The following case study on spans and layers assumes that demand and processing efficiency remains constant. This is entirely intentional so that we can focus solely upon the impact of spans and layers. Scenario A presents the 'As-Is' organizational structure which shows the resources under the existing line management structure; we then progress to Scenario B to show what cost savings can be made through operational and organizational redesign.

CASE STUDY
Spans and layers

Figure 4.1 shows how adjusting spans and layers can save an organization substantial sums of money.

Figure 4.1   Spans and layers

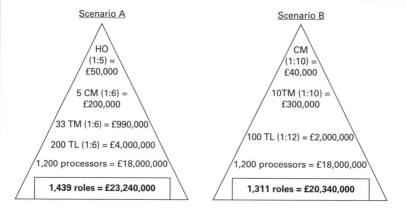

Scenario A

HO
(1:5) =
£50,000

5 CM (1:6) =
£200,000

33 TM (1:6) = £990,000

200 TL (1:6) = £4,000,000

1,200 processors = £18,000,000

1,439 roles = £23,240,000

Scenario B

CM
(1:10) =
£40,000

10TM (1:10) =
£300,000

100 TL (1:12) = £2,000,000

1,200 processors = £18,000,000

1,311 roles = £20,340,000

Notes:
Headcount reduced by 128 – down 9 per cent.
Costs reduced by £2.9m – down 13 per cent.
Layers reduced from 5 to 4.
Spans increased from 1:6 to 1:10.

Scenario A

In the existing team structure scenario, there is a team of 1,200 back-office processors (each earning £15,000 pa) who are required to complete the existing demand for the process requirement for the bank's scenario A customers. They are managed by team leaders (TLs, each earn £20,000 pa) in a ratio of 1:6 – this means that 200 TLs are required to support the processors. In turn, the 200 TLs are managed by team managers (TMs, each earn £30,000 pa) in a ratio of 1:6 – this means that 33 TMs are required to look after the TLs. Team managers also need managing and they report to centre managers (CM, each earn £40,000) also in a 1:6 ratio, hence five CMs exist. All centre managers ultimately report to the Head of Operations (HO earns £50,000 pa). Combined this generates a team of 1,439 people at a cost of £23,240,000.

Scenario B

In this scenario, assume the work demand remains constant and that the 1,200 back-office processors are still required to complete the actual work. What changes is the line management ratios. In the first instance, assume the reporting ratio increases from 1:6 in Scenario A to 1:12 – this would result in the TL population being halved. Further, if the ratio of TLs to TMs was to increase from 1:6 to 1:10, then the number of team managers would fall from 33 to 10. By increasing the spans, Scenario B has already saved 123 roles (100 TLs and 23 TMs) and now comes the layers. The pinnacle of the business will, under Scenario B, have 10 team managers reporting to them. This role could be performed by the existing Head of Operations (HO); however, for this scenario, the assumption will be that the top job will be done by one of the existing CMs, with all other CM roles and the Head of Operations role being dispensed with. In this way, the middle management layer of CM has effectively been removed, as has the HO role. This gives a much flatter, more efficient structure and means that the front-line staff are only four steps away from the top job, which in turn will help improve communication and escalation within the organization. The benefits of restructuring the operation will generate cost savings in the region of £3,000,000 pa, albeit the one-off costs of restructuring the business will need to be taken into account.

Questions

1 Reflect upon your own organization – can you identify when and where spans and layers have been adjusted to streamline the business and to save operational costs?

2 In practice, how did the business adapt to the revised organizational structure?

3 When implementing new spans and layers, what considerations need to be made with regard to the communication process and the impact upon the culture within the organization?

4 What areas within your organization do you think could benefit from the application of a programme of consolidation of spans and layers?

By deploying both process team efficiencies and spans and layers initiatives, there are significant cost savings to be made for retail banks through the centralized operations model. The programme of work needs to be carefully managed to enable each stage of the process to bed in and to give time for the respective initiatives to deliver their benefits. Extreme care should be taken to ensure that the organization is robust enough to absorb the changes and that normal service to customers is not adversely affected. All steps cannot happen at once. Careful planning is key to the successful implementation of the initiatives.

Advantages

Pulling together traditional branch-based back-office functions and locating high-volume simple activities, such as account opening, standing orders and direct debits into centralized locations meant that significant operational synergies and efficiencies could be achieved for retail banks. Through dedicated processing teams focusing upon their tasks, they could drive operational process improvements, increasing speed of production, improved consistency and quality of output. In addition, prime retail branch space (that had been taken up with non-income-generating in-house processing work) could be converted into true retail space to serve customers, leaving branch staff to focus upon customer service and retail sales. As processing teams become increasingly confident in their processing, the quality of production should increase, meaning that right-first-time levels will rise and rework will reduce. Further cost savings can be achieved through operations hierarchical restructure to simplify the organization and reduce the layers between the business.

Disadvantages

The loss of local orientated teams where one-stop-shop, end-to-end delivery can happen leads to a loss of local autonomy and control, especially when speedy decisions need to be made. Should subsequent problems arise, then it can be difficult for customers' issues to be resolved quickly. Turnaround completion times can be extended due to numerous hand-offs that may arise between the various steps of the process. In the centralized model, if errors or service failures occur, it can take time to track down precisely where the mistakes happened and subsequently it can take longer to rework the process. Centralized models can lead to bureaucracy and to lack of individual authority, which in turn can cause low morale within a command-and-control culture. The key to successful deployment of a centralized back-office model is to ensure the customer journey remains at the heart of the model, that the end-to-end process is centralized and that the culture of the retail bank is fully aligned with the future centralized model for operations.

ACTIVITY 4.2

Retail banks can manage costs through a variety of measures:

- What challenges would a retail bank face in deploying a programme of process team efficiencies and a review of spans and layers at the same time?
- Identify the benefits and shortcomings of the centralized model for retail banking operations.
- How did technology enable the growth in centralized back-office processing?
- Consider your own organization and how reorganization has led to cost savings within your business.

Offshoring retail operations

Building upon the UK centralized back-office processing model and the creation of UK call centres, the next phase in the late 1990s and early 2000s was to take retail banking operations global. Retail banks were unsurprisingly attracted by potential further cost savings of approximately 40 per cent (Independent, 2011). Retail banks simply could not ignore the opportunity to offshore their operations to Far East locations such as India and the Philippines. The primary objective was to build on the already centralized back-office and telephony operations model, but now was the time to capitalize upon wage arbitrage benefits and operations capacity management techniques to maximize efficiencies from economies of scale.

However, from the beginning, customers were suspicious and concerned, particularly in the call-handling aspect of retail banking operations. Matters became worse when stories emerged in the media of Indian call centre staff adopting English names, referring to the 'local' weather and being able to reference anything from what had happened recently in the UK soap operas to quoting the most recent football results.

Some banks took a no-offshoring stance for call centre operations from the start and played it back as a marketing competitive strength – RBS and NW led a marketing campaign that made it abundantly clear that all contact centres were domained in the UK. However, banks still extensively used offshoring teams to conduct back-office process activities on their behalf.

Advantages

Simple processes can be executed extremely well by offshore processing and call centres. Retail banks can reduce their costs significantly by utilizing the skills and services of colleagues in offshore locations. Transferral of UK back-office processing centres has been relatively problem free, with virtually no adverse media coverage. As long as the process being migrated offshore is clearly articulated, the inputs and outputs are understood, and the entire end-to-end process is migrated, then there is no reason why the offshoring model should not work. Retail banks can still make significant cost savings by offshoring their UK back-office operations. Telephony and customer contact is different. Stereotypes have been formed and it is a difficult position for UK retail banks to recover from.

Disadvantages

One of the major barriers to successful implementation of offshoring telephony-based activities is overcoming language and cultural barriers. This is discussed more fully in Chapter 6.

Santander announced in the summer of 2011 that it was creating 500 new jobs in the UK as it planned to return its India-based call centre operations to the UK. The decision was taken following adverse feedback from customers which cited the offshored business as the number one area of Santander customer dissatisfaction (BBC News, 2011). In addition, Santander confirmed that the anticipated benefits from offshoring had failed to fully materialize. Specifically, the cost of premises, exchange rate volatility and labour costs had continued to rise, making the benefits profile significantly lower than originally anticipated.

Divesting non-core businesses

Divesting is the process of removing or availing an organization of a specific activity or business division. Core businesses lie at the heart of what the organization is about and are central to the way in which it makes its money. **Non-core** businesses on the other hand are add-on businesses that, whilst perhaps being complementary to the core business, are actually additional to the company's primary operations. Following well-publicized troubles in 2014 when the discount supermarkets such as Lidl and Aldi stole market share, Tesco commenced an aggressive programme of divesting non-core businesses. In early 2016 Tesco sold off the Giraffe restaurant chain, quickly followed by Dobbies garden centres and then the disposal of coffee shop chain Harris & Hoole to Café Nero in 2016. The most recent divestment by Tesco has seen the supermarket giant sell off its in-store opticians to Vision Express (Hopkins, 2016; Cox, 2017).

Divestment The action of selling off or disowning subsidiary business interests.

Non-core Not being part of the centre or foundations of a business.

In a similar vein and from a retail bank's point of view, divesting non-core businesses relates to any activities that do not relate to banking in the primary market within which the bank operates, for example, divesting an insurance brokerage business.

In good times and periods of growth, retail banks (like the supermarkets) diversified their business into lots of other non-core income-generating activities such as life assurance and general insurance and into many non-core geographic locations, particularly the countries in emerging economies in Asia.

Divestment of non-core businesses occurs when banks look to retrench and narrow their business focus to enable them to give all their attention to core products and geographic markets – in activities that they know exceptionally well. Accordingly, they look to remove products, activities, and sometimes both, from their existing portfolio that do not relate to their core business. In doing so, the organization generates income from the sale of the divested business and reduces their operating costs, though it should be recognized that they subsequently forego the income that had been previously derived from the divested business. This will have a consequential impact upon the income side of the cost: income ratio. In deciding whether or not to divest, banks need to weigh up the impact of reducing costs and gaining capital against the loss of income generation from the non-core asset. Consider the below examples to illustrate this point:

1 In 2012, HSBC completed two major divestments to enable it to focus upon its primary business. French insurer, AXA Group, bought HSBC general insurance businesses in Hong Kong, Singapore and Mexico, whilst Hang Seng purchased similar businesses in Argentina. The combined sale generated almost $900m for HSBC. Chief Executive Stuart Gulliver said, 'It will enable us to focus our capital and resources on the growth of our core businesses, including the building of our broader wealth management capabilities' (BBC News, 2012a). In this case, divestment has enabled HSBC to retain its focus on its core domestic market and to generate sufficient funding to exploit the wealth management segment.

2 In a more recent non-core asset sale, Barclays sold its entire loss-making Italian business of 85 branches to Mediobanca for a loss of £258m. Chief Executive Jes Staley said: 'Accelerating the rundown of Barclays non-core is a key part of our strategy to close the gap between the group's returns and those in our strong core business' (Shapland, 2016). Barclays made a loss on the deal, but it was still the right thing to do for the organization. Barclays offloaded an under-performing 'asset' so that it could focus upon its traditional market, rather than be distracted with running operations elsewhere in central Europe.

3 Insurance company Direct Line (who also owned Churchill, Green Flag and Privilege insurance) was divested by RBS in 2014 (BBC News, 2012b; Grierson, 2012). Citizens Bank in the United States was another significant disposal that happened in 2015 (BBC News, 2015). Both divestments were made in an attempt to restore the bank's capital position. Though both respective businesses were profitable, they were seen as non-core businesses. In the case of Direct Line, RBS was offloading non-core general insurance products from its portfolio, and in the case of Citizens Bank, it was outside the geographic scope of RBS's traditional core UK domestic market.

   In this case, RBS needed to restore its precarious capital position. This led RBS to dispose of two perfectly well-performing non-core businesses, so that the bank could improve its capital reserves position, whilst simultaneously enabling the organization to spend more time focusing upon its core domestic banking activities. From an investor's perspective, however, the question is whether the divestment of performing assets may be seen as short-termism and that perhaps in the long run it would have been more prudent to hold on to performing assets that would have continued to add shareholder value, even though they might be perceived as non-core businesses.

Advantages

Divesting non-core businesses can generate large amounts of capital relatively quickly, though the timing of the disposal is key to generating returns on investment. If timed well, not only can capital gains be made, but almost immediately the ongoing operational costs can be removed from the cost side of the cost-to-income equation. Further, by removing non-core businesses from the organizational structure, the company can focus a greater amount of time on the markets and products that it knows best. Distractions are removed.

Non-core divestment should be considered when a retail bank needs funding to manage its core operations and to expand into markets that it believes to be core to its future success. If a bank is in a precarious position financially, it can raise capital through the sale of a non-core business. If a non-core business is struggling and is beginning to drain other resources within the parent organization, then divestment, even at a loss, may well be the right thing to do.

Disadvantages

Divestment of non-core business usually happens after a blip in the performance of the parent business. The problem can then be selling the asset at a fair and reasonable price. As the market becomes aware of any impending problems facing the parent company, so realizing the maximum value for the asset in troublesome times can be difficult. The extent of the financial position faced by the parent company will determine whether the disposal realizes a good market price or if it is treated as a fire sale. The danger here is that well-performing assets are offloaded in the myopic desire of the parent company to return to core business only. Irrational decisions can be made as desperation creeps in.

Branch closures

The traditional cornerstone of retail banking, the branch network was once seen as the very physical embodiment of a bank's power and security. The main players held prominence in every high street and every community, with commanding sandstone buildings decorated with pillars and towers, providing public reassurance of the institution's strength and stability. But in recent times all has changed for the branch network. Some would argue that the demise of branches has been a long time coming, with many outlets failing to turn sufficient profit to afford to keep the lights on, let alone pay for the substantial number of staff that reside within them. The European Banking Federation reported that 9,100 branches were closed during 2016, bringing the total number of branches closed since 2008 to a staggering 48,000 (around a 20 per cent reduction). The report also highlights how this can have a direct impact on the cost-to-income ratio, stating, 'With many customers embracing electronic payments and digital and mobile banking and interest rates at rock bottom, banks have slashed their costly brick-and-mortar outlets to save costs' (Rumney, 2017).

Sale and leaseback – capital generation and cost impact

Retail banks have traditionally held much of their capital in their physical branch premises, their operational centres and their head office buildings. The process of **sale and leaseback** enables retail banks to relinquish tied-up capital and enable funding of other retail bank initiatives, or to simply hold more capital reserves. Whilst the process of selling off property assets is a great way to generate liquid capital, there is a consequence. The consequence is that the subsequent lease-back agreement will add cost to the bottom line of the retail banks' business activities. Whilst selling off assets such as premises can therefore generate much-needed liquidity at times where funding is limited, this will add cost to the retail bank.

To complement Lloyds Bank's future programme of 200 branch closures, saving £400m per year, Lloyds created two sale and leaseback deals in 2016. First was for 44 branches that were sold to Aprirose for £39.5m in 2016 and the second deal was for a further 40 branches that were sold for £34m. Capital proceeds from the sale enabled Lloyds to reduce the extent of taxpayer ownership of the bank. All branches were agreed to be leased back on 15-year deals (Morgan Pryce, 2017).

Sale and leaseback   The sale of an asset or group of assets, that the seller then immediately rents back from the buyer, thereby raising cash and enabling an allowable tax deduction.

External trends and influences upon customer transactions

Whilst we are aware of the emergence and growth of alternative channels such as call centres and internet banking, retail banks have blamed branch closures squarely on the shoulders of customers who have chosen to defect to other channels. But is this fair? Did customers fall out of favour with branches or were they in fact pushed towards the door? The truth is, it is a bit of both, with a dash of technological innovation added in for good measure.

By being provided with an increased range of distribution channels customers were empowered to transact as they wished. Retail banks in the late 1980s extolled the virtues of 'Martini Banking', a term synonymous with the alcoholic beverage of the same era that promoted the rather catchy strapline, 'any time, any place, anywhere'. Yet perhaps retail banks had a slightly different agenda – it was not simply the wish to provide customers with increased choice that underpinned the business rationale to create new channels. Customers were not defecting in their droves to other financial institutions, nor were they unhappy with the service being provided by their branches. So what then was the underlying reason? Retail banks were well aware of the cost-to-service transaction cost in branches being many times more expensive than that of a call centre, online or through a digital application. Perhaps this is a more logical explanation as to why retail banks sought to create alternative channels in the first place and why front-line staff were actively encouraged to promote the virtues of the Martini banking approach.

The cost per transaction via branch is significantly higher than self-service channels. The overheads associated with running a branch network mean that the cost per transaction is far higher than that of a call centre and even more again than that of digital banking. It is quite simply the case that branches are not a sustainable model for conducting transactions any longer. Branch staff have to be commended for doing a tremendous job of enticing customers away to alternative channels. Indeed, the only reason most people need to go into a branch to transact nowadays is to pay in a cheque and even then there are smart ATMs that can do that for you.

Recent technology developments and social pressures are revolutionizing the traditional way of conducting personal and business transactions by way of cheques. Whilst cheques (as a simple form of Bill of Exchange) were originally seen as an innovative and convenient way of making payments for goods and services, they have also been subject to criticism due to lengthy clearance times and archaic in terms of having to hand write the cheque and to then check off the paid cheques to bank statements and to cheque book stubs. In the digital age, customers demand a quicker and more efficient way of making payments, whilst still enabling traditionalists to use cheques as their transactional medium of choice.

With effect from 30 October 2017, the Cheque and Credit Clearing Company (C&CCC) has launched a multifaceted approach to overhauling the cheque clearance process in the UK.

A phased rollout of new, image-based clearing was introduced where banks can now digitally image cheques and the images can be sent electronically to the originator's bank for settlement within 24 hours.

Customers will not notice much difference, other than the fact that participating banks will enable funds to become available quicker than before – it is anticipated that, 'at some stage in the second half of 2018, all of the UK's banks and building societies will clear all cheques via the Image Clearing System and only then will customers consistently benefit from the faster timescale' (Cheque and Credit Clearing Company, 2017).

Until then, two clearing systems will operate in parallel, which means that some cheques that customers write or pay in will be cleared more quickly via the Image Clearing System, and some will clear to the existing, six-weekday timescale through the paper-based system.

For the time being, customers who continue to write cheques do not need to do anything differently and their cheques can continue to be used in exactly the same manner today as they have been used in the past. Some UK retail banks such as Barclays have tested self-cheque imaging via mobile phone applications, but as yet, none of the major UK retail banks have formally launched a UK self-scanning service for processing cheques.

As far back as 1967, the migration to low-cost alternative channels writing was on the wall. With the creation of the first ATM, customers had their first positive alternative choice for obtaining cash. As reported in *Chartered Banker* (Batiz-Lazo, 2016), 'it was bankers' concerns with rising labour costs that drove the search for a solution'. The important point here is that customers were not looking for an alternative way to gain access to their cash; it was the banks' desire to reduce costs that led to ATM and indeed subsequent channel innovation. As the years rolled by, branches would lie empty, bereft of customers, as cashiers looked out of the windows to see queues at their ATMs. (Bizarrely, in the early 1990s, I can recall our chief clerk suggesting that we shut the ATM at lunchtime so that we could drive some footfall into the branch and sell telephone banking to the customers in order to hit our target number of referrals that had been handed down to us from head office. Complete madness and perhaps an early sign of how targets and sales would ultimately drive the wrong behaviours in bankers in years to come!)

Since the dawn of the ATM, many more new technologies have emerged, all adding to the empowerment of customers and enabling the ease of 'self-serving' their own transactions. Chapter 8 covers the evolution of new technologies in more detail; however, it is fair to say that retail banks have reacted quickly to emerging technologies to develop innovative solutions to meet the needs of customers. The growth in mobile telephony both in terms of the power of mobile devices and the development of the supporting mobile network infrastructure has created a major channel enhancement and opportunity for retail banks to create innovative self-execution of simple transactions for customers. Alternative methods of making payments have also enabled greater customer autonomy, eg PayPal (now owned by eBay) which created a very intuitive customer application to enable payment for goods and services without the need to visit a bank. More recently contactless payments have led to customers flashing their phones at countertop terminals to pay for coffee and newspapers. Though by no means an exhaustive list, all such initiatives have led to less reliance upon branches and indeed less need for transactional banks. The BBA reported that 40 million mobile and internet transactions were conducted each week in 2013, with around 1,800 transactions per minute being conducted via smartphones (Hyde, 2014).

In 2015, *Chartered Banker* magazine reported that spending on mobile devices would increase fourfold to £53.6bn by 2024. The subsequent impact upon sales is even more dramatic – doubling to £112bn, which would equate to an additional demand of 30,000 stores, rising to 48,000 in the next decade (Chartered Banker, 2015).

The costs to service customer transactions per channel are noted below and this helps us understand why retail banks led the charge to encourage customers to use alternatives to branches to complete transactions (CEB TowerGroup, 2012):

- call centre $4.04;
- branch $4.00;
- ATM $0.61;
- mobile $0.19;
- online $0.09.

Prima facie, it would therefore seem that simply moving transactions from branches to lower-cost alternatives would in itself provide the justification and impetus that would lead to many branch closures, but it is not quite as simple as that. There are two main challenges that retail banks face in addressing the drive to migrate transactions to low-cost channel alternatives.

First is recognition that many of the transactions conducted via mobile and online banking are additional transactions and not direct replacements, ie over-and-above transactions that arise due to the convenience of the user interface, rather than direct substitute transactions from branch-based activity. The relationship between the channels is not always direct, so modelling the potential cost savings is not always accurate and can only truly be realized when branch closures and human resources savings actually happen.

Second is the offsetting of branch closures against the potential to drive income from the customer base. Whilst the cost savings that can be achieved from closing branches and making staff reductions can be substantial, consideration has to be given to the impact side of the cost-to-income ratio when taking such a drastic step. The cost savings from branch closures have to exceed the income that could have been generated and that may well be lost from the customers affected by the retail bank branch closures. Cutting costs through branch closures may have a quick impact on the cost side of the cost-to-income ratio, but the loss of potential income for years to come may well mean that they are more advantageous to hold on to.

Deloitte reports that the average branch closure generates £200,000 in cost savings and when extrapolated up to a branch closure programme of 500 outlets, this would lead to savings of around £100m a year. On the cost side, this is a substantial number, but it has to be considered in the wider context of the cost-to-income ratio – eg the equivalent income requirement would be a 100 basis point interest margin on a deposit book of £10bn [to create £100m of income] therefore the retail bank needs to weigh up the potential costs savings through branch closures vs income potential that could come from the savers that have invested money in the bank (Deloitte, 2014).

As transactions continue to migrate to lower-cost channels, the need to retain as many branches has fallen drastically. In many cases it is far easier to realize cost savings through reducing staff numbers and branches, rather than to try to derive more income from a stagnant marketplace. This has been exacerbated further by current market conditions, which means that making 100 basis points interest margin on deposits to derive such an income stream is particularly difficult at times where bank base rates have been held at 0.5 per cent or lower since March 2009 (Bank of England, 2017).

Branches may well still have a role to play in the future of retail banking and that will be discussed in chapters yet to come, but there is no getting away from the fact that 2,000 outlets have closed in the UK since 2010 and we can expect more closures still to come (Wallace, 2015).

RBS continues to perceive branch closures as an essential part of its cost-cutting programme. Chief Executive Ross McEwan confirmed this to the BBC:

the cuts will be 'huge, and unfortunately there will be job losses amongst that. Branches have been closing and will continue to close. The shape of a branch is changing, and what people do in a branch is changing.' McEwan plans to cut £750m of costs this year (BBC News, 2017; Stephanou, 2017).

Advantages

Branch closures are a very public sign of a cost reduction programme that is being implemented by a retail bank. By closing retail branches, banks can realize substantial amounts of money through a variety of means. First, if the retail bank premises are owned, then capital gains can be achieved through the sale of the commercial property. Second, the operational costs associated with running the branch will also be saved (rates, heating, lighting, etc), and finally, the associated staff costs are relinquished. Retail banks have witnessed mass migration of transactions to alternative channels, meaning that the nature and design of the branches of the past are no longer needed today. Irrespective of how or why customers moved to alternative channels, retail banks no longer need to have prime retail assets tied up to meet customers' transactional needs. From a shareholders' point of view, it is quite simply poor use of capital to have scarce sources of capital funding tied up in assets that are effectively non-performing or are being underutilized. That is not to say that retail bank branches are dead – far from it – but they will more likely exist in a completely different configuration to serve the future needs of customers and they will be radically redesigned to become the branch of the future.

Disadvantages

Branch closures are contentious and emotional – especially when many retail banks are adopting a similar approach to reduce their branch networks at the same time. The impact on small communities can be devastating, with the loss of the last bank in town leading to some people effectively becoming cut off from being able to conduct banking activities. Retail banks need to take the long-term view, taking into account the potential loss of future income, before implementing their branch closure programmes. The negative public reaction to branch closures needs to be managed carefully and sensitively in order to mitigate brand damage. However, it is important to provide context here. It is not only banks that are vacating the high street. The digital age has already caused electrical stores (for example Comet), music stores (for example HMV) and travel agents (such as Thomas Cook) to all vacate retail premises throughout the UK.

Other costs

As we have seen, there are many ways in which retail banks can reduce their operational costs. In addition to the strategies presented above, there are many more tactical, specific cost savings that retail banks can make, for example closer management and control of day-to-day staff expenses, such as restricting travel and increasing use of audio/video conferencing. Management of suppliers is another area where significant cost savings can be made. An efficient, well-managed procurement process can often bring additional savings to banks, where not only the product or service in question can be improved, but the price could be better too.

Whilst reducing spend on sponsorship and marketing activities, retail banks need to be cautious not to impact customers in an adverse manner. In late 2013, Coutts Bank decided to withdraw the annual issue of leather-bound diaries to their customers. This created a major customer revolt and led to Coutts having to swiftly renege on their intention to withdraw their diaries (Arnold, 2014).

Costs summary

Retail banks have many opportunities to save costs, from very small right the way through to the huge cost savings that can be derived through organizational redesign. What is important is for retail banks to engender a culture of ongoing cost control and cost management. Everyone is accountable for every penny spent in the organization within which they work. Ask yourself every day, if it was your money, would you spend it in the way you propose to? Retail banks have to actively seek out wasteful activities and behaviours and eliminate them. They need to identify manual, labour-intensive processes and automate them. They should also look at the customer journey and simplify the end-to-end experience from a customer perspective and remove activities that add no value. There is a perception that reducing costs means reducing people in retail banking and, whilst partly true, not all costs are people related. What we have to focus on is reducing people costs that are associated with non-value-adding activities and then redirect our resources to activities where true value lies.

Costs are a fundamental part of running any business, not least a retail bank. It is our responsibility to ensure we control our day-to-day costs and expenses in line with our plans to drive income. Certain costs have to be incurred to grow the business, but we have to ensure all plans to drive income have a fair representation of the costs involved so that we continually focus and balance both sides of the cost-to-income ratio prudently.

ACTIVITY 4.3

- Consider the current cost-cutting strategies being deployed within your own bank. Identify two strategies that focus upon reducing costs, eg centralization, restructuring, offshoring, divestment and branch closures.

- What operational costs are being impacted? Eg human resources, operational costs or technological costs.

- What are the immediate benefits to the retail banks and what if any long-term implications might this have upon the organization?

- What alternatives do you think your bank could have considered as a way to impact the cost-to-income ratio and why?

Retail banking strategies for managing income

This section retains focus upon retail banks, how they manage their income today and how they will make money in the future. It is important to be aware that investment and commercial banks such as Morgan Stanley generate revenues through a variety of other means such as investment banking advice, brokerage and asset management. Goldman Sachs support clients with trading stocks, bonds, commodities and currencies.

Retail banking products and design

Retail banking products are generally straightforward and form basic functions to meet the needs of retail banking customers.

Retail banking products

Current accounts – used to make payments through a variety of convenient methods such as debit card, cheque book, standing orders and direct debits. Interest is seldom paid. Overdraft facilities are available if needs be.

Savings accounts – a safe place to put money aside for a future large purchase or investment.

Credit cards – a convenient way to make payments for goods and services at home and abroad. Interest-free periods of up to 54 days would be the norm at which time the entire balance should be repaid, otherwise debit interest rates would apply to any outstanding balance.

Personal loans – unsecured personal loans of up to £25,000 can be granted subject to affordability, to enable personal purchase of items such as cars, home improvements and holidays.

Mortgages – home purchase loans, typically taken out over a period of 25 years or more, mortgages are secured against the property, thus alleviating some of the risk that the lender faces. That said, no amount of security ever makes a bad lending proposition good.

Retail banking products are that simple. Fundamentally, there is nothing much between them. The core facets will always be generic and will always at their core be similar; however, the bells and whistles that product designers can attach such as incentives, interest rates, fees and value add-ons can all determine which products achieve 'Best Buy' status. Retail banks can flex the different components of product design in the same way as a graphic equalizer is used to delicately manage the sound output for a music system – but they cannot deliver all the benefits to all customers all of the time, otherwise there would be no profit margin to be had. It comes down to the desired market positioning and the offer that each of the respective retail banks wants to make to customers. Go high on interest payments, go low on add-ons. Go high on customer service, go low on interest offers. The choices are almost endless, and it falls to each and every retail bank to make their respective decision as to which product attributes it wants to major on and what customer segments it wants to target. This will determine how the product should be priced and positioned and, most importantly of all, how much income the product will generate for the retail bank.

Product design governance

Retail bank products are overseen by the Financial Services Conduct Authority with key product design features being governed via a series of modular handbooks, the most relevant being the *Banking Code of Business Standards* (BCOBS). The Code covers guidance on many aspects of product design including how firms should explain the applicable interest rate, how banks should use clear language that avoids the use of jargon, and ethical principles about being fair to customers including the provision of post-purchase cooling-off periods. Further handbooks covering the insurance and mortgage parts of banking are also part of the consolidated FCA Handbook.

> **REGULATION**
>
> For updates on the FCA Handbook and component sourcebooks, check here:
> https://www.handbook.fca.org.uk/handbook

Product innovation – individual retail bank competitive advantage vs collaborative mass-market progression

Product innovation is one way that retail banks can attract new customers and obtain vital market share within the competitive retail banking marketplace. One such way to do this is by capitalizing on evolving and emerging technologies, integrating them within retail banking products. To do so as an early adopter could generate competitive advantage, though achieving long-term sustainable competitive advantage is a different matter altogether. In July 2015, the contactless system provided by Apple Pay was introduced in the UK, enabling customers to make transactions via their smartphone and without physically having to use their contactless cards. At the time of launch, many banks worked together to help deliver Apple Pay to the mass market – no single bank was able to command uniqueness or competitive advantage. NatWest, Royal Bank of Scotland, Nationwide, Santander, Ulster Bank, MBNA and American Express all came to market on the opening day to create a collaborative approach to help launch Apple Pay progressively and seamlessly to the UK general public – irrespective of which retail bank they held their account with (Williams, 2015).

Product innovation cost vs benefit of proposition

Product development is costly, not only in terms of the investment creating new products; the associated marketing budgets required to bring new, innovative products to market adds further costs. All associated costs of developing products, including promotion, marketing, on-boarding and managing the accounts thereafter have to be considered when weighing up the value the new product will bring to the retail bank. The proposition needs to be unique enough and not readily copiable so as to deliver a sustainable competitive advantage and therefore a valuable income stream for the retail bank.

Advantages

Product innovation can lead to gains in market share and ultimately increased income and profitability. Retail bank brand value can be enhanced through successfully bringing new products to market. Banks that can align their products to the changing needs of the external environment, such as adapting to new technologies and aligning with social changes, are best placed to be successful. Conversely, misinterpreting the external market will lead to loss of early adoption benefits and may be difficult to recover from.

Disadvantages

Retail bank products are readily copiable, with no real opportunities to hold patents and copyrights over the intellectual property that underpins the product design. This means that for the early adopters, they carry the risk of the new product failing to achieve its intended market success (as well as the potential rewards). Even if the product is a success, there are very few, if indeed any, barriers that prevent the competition from being able to mimic the product. The costs of later entry will be far lower than that of the original innovating bank. Furthermore, any foibles that have emerged in the early adoption stage can be avoided by the followers.

Interest rate margins

How banks make money through interest rates

Banks traditionally derive most of their income through the difference between the interest they pay to customers for their deposits and the interest that they charge borrowers for loans and advances. This is known as **net interest margin** (NIM). The NIM is therefore the gap where banks realize their interest earnings. Whether market rates are high or low, it makes no real difference to banks; what matters is the differential between what interest is earned and what interest is paid out. NIM spread is therefore critical to a bank's profitability.

> **Net interest margin**   The difference between the interest income made by banks (usually on loans and advances) and the amount of interest paid out (to their depositors and lenders).

When market interest rates rise, the bank funding costs also rise (including the costs of interest payments payable on deposits) therefore there is not always a direct correlation between higher interest rate and higher interest rate margins. Another key dynamic is the phasing or time differential that exists between the typical repayment period of loans versus the anticipated call period for customer deposits to be repaid. Banks will usually make loans that have a longer maturity period than that of the deposits that they hold on behalf of customers.

In times of low market interest rates, you would be forgiven for thinking that banks would struggle to achieve sufficient NIM to survive, but that is not quite the case. In practical terms, as market interest rates get closer to zero, banks find themselves in a quandary – deposits still need to have interest paid (though there are cases of negative interest rates being charged for deposits in developed countries such as Germany) which means the NIM will narrow and the only way to expand the gap is through flexing and increasing the loan and advances interest rate side of the equation.

Managing interest rate income following the global banking crisis

At the peak of the global banking crisis, the swap rate (which measures the cost to banks) was 5.26 per cent, whilst the mortgage rate was 6.08 per cent – the spread or margin equalling the difference between the two being 0.82 percentage points. Within a year of the banking crisis the margin had almost trebled to 2.43 percentage points (swap rate for fixed-rate deals dropping to 3.29 per cent with average mortgage rate falling marginally to 5.72 per cent). This means that the bank's profitability on fixed-rate home loan advances had increased threefold (Winnett and Wallop, 2009). Customer perceptions following the massive investment of taxpayers' money would have been that any and all potential savings would have been passed on to customers; however, in reality banks were not passing on the benefits to customers, preferring instead to either withdraw from the mortgage market completely or to try to recoup losses of the past and/or offset and offer higher savings rates through the enhanced NIM they could achieve post-crisis.

Whilst previously high-interest-rate loans will have been replaced with lower-rate loans, the cost of funding has been exceptionally low, with some savings accounts, such as HSBC's Flexible Saver Account, offering depositors 0.01 per cent interest (HSBC, 2017).

In the United States, J P Morgan Chase reported that the NIM during the period 2005–2010 averaged 2.95 per cent, yet in 2014, six years after the banking crisis, the NIM had narrowed to 2.18 per cent. The sensitivity of the spread was highlighted by the stark fact that if the NIM could expand by just half a per cent, this would lead to an increase in J P Morgan's earnings of $10bn (Economist, 2015).

The movement of low market interest rates to higher interest rates brings a further threat to retail banks – especially after a sustained period of low interest rates. Whilst it is tempting for banks to maximize the NIM when market rates rise, the process of doing so needs to be managed carefully and sensitively. If customers have been borrowing on a variable interest rate product, they may well struggle to meet the increased payments that higher interest rates will inevitably bring. Borrowing customers have enjoyed low interest rates since the banking crisis of 2008, but the days of low interest rates will not go on forever and customers and banks need to prepare for the upturn in market interest rates that will inevitably come in the future. High interest rates do not necessarily mean good news for banks – managing loan defaults, making provisions and impairments for doubtful debts and dealing with subsequent bad debts are not what retail banks want.

Advantages

The spread of net interest margin is fundamental to how retail banks generate profits. It is the expression of the difference between the average interest charged to borrowers versus the average interest paid out to depositors. NIM exists whether market rates are high or low, so there is always the opportunity for banks to make money. It's just a question of the extent of the scale of the margin. Retail banks can choose where they price their product range and accordingly they are in control of the NIM spread that they offer. Banks that offer market-leading interest rates will have finer margins (aiming to attract greater market share), whilst other banks will have broader NIM, but may well struggle to acquire market share.

Disadvantages

NIM changes relatively slowly, but banks need to constantly monitor the marketplace, delicately reviewing, adjusting and balancing their exposure and potential movement of their variable market interest rate deposits and against the range of fixed-rate savings and loan products that they have in their portfolio. Should market interest rates rise rapidly, banks may be left with an array of fixed-rate products that could move from being profit generating for the bank to being a cost.

Fee income

Whilst interest margin has been the foundation upon which retail banks have generated income in the past, increasing fee income has become a primary source of revenue for banks. Fees or commission payments exist in two main forms. The first is purchase fees (or commission payments) for a service or product that customers wish to purchase, and the second is penal fees that relate to breach of a contractual agreement between the retail bank and its customers.

Purchase fees

Purchase fees relate to the up-front and ongoing fees, charges or commission earnings that retail banks earn from the sale of financial products. All fees, charges and commission earnings should be clearly stated prior to the customer signing the agreement form.

1 *Packaged current accounts* – in the mid-1990s, a new current account phenomenon began and swept across retail banking in the UK: packaged current accounts. For payment of a regular monthly fee, current account holders were offered (though this is not an exhaustive list) myriad benefits including free annual travel insurance, mobile phone insurance, extended warranty on electrical goods, lost key insurance, car breakdown cover, a lost card protection service, airport travel lounge access, and 2 for 1 sports and adventure activities.

   Traditional current accounts enabled customers to make payments through a variety of means such as cheque, debit card, standing order and direct debit. Customers would typically have their regular salary paid into their current account and the balance would inevitably drop on a monthly basis, as mortgages and bills were paid, with surplus current account balances being moved elsewhere to attract better rates of interest. Typically, balances would fall almost to zero before the monthly cycle began again. From a retail bank's perspective, traditional current accounts cost money to operate. Processing transactions costs banks money, producing cheque books and cards costs banks money, opening branches costs money, yet the banks were determined to keep the image of free banking. The only opportunity to make money from traditional current accounts was via the NIM, yet the opportunities to do so were very limited as the balances held in current accounts were usually very low. The desire was to build on and turn the traditional current account into a mass-market, regular fee-income-generating machine. However, there had to be a perceived value-add for the customer, hence where the variety of innovative 'benefits' came from. Through intensive marketing and staff sales incentive schemes, retail banks embarked upon mass-conversion programmes to transition as many traditional current account customers over to packaged accounts as possible. Every 100,000 traditional current account customers that a retail bank could convert to a packaged current account would generate £0.5m per month of additional revenue for the bank. The net profit would come from the degree to which customers would go on to use the packaged benefits.

With hues not dissimilar to the mis-selling of Payment Protection Insurance, almost two decades on, the package account is under severe scrutiny by City watchdogs. The undertones of bank greed, selling inappropriate products, not being honest, not disclosing that cheaper products were available, aggressive sales targets and incentivizing staff to sell all give rise to the concern that packaged accounts could be the next PPI. Customers are raising many concerns about mis-selling, citing the inability to use certain 'benefits' of the package account, concerns that they never actually signed up for a packaged account, and in some instances that they cancelled the packaged account but it was never converted back to a traditional current account. At the time of writing, the Financial Ombudsman Service receives 1,000 new complaints about packaged accounts each week.

Packaged accounts, which were intended to be an income-generating product, may well become the next PPI headache for retail banks. With PPI claims set to cease in the summer of 2019, expect the new claims businesses to move on and turn their attentions to packaged accounts and the refunding of fees.

2 *General insurance* – since the mid-1980s general insurance products such as car, travel, house buildings and house contents insurance have been made available via retail banks. Retail banks focused upon cross-selling insurance products within branches as they earned a **brokerage** commission payment from the underwriting insurance company for every policy that was taken out by the customers. This was a valuable source of additional income for retail banks and was essentially risk-free. Insurance policy commission earnings were not only profitable to retail banks, but had no impact upon interest margins – all earnings went straight to the bottom line of profitability. Furthermore, the insurance company that was underwriting the policy carried all the risk should there be any subsequent claims made.

Brokerage   Providing a service or introduction that generates fee income.

3 *Life assurance* – in a similar vein, in the late 1980s banks acted as introducers to large life assurance companies. Many retail banks forged tied arrangements with specific life assurance organizations, for example, Bank of Scotland with Standard Life. This meant that whenever a mortgage lending product was sold by the bank, the adviser could introduce the life assurer to arrange a repayment product (for interest-only mortgages and life cover to protect the customer, should the work happen to protect the mortgage advance for the lifetime of the loan). This became another fruitful non-interest-earning aspect of retail bank earnings. The role of the tied life assurance company partnership expanded further in the late 1990s to include the provision of investment advice and personal pension planning. This led to even more commission earnings for retail banks, with seemingly no to little risk attached for the retail banks. The selling of life assurance-related products had become a primary source of income for retail banks. Yet by 1998, tied relationships were beginning to prove troublesome as the arrangements restricted banks from being able to offer better products from other organizations. Bank of Scotland sought to get around the tied relationship through the creation of their own independent life insurance company to work around the Financial Service Act legislation (Verity, 1998).

4 *Payment Protection Insurance (PPI)* – linked to the sale of both secured mortgages and unsecured personal loans and credit cards, PPI was designed with very good intentions in mind – to help customers repay indebtedness should they be unable to repay the loan due to illness, unemployment or death. After all, the customer would go on to insure the asset they buy, whether it be a home, a holiday or a car, so why should they not insure the debt that they were taking on? Surely that would make sense. Furthermore, all aspects of the associated insurance, interest payable, any arrangement fees and the annual percentage rate payable had to be transparently detailed on the Consumer Credit Act paperwork before being signed. Line by line, all aspects of the loan had to be detailed. On the face of it, PPI was a good product, if it was sold to those customers who genuinely had a need for it. But here begins the rub. PPI was extremely lucrative for retail banks, generating significantly more commission earnings than any of the general insurance products. Consequently, the income that could be generated from selling PPI led to the emergence of pan-industry sales malpractices. Blinded by the potential of dazzling profits, senior management led the charge through incentivization of retail bank staff to sell PPI. Greed overtook trust and ethics. Customers

were no longer thoroughly assessed for PPI eligibility and suitability. During the late 1980s and 1990s, weekly tracking of PPI to loans sold became the dominant metric in many retail banks. If numbers were not achieved, consequences would follow – not least cash bonuses would be lost. Staff tea room leader boards became commonplace to show sales performance; humiliation and retraining would follow if your respective numbers were not up to scratch and you didn't want to let your team down. Inappropriate behaviours crept into all areas of retail banking that would ultimately lead to the PPI bubble bursting. Various innovative tactics were deployed by salespeople, including suggesting to customers that their loan application would be more likely to succeed with the insurance added than without it. In other cases, PPI was not even mentioned and would simply be assumptively sold and added to the loan documentation. From personal experience, I can even recall some call centre staff deliberately incorrectly keying personal loan applications so that they would be declined by the system, rather than achieve a perfectly good loan sale without PPI. To do so otherwise would have been detrimental to the call centre operators' PPI to loans sold statistics. More madness, but poorly thought out performance measures inevitably drive weird behaviours.

It would be almost a decade later that the issue of mis-selling PPI would truly come back to bite the retail banks. In 2008 the catalyst was a report issued by consumer group Which? that reported that one in three PPI customers may never be able to make a claim. The report went on to add, 'If you have a loan and think you might have been mis-sold PPI, now's the time to fight back. Compensation could be just a letter away' (Which? 2008). In the summer of 2008, the Financial Ombudsman formally requested the Financial Services Authority to investigate how banks were handling PPI-related complaints. In October 2008 Alliance & Leicester (£7m) became the first of many retail banks to be fined for mis-selling PPI.

Between 1990 and 2010, £44bn of PPI policies were sold, though the actual extent of mis-sold policies is unknown (Dunkley, 2016). Most current figures show that a total of £250.5m was paid in July 2017 to customers who complained about the way they were sold payment protection insurance, bringing the amount repaid since January 2011 to £27.9bn (FCA, 2017). Almost three-quarters of all PPI policies have now been repaid.

Whilst in many cases PPI may well have been entirely appropriate for some customers, the understandable uproar and furore that has taken place since 2008 has been overwhelming. For retail banks the PPI scandal has been devastating, not only in purely monetary terms through refunds that have had to be made, but also for setting up operations to investigate claims and to make the actual refunds themselves.

Another major cost to be considered in the PPI debacle was that of fines levied by the Financial Conduct Authority, the most recent being Lloyds Bank, who received the largest ever retail fine of £117m in June 2015 for failing to treat their customers fairly when handling PPI complaints between March 2012 and May 2013 (FCA, 2015).

PPI, combined with the impact of the financial crisis of 2008, has led to the destruction of trust and confidence in UK retail banks. PPI originally provided a positive additional source of income to banks. It should only ever have been seen as a secondary contributory flow of income but greed set in. PPI became a primary goal, a key performance metric. Customers were abused and in many ways so too were retail bank staff. PPI as a source of income came to an abrupt end and instead became a cost in so many different ways.

ACTIVITY 4.4

PPI mis-selling has eroded customer trust:

- What steps can banks take to rectify the position?
- What lessons has the financial sector in the UK learnt from the PPI experience?
- Are there any other similar PPI-type skeletons in retail bank closets?

Penal fees

One of the most controversial ways of banks making income is through the penalty charges they levy against customers for overdrawing their current accounts or breaching an agreed overdraft facility. The controversy stems from three main areas:

1 Fairness of the charge levied – does the amount of the fee seem to be appropriate for the extent of the breach? In some cases people have been charged £39 for being just £1 over an authorized overdraft limit. The Office of Fair Trading is currently hearing a test case that will ultimately decide whether these charges are, or are not, fair (Lowe, 2018).

2 Extent of the penal charge – does the fee charged accurately reflect the actual cost of the work involved in taking the remedial action? Customers are entitled to value for money and not a punishment levy.

3 The retail bank's ability to take the fee out of the customer's account whether the customer disputes the fee or not.

Whilst penal fees do generate income for UK banks, it should be contextualized that many current account customers in the UK still enjoy free banking. They are able to conduct transactions, make payments in and out of their accounts via debit card, cheque, direct debit or standing order. Further, customers can use digital banking to keep track of their money and use ATMs to get cash 24/7. Branch staff are available for face-to-face discussions and call centre staff are there to support customers too. All for free.

In the United States, penal fees are even more aggressive than in the UK. As well as overdraft fees, fees can be charged if a customer's balance falls below a minimum threshold. Customers also have to pay transaction fees every time they use an ATM owned by a financial institution other than that of the account holding bank.

The big three US banks – J P Morgan Chase, Bank of America and Wells Fargo – earned more than $6.4bn in overdraft and ATM fees in 2016 (up by $300m on 2015 – J P Morgan Chase increased their ATM transaction fees by 50 cents at the end of 2015). This equals around $25 for every adult American (Long, 2017).

US banks also regularly charge a form of purchase fee or 'maintenance fees' just to keep customers' bank accounts open. In 2016 the Big 3 generated a further $2.3bn of revenue from this form of fee.

In summary, income can be generated in several ways, primarily through net interest margin and fees. In practical terms, a review by the Office of Fair Trading (OFT) found that during 2007–2011, banks made an average of £139 per year on each current account (this compared to £152 per account in 2006). Of this, £60 related to net credit interest income and £29 was from unauthorized overdraft fees (Oxlade, 2013). Whilst overdraft fees had fallen and saved customers £928m, the OFT still believes that charging structures remain too complex.

How banks will make money in the future

Retail banks need to actively look for innovative ways to identify and create sources of income. Traditional interest earnings will continue to provide a good and consistent source of revenue, but with continued low rates and increased competition, the spread of the net interest margin is more likely to narrow than open, thus limiting the opportunity to make extremely large profits from deposits and advances. Fees will continue to provide complementary income for banks; however, banks need to charge fairly and see that customers get value for money from the services provided. In the Santander 123 case study that follows, you will learn how banks have to react to customer needs and feedback, be agile to adjust their pricing policy, and dynamic to change the design components of the products. Bankers must resist the temptation to charge exorbitant purchase and penal fees. The impact of all pricing decisions should not only be assessed against value to the organization's bottom line, but against the potential impact upon customers. As we have seen, failure to do so may lead to short-term revenues, but ultimately long-term reputational damage, litigation and compensation.

ACTIVITY 4.5

Generating income is a fundamental part of running a business:

- What innovative ways has your organization identified to drive income?

- Explain the advantages and disadvantages of taking an innovative approach to drive new forms of income streams.

- Is there any threat of future reputational damage from new income-generating activities that are happening today?

Speed with which banks can change to meet customer needs

Banks, like any other retail organization, have to be able to adapt to changes in social interests, technology enhancements, changes in the economy and turbulence in the political arena. Further, they have to be able to adjust and adapt to the immediate pressures of the competitive environment – to respond to the threat of new entrants as well as the moves made by the existing players as they all strive for market dominance. Banks are typically embroiled in internal governance and policy forums. Decision making can be complex, committee-based and cumbersome, often with management layers trying to add value and pre-empt the views of the senior management. The process of bringing new products to market is not typically slick or dynamic. Banks can, however, still choose the pace at which they wish to evolve and change and they can prioritize where they wish to invest their financial and human resources. Different markets offer different opportunities and banks can choose which opportunities they want to take the lead on, which they want to follow and which they want to avoid altogether. As we will see in the case study that follows, some banks act opportunistically, ready to strike when an opportunity arises. Others wait, stealthily considering their position, but nonetheless fully aware of what is going on and perhaps are happy to follow.

Then there is the counter-reaction strategy; when customers defect due to a change in bank policy or pricing, the detrimental impact on the organization may lead to a reversal or softening of the bank's position. Banks need to act quickly to avoid haemorrhaging customers. This is precisely what happened with Santander 123 and whilst the organization did not reverse the original increased charges to their flagship product, they instead created a new, aggressively priced 'lite' product. It took six months to bring the defensive (anti-customer defection) strategy Santander 'lite' product to market. Six months is a quick turnaround time when you consider everything Santander had to do. From the initial change in pricing policy of the original 123 product, the organization had to listen to adverse customer feedback and learn from the comments, and they had to watch on as Tesco Bank repriced their competitor product and took market share. Then Santander had to consider product redesign and deal with the complexity of new product integration on the Santander IT systems. The product had to be serviceable in branches, in call centres and over the internet. Both internal communications and product launch via marketing and promotion campaigns all had to be prepared. Six months is an impressive achievement.

CASE STUDY
Santander 123

The following case study combines all facets of retail bank income generation: innovative product design, interest margins and fee income. Santander 123 is one of the most complex and innovative current accounts available in the UK financial marketplace. The fact that 123 is a current account is almost lost in the vast combination of additional benefits and conditions that are wrapped around the core product offering.

Santander 123 was launched in the spring of 2012. The core current account offer includes traditional facilities such as:

- contactless debit card;
- cheque book;
- arranged overdraft facilities;
- set up direct debits and standing orders;
- transfer money and pay bills online including faster payments.

123 specific features:

- provides cashback on your household bills:
    - 1 per cent on water, council tax and Santander mortgage payments;
    - 2 per cent on energy bills; and
    - 3 per cent on phone, broadband, mobile and TV;
- pays interest on credit balances.

Three conditions apply:

- £2 monthly fee;
- £500 minimum pay-in per month (not switched from another Santander account);
- two active direct debits that pay the household bills.

The Santander 123 current account was proclaimed as the saviour of the Santander brand. Seven years ago, against the backdrop of the financial crisis combined with tricky integrations of Alliance & Leicester and Bradford & Bingley, Santander was trailing in the customer services polls, with 62 per cent of customers rating it 'poor'. By August 2015, the success of its highly innovative 123 account meant Santander was near the top of the customer service charts, with 81 per cent now rating it 'great' (Lewis, 2015).

The 123 account initially offered savers extremely good returns on their money. Santander was offering a higher interest rate than almost all savings bonds and ISAs. (Santander had the lowest NIM of all retail banks during the 2012–2014 reporting period covered by the Competition & Markets Authority's Retail Banking Market Investigation report of 14 August 2015.) More than 78,000 current account holders used the Current Account Switching Service (CASS) to move to Santander between April and June 2014 alone (Christie, 2015).

In September 2015, Santander announced (with not a lot of reasoning why) that the monthly fee was to be increased from £2 to £5, with the changes taking effect from January 2016 (Osborne, 2015). Tesco Bank seized the initiative and announced the following day that they would be removing their £5 monthly current account fee for customers that deposited less than the threshold £750 (Lawrie, 2015).

As a result of the proposed increase in monthly fees, the last three months of 2015 saw the number of current account switchers joining Santander fall away dramatically. In July 2016 Santander took remedial action to reinvigorate its 123 product range by introducing a 'lite' 123 account, which charges a £1 monthly fee and entitles customers to cashback and preferential rates, but does not pay interest on credit balances (Boyce, 2016).

Santander is currently offering market-leading interest rates to its customers. At the time of writing, the interest rate on offer was 1.50 per cent AER/1.49 per cent gross (variable) payable on your entire balance up to £20,000 (Santander, 2017). Whilst this is out of sync with the Bank of England base rate (which has been constantly hovering at around 0.25–0.5 per cent for the last decade) Santander must be able to generate sufficient interest margin between its lending products and the aggressively priced 123 current account to ensure there is sufficient margin to turn a profit. Further 123 loss leaders include the payment of cashback incentives to customers who pay their bills through the cashback mechanism. The interest and cashback costs are offset from two main aspects. First is to ensure that substantial monthly inward credits are received in to the customer's bank account. Second is the surety of regular fee income. Whilst the extent of interest payable to customers can fluctuate depending on the daily balance held in the current account, Santander can avoid the complexity of trying to drive interest rate margin income by swapping out the potential for tight interest rate income for a steady flow of fee-based income instead.

Bank accounts can be cloned easily and RBS has created a very similar type of account to Santander. RBS Reward pays 2 per cent cashback on seven types of household bills paid by direct debit. RBS offers a range of cashback accounts: Reward for £2 per month, Reward Silver for £12 per month and Reward Platinum for £25. All offer 2 per cent cashback plus an ever-increasing number of additional lifestyle benefits such as mobile phone insurance, travel insurance and car breakdown cover.

As has been evidenced within the case study, customers are sensitive to the increase in fees and they instantly vote with their feet. If customers feel that fees or increases in fees are unjustified, then they simply walk away. Retail banks have to be extremely cautious when considering revising the pricing strategy for their complex packaged accounts.

Questions

1 What are the cost-to-income implications for introducing an innovative product such as Santander 123?

2 How does the NIM and the monthly fee add value to Santander? What alternative ways of driving income could Santander have considered?

3 How do you think customers reacted when the monthly fees were suddenly increased?

4 What risks does a retail bank face in launching an innovative product?

5 How do you view the opportunistic stance taken by Tesco Bank? Can you compare this to a broad modern-day retail scenario where a competitor has taken advantage of an emerging opportunity?

6 Consider your own bank; what innovative products have been introduced recently? How do you think the pricing (NIM and fee) strategy positions the product and what other benefits exist to entice customers? Do you believe there is a sustainable competitive advantage for this product?

Chapter summary

- Cost-to-income ratios are vital efficiency measures that are used to assess the current and past performance of organizations.

- Retail banks can choose how to deploy a range of strategies to address cost management and to derive income.

- Retail banks are extremely complex businesses and they ebb and flow through periods of growth and retrenchment.

- Retail banks have to adjust to the changing demands of customers and have to respond to the evolution of technology and new social norms.

- For every hard pound earned, the organization has to ensure its costs are not growing at the same rate.

- Taking a myopic view that might generate substantial short-term income, but does not align with what customers need, will only come back to bite you another day.

- Avoid the temptation of trying to take sugar-coated short-cuts to drive income.
- Do not fall into the trap of implementing cost reduction programmes before fully considering the implications to customers in the first instance.
- Retail banking is all about customers and what we do to serve them. Our raison d'être is to serve customers well – nothing short of that will do.
- All plans to reduce costs and generate income must always be considered with the customer in mind. Is what I am planning to do going to adversely impact upon my customers today or in the future? If the answer is maybe or yes, then don't be tempted to do it, even though to do so in the short term might temporarily boost one side of the cost-to-income ratio.

Objective check

1 What are the challenges that retail banks face? How does the cost-to-income ratio help us understand these challenges?

2 How can the cost-to-income ratio be used to explain a retail bank's efficiency?

3 How can you strategically influence the cost and income components of the cost-to-income ratio?

4 How can banks make more income in the future?

5 What are the limitations of some of the strategies deployed by retail banks to influence the cost-to-income ratio?

6 Are banks able to change quickly to meet customer needs? What might stand in the way of fast-paced change?

7 What factors need to be taken into account when considering the cost versus benefit proposition of product innovation in banks?

Further reading

Barclays (nd) Future of cheques: Pay in cheques with your Barclays mobile app [online] https://www.barclays.co.uk/ways-to-bank/mobile-banking-services/future-of-cheques/ [Accessed 23 July 2018]

Boston Consulting Group (2008) Banking on lean advantage [online] https://www.bcg.com/documents/file15159.pdf [Accessed 22 September 2017]

Christie, S (2015) Packaged bank accounts: Could you get a £1,500 refund?, *The Telegraph*, 28 May [online] http://www.telegraph.co.uk/finance/personalfinance/bank-accounts/11630332/Packaged-bank-accounts-could-you-get-a-1500-refund.html [Accessed 7 October 2017]

Deloitte (2011) Shared services handbook: Hit the road [online] https://www2.deloitte.com/content/dam/Deloitte/dk/Documents/finance/SSC-Handbook-%20Hit-the-Road.pdf [Accessed 22 September 2017]

Economist (2013) Administer with care, 29 June [online] https://www.economist.com/news/finance-and-economics/21580164-low-interest-rates-are-squeezing-banks-profits-higher-ones-may-do [Accessed 3 October 2013]

Evans, R (2011) PPI: Timeline of the mis-selling scandal, *The Telegraph*, 5 May [online] http://www.telegraph.co.uk/finance/personalfinance/insurance/incomeprotection/8495161/PPI-timeline-of-the-mis-selling-scandal.html [Accessed 7 October 2017]

Marous, J (2015) Mobile banking usage to double, *The Financial Brand*, 10 August [online] https://thefinancialbrand.com/53431/global-mobile-banking-usage-study/ [Accessed 1 October 2017]

Osborne, H (2012) PPI exposé: How the banks drove staff to mis-sell the insurance, *The Guardian*, 8 November [online] https://www.theguardian.com/money/2012/nov/08/ppi-expose-banks-drove-staff-mis-sell-insurance [Accessed 7 October 2017]

References

Arnold, M (2014) Banks must cut costs but remember what their customers want, *Financial Times* [online] https://www.ft.com/content/a3fbfd2e-5873-11e4-942f-00144feab7de [Accessed 22 September 2017]

Bank of England (2017) Changes in bank rate, minimum lending rate, minimum band 1 dealing rate, repo rate and official bank rate [online] http://www.bankofengland.co.uk/statistics/Documents/rates/baserate.pdf [Accessed 1 October 2017]

Batiz-Lazo, B (2016) The dawn of digital banking, *CB Magazine* [online] https://charteredbankermba.bangor.ac.uk/documents/EF2017CBMagazineApr_May2016lo-res-44-45.pdf [Accessed 1 October 2017]

BBC News (2011) Santander brings call centres back to UK [online] http://www.bbc.co.uk/news/business-14073889 [Accessed 22 September 2017]

BBC News (2012a) HSBC sells off insurance businesses to AXA and QBE, 7 March [online] http://www.bbc.co.uk/news/business-17283134 [Accessed 28 September 2017]

BBC News (2012b) RBS confirms it will sell off Direct Line Insurance, 14 September [online] http://www.bbc.co.uk/news/business-19596192 [Accessed 28 September 2017]

BBC News (2015) RBS sells remaining stake in US bank citizens, 30 October [online] http://www.bbc.co.uk/news/business-34673153 [Accessed 28 September 2017]

BBC News (2017) Royal Bank of Scotland losses more than treble to £7bn [online] http://www.bbc.co.uk/news/business-39074461 [Accessed 28 September 2017]

Boyce, L (2016) Santander launches 123 'lite' current account costing £1 a month to step up its game in the battle for new customers, *This is Money*, 21 July [online] http://www.thisismoney.co.uk/money/saving/article-3697776/Santander-launches-123-lite-current-account-costing-1-month.html [Accessed 1 October 2017]

CEB TowerGroup/PWC (2012) Rebooting the branch: Reinventing branch banking in a multi-channel, global environment [online] https://www.pwc.com/us/en/industries/financial-services/library/viewpoints/reinventing-branch-banking-network.html [Accessed 1 October 2017]

Chartered Banker (2015) Mobile spending to top £53bn by 2024, June/July Cheque and Credit Clearing Company (2017) About cheque imaging: Phase roll-out began [online] https://www.chequeandcredit.co.uk/cheque-users/businesses/cheque-imaging/about-cheque-imaging-phased-roll-out-began [Accessed 23 July 2018]

Christie, S (2015) Is Santander that much better than the rest? *The Telegraph*, 3 February [online] http://www.telegraph.co.uk/finance/personalfinance/bank-accounts/10958488/Is-Santander-123s-current-account-really-that-much-better-than-the-rest.html [Accessed 1 October 2017]

Competition & Markets Authority (2015) Retail banking market investigation, 14 August [online] https://www.gov.uk/cma-cases/review-of-banking-for-small-and-medium-sized-businesses-smes-in-the-uk [Accessed 3 October 2017]

Cox, J (2017) Tesco to sell opticians business to Vision Express, *The Independent*, 19 April [online] http://www.independent.co.uk/news/business/news/tesco-vision-express-opticians-business-sell-matt-davies-a7690376.html [Accessed 28 September 2017]

Credit and Cheque Clearing Company (2017) Details announced for the introduction of a faster, industry-wide, image-based cheque clearing system [online] https://www.chequeandcredit.co.uk/press-release/details-announced-introduction-faster-industry-wide-image-based-cheque-clearing-system [Accessed 24 August 2018]

Deloitte (2014) Banking disrupted how technologies are threatening European banking model [online] https://www2.deloitte.com/content/dam/Deloitte/pt/Documents/financial-services/dttl-fsi-uk-Banking-Disrupted-2014-06.pdf [Accessed 30 September 2017]

Dunkley, E (2016) Banks braced for additional £22bn in PPI claim payouts, *Financial Times*, 4 April [online] https://www.ft.com/content/ebb83a38-f7fa-11e5-96db-fc683b5e52db [Accessed 7 October 2017]

Economist (2015) Aiming for the net [online] https://www.economist.com/news/finance-and-economics/21657426-banks-once-dreaded-rate-rises-are-they-right-look-forward-them-now-aiming [Accessed 3 October 2017]

FCA (2015) Lloyds Banking Group fined £117m for failing to handle PPI complaints fairly, 5 June [online] https://www.fca.org.uk/news/press-releases/lloyds-banking-group-fined-%C2%A3117m-failing-handle-ppi-complaints-fairly [Accessed 7 October 2017]

FCA (2017) Monthly PPI refunds and compensation [online] https://www.fca.org.uk/news/ppi-monthly-refunds-compensation [Accessed 7th October 2017]

Grierson, J (2012) RBS to sell off Churchill and Direct Line insurance arm, *The Independent*, 14 September [online] http://www.independent.co.uk/news/business/news/rbs-to-sell-off-churchill-and-direct-line-insurance-arm-8138751.html [Accessed 28 September 2017]

Hopkins, J (2016) Tesco mega-sale of sideshow businesses goes on with £217m disposal of Dobbies Garden Centres, *This is Money*, 17 June [online] http://www.thisismoney.co.uk/money/markets/article-3646474/Tesco-continues-flog-non-core-businesses-sale-Dobbies-Garden-Centres-investors-217million.html [Accessed 28 September 2017]

HSBC (2017) Interest rates [online] https://www.hsbc.co.uk/1/2/hsbc-interest-rates [Accessed 3 October 2017]

Hyde, D (2014) Banking technology brings 'seismic decline' in branch transactions, *The Telegraph* [online] http://www.telegraph.co.uk/finance/personalfinance/bank-accounts/10733432/Banking-technology-brings-seismic-decline-in-branch-transactions.html [Accessed 1 October 2017]

Independent (2011) UK firms decide it's time to hang up on Indian call centres [online] http://www.independent.co.uk/news/business/analysis-and-features/uk-firms-decide-its-time-to-hang-up-on-indian-call-centres-2309558.html [Accessed 22 September 2017]

Lawrie, E (2015) Banks battle for customers: Tesco scraps £5 current account fee after Santander slaps 150% charge hike on customers, *This is Money*, 15 September [online] http://www.thisismoney.co.uk/money/saving/article-3235271/Gloves-Tesco-Bank-scraps-5-current-account-fee.html [Accessed 7 October 2017]

Lewis, M (2015) Should you ditch Britain's best bank account? *The Telegraph*, 13 October [online] http://www.telegraph.co.uk/finance/personalfinance/bank-accounts/11927222/Should-you-ditch-Britains-best-bank-account.html [Accessed 1 October 2017]

Long, H (2017) Big banks rack up $6.4 billion in ATM and overdraft fees, *CNN Money*, 22 February [online] http://money.cnn.com/2017/02/22/investing/atm-overdraft-fees-rise/index.html [Accessed 7 October 2017]

Lowe, J (2018) Unfair and fair charges, *Bank Account Advice*, 26 February [online] http://www.bankaccountadvice.co.uk/unfair-and-fair-bank-charges.html [Accessed 10 April 2018]

Money Week (2013) Cost/income ratio [online] http://moneyweek.com/glossary/cost-to-income-ratio/ [Accessed 1 October 2017]

Morgan Pryce (2017) Lloyds Bank Branches, sale and leaseback details [online] http://www.morganpryce.co.uk/news/lloyds-bank-branches-sale-and-leaseback-deals [Accessed 1 October 2017]

Osborne, H (2015) Santander to increase 123 account fees, *The Guardian*, 14 September [online] https://www.theguardian.com/money/2015/sep/14/santander-increase-123-account-fees [Accessed 7 October 2017]

Oxlade, A (2013) Banks make average of £139 a year on each current account, *The Telegraph*, 25 January [online] http://www.telegraph.co.uk/finance/personalfinance/bank-accounts/9825998/Banks-make-average-139-a-year-on-each-current-account.html [Accessed 7 October 2017]

Rumney, E (2017) EU banks close branches, cut jobs as customers go online, *Reuters*, 12 September [online] https://uk.reuters.com/article/uk-europe-banks-closures/eu-banks-close-branches-cut-jobs-as-customers-go-online-idUKKCN1BN2DU [Accessed 29 September 2017]

Santander (2017) 123 Current Account [online] http://www.santander.co.uk/uk/current-accounts/123-current-account [Accessed 1 October 2017]

Shapland, M (2016) Barclays sells its Italian banking business to Mediobanca for a £258m loss, *This is Money*, 30 August [online] http://www.thisismoney.co.uk/money/markets/article-3765212/Barclays-sells-Italian-banking-business-Mediobanca-258m-loss.html#ixzz4u0fm5eCz [Accessed 28 September 2017]

Stephanou, A (2017) RBS Loses £7 billion in a year, *Currency Solutions*, 24 February [online] https://www.currencysolutions.co.uk/news/RBS-Loses-7-billion-in-a-Year.html [Accessed 28 September 2017]

Verity, A (1998) Bank of Scotland launches life office to bypass Act, *The Independent* [online] http://www.independent.co.uk/news/business/bank-of-scotland-launches-life-office-to-bypass-act-1175480.html [Accessed 7 October 2017]

Wallace, T (2015) Thousands more UK bank branches could face closure, *The Telegraph*, 14 September [online] http://www.telegraph.co.uk/finance/newsbysector/banksandfinance/11863736/Thousands-more-UK-bank-branches-could-face-closure.html [Accessed 28 September 2017]

Which? (2008) One in three with PPI may find it worthless, 28 May [online] http://www.which.co.uk/news/2008/05/one-in-three-with-ppi-may-find-it-worthless-144107/ [Accessed 7 October 2017]

Williams, R (2015) Apple Pay: Everything you need to know, *The Telegraph* [online] http://www.telegraph.co.uk/technology/apple/11720595/Apple-Pay-Everything-you-need-to-know.html [Accessed 3 October 2017]

Winnett, R and Wallop, H (2009) Banks triple profit margin on mortgages, despite low interest rates, *The Telegraph*, 10 September [online] http://www.telegraph.co.uk/finance/personalfinance/borrowing/mortgages/6163205/Banks-triple-profit-margin-on-mortgages-despite-low-interest-rates.html [Accessed 3 October 2017]

Disruption in the market

INTRODUCTION

The latter part of the 20th century and the early part of the 21st century have witnessed the proliferation of new retail financial institutions. Just as in aviation and the grocery markets, new entrants such as easyJet and Lidl come along and shake up their respective markets. Within retail banking, high-profile new entrants are beginning to emerge whilst many others are waiting in the wings, ready to take advantage of the current vulnerabilities of the traditional banks. Whilst they may face high barriers to entry, in terms of capital and regulatory requirements, they come to the market unbridled with negative perceptions and offer a freshness and innovative customer proposition. This chapter will look at the market conditions which led to the emergence of new banks, how they have developed, what their impact has been and what challenges they will face in the future.

Four main groups of new players have emerged over the past 30 years or so. Supermarket banks arrived first, then challenger brand banks, followed by **fintechs** and substitute banks. This chapter focuses on the conditions which gave rise to the evolution of each and how they have grown and changed the financial landscape.

Fintech An abridged expression, related to technology used behind the scenes to support and underpin financial institutions. Now in the 21st century, the term has grown to mean any technological innovation in the financial sector and relates to a new genre of innovative financial service providers that have begun to disrupt the traditional financial services marketplace through direct provision of their services to customers.

LEARNING OBJECTIVES

By the end of this chapter you will be able to:

- evaluate and explain the underlying drivers that gave rise to the evolution of supermarket banks, challenger brand banks, fintechs and substitute banks;

- differentiate between the retail banking propositions offered by supermarket banks, challenger brand banks, fintechs and substitute banks;

- reflect upon the impacts and threats that supermarket banks, challenger brand banks, fintechs and substitute banks have upon traditional retail banks;

- elaborate upon the opportunities and challenges that lie ahead for supermarket banks, challenger brand banks, fintechs and substitute banks.

Supermarket banks

The evolution of supermarket banking in the UK commenced in the late 20th century, with both Sainsbury's Bank (a joint venture between Bank of Scotland and J Sainsbury plc) and Tesco Bank (a joint venture between Royal Bank of Scotland and Tesco) launching their new organizations in 1997.

Market conditions

The freshness of the supermarket brands, combined with a ready-made retail branch/store network (no need to establish a costly high street presence, many open 24 hours a day, 7 days a week and with extensive car parking facilities too) and extensive marketing resources, made the marriage of financial services and grocery retail a very powerful one. Financial products sit very nicely in high-footfall outlets, with key product placement within the shopping aisles; pet insurance in with pet food, travel insurance in with sun cream and credit cards in with high-value products in the electrical aisles. Even car insurance is appropriately positioned in the supermarket filling stations. By offering simple loan, credit card and savings products, (without the excessive costs of the traditional retail banks) the supermarket banks often offer the best-buy deals in the marketplace.

Supermarket customers have been used to collecting points and gaining bonuses through loyalty card schemes such as Nectar (Sainsbury's) and Clubcard (Tesco). The loyalty schemes would now be expanded to encompass the financial products in a retailer's product portfolio.

Supermarket banks have severed their ties with their traditional retail bank partners and have stepped out on their own. In 2008, Tesco Personal Finance became a wholly owned subsidiary of Tesco and on 1 June 2009 was rebranded as Tesco Bank; Sainsbury's Bank cut its ties with Lloyds Banking Group in May 2013 (Neville, 2013).

The supermarket banks have been largely unaffected by the financial crisis of 2008 and they have also avoided the negativity of past mis-selling of products such as PPI. Yet perhaps surprisingly, a survey completed by Money Supermarket in 2012 found that only 4 per cent of UK adults would trust a supermarket brand more than a bank, compared to 27 per cent who said they would trust a traditional banking brand more than a supermarket. A further one in five said that they would not trust a supermarket brand at all to look after their finances (Money Supermarket, 2012). Three years later, Money Supermarket refreshed their survey and the position remained unchanged with Kevin Mountford, head of banking at Money Supermarket, summarizing, 'The traditional players [retail banks] still have the monopoly on the banking scene when it comes to consumer trust, with many people perhaps naturally cautious about the expertise and capability of new entrants' (Stevens, 2015).

The supermarket banks continue to build on their reward schemes, innovate new products and adapt to the needs of their customers. Tesco have created their own payment app, known as PayQwiq, to replace their previous system. The new app will let customers store both their debit and Clubcard details and enable them to pay contactlessly for purchases of up to £400 (Atkins, 2016).

ACTIVITY 5.1
Could history repeat itself?

- Perhaps a modern-day equivalent, joint venture approach could happen between the fintechs and traditional retail banks in the next chapter of the retail banking story. What pros and cons do you foresee with this approach?

- Evaluate what core competencies the supermarket banks have and how they can use these facets to retain and develop their competitive position within the financial services market.

- The public perception of the traditional banks still holds them in a more trustworthy position than the supermarket banks – why should this be? What do the supermarkets need to do to overcome this position?

Retail supermarkets had been growing fast and had extensive experience of diversifying into many different businesses including the sale of petrol, in-store opticians, clothing and electrical goods. Supermarket retail outlets have adapted to local market conditions to create various retail store designs to meet the needs of both city centre and rural community customers. In addition, the supermarkets have retained their superstores and the megastores for shopping malls and out-of-town retail parks. Further, supermarkets moved into direct catalogue and internet sales. Far from going entirely faceless and moving from bricks to clicks, the supermarkets created internet/home delivery grocery services. Even the product range was adapting, with most supermarkets offering low-cost value products, maintaining their standard range and developing their high-end premium products to compete with the recognized traditional primary high street brands.

The evolution

Supermarket banks were initially set up as joint ventures between recognized traditional banks and supermarkets with the collaborations expected to maximize the experience and market potential from the respective partners:

- Tesco Personal Finance originated via a joint venture between Royal Bank of Scotland and Tesco on 1 February 1997. Similarly, Sainsbury's Bank was formed by a joint venture between Bank of Scotland and J Sainsbury plc only days later on 19 February 1997.

- Marks & Spencer had been involved with financial services since 1985, originally developing its own Chargecard, though only in 2000 did M&S start to accept payments from Visa and Mastercard (Cope, 1999). M&S Money evolved in 2003, before M&S sold its sub-brand to HSBC in 2004.

- In 2013 Barclays joined forces with Asda to create Asda Money (BBC News, 2013a). Since 2014, Barclays has opened eight 'Essentials branches' in Asda stores throughout the UK. The outlets provide self-service convenience with the support of bank staff during the day.

The collaborations led to the creation of individual 'new' banks with their own banking licences. Supermarket banks operate on a non-traditional basis – without cashiers – and they are creative in their use of retail space in their shopping locations. Car parking, longer opening hours, brighter, more vibrant environments make supermarket banking a desirable option for customers. Both Sainsbury's Bank and Tesco Bank became wholly owned subsidiaries of their parent supermarkets in 2014 and 2008 respectively.

Initially focused on a simple product offering, avoiding the costly money transmission accounts, the new players focused upon market-leading high-interest-earning savings accounts, credit cards and personal loans. Mortgages followed later, as did a raft of simple insurance products.

CASE STUDY
Tesco Bank

Originally branded as Tesco Personal Finance, the joint venture between RBS and Tesco witnessed the coming together of two UK domestic giants in their respective fields of expertise. Both parties brought core competencies, skills and knowledge to the table; RBS with its experience in financial product development combined with managing extensive financial operational businesses, and Tesco adding marketing and branding flair along with access to a huge customer base. But Tesco had more than just access to millions of customers. It held valuable information about them. Whilst supermarket loyalty schemes were not new, Clubcard was introduced in 1995 at a time when the digital age and computerized research were in their ascendency. Clubcard enabled Tesco to gather shopping behaviour patterns and in turn target offers and promotions to specific customer groups. Commenting upon the importance of Clubcard as the single most significant factor driving the success of Tesco, Sir Terry Leahy stated, 'I knew the whole industry's structure would never be the same again' (Winterman, 2013). Within one year, Tesco became the UK's number one supermarket.

Tesco now understood its customers and its desire to address customer needs brought innovation to both the product range and the way in which products were distributed. Tesco developed multiple levels of product, with the 'Value' range being introduced in 1993 and 'Finest' five years later in 1998. Further, Tesco adapted its store design to meet the needs of different customer groups, creating:

- Tesco Express: launched in 1994, these outlets are designed to be convenience stores. Designed to meet the needs of local communities, ideal for short shopping visits. They seldom carry the 'Value' product range.

- Tesco Metro: launched in 1992 and typically serving city centre, urban communities, usually larger than Express stores with an extensive range of primary product brands as well as some of Tesco's premium product range too.

- Tesco Superstore: intended for frequent, one-stop-shopping experiences, these standard-sized supermarkets carry a wide and diverse range of primary and secondary as well as the entire range of own brand products. Further, Superstores have in-store bakery and/or fishmonger and butchery counters. In addition, some Superstores also stock a selection of stationery, electrical goods and clothing lines.

- Tesco Extra: introduced in 1997, this is a hypermarket format that in addition to all levels of groceries, includes a vast array of white and electrical goods, DIY products, furniture, clothing, toys and financial services.

Tesco Bank Timeline

1997
February: Tesco Personal Finance is launched as a 50:50 joint venture with RBS.
July: first credit card is launched.
August: personal loans, savings and home insurance products are introduced.
2002: eight new products, including car, pet and travel insurance.

2004: in-store travel money service is created.

2008: Tesco becomes sole owner of Tesco Personal Finance on 19 December.

2009: on 1 June, Tesco Personal Finance becomes Tesco Bank.

2010: sales incentives are removed from front-line staff and additional call centres are opened in Newcastle and Glasgow.

2012: mortgages are introduced to the product range. All banking products have been migrated to Tesco Bank systems – now serving 6 million customers.

2013

June: introduction of Box Insurance for young drivers to keep costs down and to encourage responsible driving.

November: 300 new colleagues recruited in advance of current account launch.

2014

June: Tesco bank launches its current account and mobile banking app.

June: Tesco wins What Mortgage – Best Direct Lender Award. (Corporate.tescobank.com/20/about-us/history)

The supermarket banks have not had it all their own way. They have found that they too are not immune to the threat of fraudsters. Tesco Bank suffered from a cyberattack incident in November 2016 affecting 9,000 customers with £2.5m being stolen. Subsequently all payments were frozen for 24 hours whilst the incident was investigated and resolved (Treanor, 2016; Arthur, 2016).

Questions

1 What did the respective joint venture partners of Tesco Personal Finance contribute to the original arrangement? What modern-day partnerships do you think could be forged to drive the financial services marketplace forward?

2 What value did the respective partners get from the original joint venture, ie what did RBS and Tesco gain?

3 Supermarket in-store banking brings many benefits for customers. Identify the key areas where the supermarket in-store branch model is more compelling than the high street retail banking branch model.

4 How could the performance of the grocery business impact upon the customers' perception of the supermarket banks?

The current position

Supermarket banks continue to build their banking knowledge and experience through joint ventures with financial sector partners, before acquiring the businesses as wholly owned subsidiaries and subsequently developing their product range and method of distribution further. Most recently Asda has partnered with Freedom Finance to provide access to a wide range of personal loan providers. Brian Brodie, Chief Executive of Freedom Finance, said, 'This is the first time a panel-based lending approach has been applied to a UK retail loan offering. It widens the market space for Asda Money, who will now be able to say yes to more customers' (Jones, 2017a).

Brodie added:

> It is our mission to help as many customers as possible secure the funding
> needed to realize their dreams and ensure we deliver on our promise of great
> customer outcomes. This joint venture will significantly increase the number
> of personal loan approvals that Asda Money will be able to provide to its
> 19-million-strong customer base. By bringing together the strength of the Asda
> brand and the experience of Freedom we will truly deliver a market-leading
> loan proposition for Asda versus their competitors (Jones, 2017a).

This is not the first time Asda has worked strategically with financial partners. In 2013 Barclays announced that it would be closing four branches, which would be relocated to four Asda stores. Since then, Barclays has grown its 'Barclays Essentials' branches in to eight Asda store locations, providing convenience banking through plenty of car parking, late opening hours and a variety of self-service machines.

Supermarket banks have remained focused and have chosen not to try to compete on all aspects of retail banking, deciding when and how they want to enter specific market segments. They have aligned their core grocery retail business with their financial product offering. The two distinct, yet complementary businesses have alignment from a customer segmentation perspective; pet food shopping has pet insurance product promotions, suntan creams are aligned with travel insurance promotions, electrical goods are complemented with credit card and personal loan promotions and so on.

Cost of entry to create an expanded branch/store network remains low, as the supermarkets are not burdened with legacy high street infrastructure, rather they can create in-store banking areas in key locations; this is complemented with effective supermarket bank product placement in the retail stores.

Technology infrastructure costs are low, with new forms of delivery such as cloud-based apps making it easy for supermarket banks to bring new products to market.

Customers generally have a positive perception of supermarkets. They have not been adversely affected by the financial crisis of 2008, nor do they suffer from negative 'fat-cat, greedy banker' connotations that are synonymous with the traditional retail banks.

Threat and impact

Supermarket banks are now well established, having gained significant numbers of customers in their first decade or so of operation. They are well positioned to use their known and trusted brands and their extensive customer data, and to leverage their banking franchises through their vast distribution networks. Whilst largely unaffected by the financial crisis of 2008, many would say supermarket banks are more trusted than the traditional banks; however, extreme care needs to be taken. Should the primary brand be adversely affected, then the financial side of their operations may be tarnished too. When the news broke that Tesco Everyday Value Spaghetti Bolognese contained 60 per cent horsemeat (BBC News, 2013b) and that their Everyday Value Beefburgers had 29 per cent horsemeat (Silverman and Philipson, 2013), the systemic impact of the news could have led to brand association contagion for the financial services business that carries the same name. In a similar vein, Tesco has paid £129m to the UK's Serious Fraud Office following false accounting between February and September 2014. Tesco overstated its profits by £300m by bringing forward payments from its suppliers to enhance results. The Financial Conduct Authority instructed Tesco to set up a compensation scheme for people who purchased shares based upon the erroneous results. Tesco estimates that the cost of settlement will be in the region of £235m (Pratley, 2017; Williams-Grut, 2017). As the traditional banks suffered and continue to suffer with trust-related issues, the supermarket banks need to protect both their bank and their core brand from adverse publicity.

ACTIVITY 5.2

- What lessons could your bank learn from the supermarket bank experience? How might this help your organization grow in the future?

- Is there an opportunity to differentiate retail financial products in the same way as the grocery business does for various customer segments and demographic groups within supermarkets?

- Could retail branches be designed in a similar way to the grocery store formats? What could the equivalent retail branch network look like?

New challenger brand banks

New challenger brand banks started to appear towards the end of the 20th century and into the beginning of the 21st century. Metro Bank became the first independent bank to appear on the high street in over 100 years, when it opened its Holborn store in 2010. As many of the traditional banks look to withdraw from branch-based banking, new brand banks are looking to acquire new stores. Both Virgin and Metro have aspirations to expand their physical store presence in the UK in the years ahead.

Market conditions

At the end of the 20th century, even before the banking crisis had struck, traditional banks were becoming tarnished with accusations of greed and mismanagement, being seen as inept and untrustworthy, thinking only of themselves and not customers. Some would say they were negligent; others would say they just buried their heads in the sand and didn't appear to care about anything other than profits. Whichever way you cut it, the traditional banks had a long way to go to regain the confidence of the general public. Customers were looking for something new, something vibrant, something that would shake up the old cronies and the old regime.

The creation of new banks by organizations that were synonymous with success and which had core competencies in innovation and brand development into diverse markets was on the horizon. They could see the potential of leveraging their brand and taking lucrative market share from the traditional players. They had the vision and customer inertia was on their side; if only they could capitalize on both factors, they could achieve significant and complementary income streams from the financial services.

The evolution

As the traditional banks have struggled to deal with the outcome of the 2008 financial crisis, in terms of reputational damage, payment of compensation and internal reorganizations, challenger banks such as Virgin Money have been significant beneficiaries.

CASE STUDY
Virgin

Virgin is made up of around 400 operations; comprising a myriad of businesses owned through a complex range of offshore trusts and overseas holding companies.

Virgin's primary branded firms are Virgin Atlantic, Virgin Money, Virgin Media and Virgin Trains – all of which have other major shareholders. In many cases the Virgin brand is simply licensed to a company that has purchased a subsidiary from Richard Branson himself. These include Virgin Mobile USA, Virgin Mobile Australia, Virgin Radio and Virgin Music (now part of EMI). In return, as the licence holder of the Virgin brand, Richard Branson receives annual or triennial fees that amount to hundreds of millions over time.

At a similar time to the arrival of supermarket banks in the late 1990s, new non-traditional banks were emerging. First to come to the fore was Virgin Direct. Launched in 1995, Virgin Direct had the brand and the experience of diversification behind them, and partnered with Norwich Union to initially launch a niche PEP product. Virgin Direct took over 4,000 calls on its first day of operation and within a month had more than £40m invested.

Virgin maintained a focus on niche financial products for several years, such as pensions, ISAs and TESSAs. One account was launched in partnership with Royal Bank of Scotland in 1997. In 1997 AMP bought out Norwich Union's stake in Virgin Direct. In 2001, RBS bought out Virgin's stake in the One Account.

Virgin Money credit cards and personal loans were launched under the Virgin Money banner in 2002.

2004 was a turning point for Virgin Money as the organization became a wholly owned subsidiary of the Virgin organization by acquiring the 50 per cent stake owned by AMP for £90m. Various insurance products were introduced including car, home, travel and pet insurance.

On 8 January 2010, Virgin Money announced that they had acquired Church House Trust for £12.3m. This gave Virgin Money a small but very important foothold in the UK retail banking market. Though Church House Trust had no branches, it provided Virgin Money with a much-craved-for UK banking licence.

Numerous industry awards followed over subsequent years and investment in Virgin Money as a financial brand was heavily promoted.

In 2011 Virgin Money became the primary sponsor of the London Marathon.

2012 saw Virgin Money acquire the ill-fated Northern Rock business, which was quickly backed up by the sponsoring of Newcastle United Football Club. Virgin Money introduced its lounges for customers, offering a relaxed environment, with free refreshments and Wi-Fi for all members.

18 November 2014 was another momentous day for Virgin Money when it became listed on the London Stock Exchange. The capital raised enabled Virgin Money to repay the UK government £50m for the acquisition of Northern Rock. Richard Branson made £85m from the public sale.

In 2014, Chief Executive Jayne-Anne Gadhia said, 'The days where you have branches where customers stand in queues for transactional banking are over.' The CEO went on to point out that Virgin Money is in a different situation to the high street giants, as the lender only has 75 branches and is committed to keeping all of them open (Salmon, 2014).

Virgin Money's website provides a fascinating insight into and comparison between the vision of traditional banks [Fred Goodwin at RBS] and that of an entrepreneur like Sir Richard Branson. Jayne-Anne Gadhia recounts a presentation made by the former RBS Chief Executive in 2000 where he said, 'he was sure that there were no new innovations left in financial services' (Gadhia, 2015). Yet six years earlier Jayne-Anne Gadhia had met Sir Richard Branson and he was talking about taking people into space – maybe even building a hotel up there! The difference in visionary leadership was stark and compelling. People become engaged, they are inspired and they dare to believe. Innovation has to be led, there needs to be the germination of an idea or concept to excite, motivate and challenge people.

To complement the Virgin Money network of 75 branches, seven innovative Virgin Money Lounges have been introduced throughout the UK. Initially created from utilizing surplus office space in Virgin Money's illustrious St Andrew's Square premises, the Virgin Money Lounge concept is now credited as a major driver of materially greater sales in the neighbouring branches.

Whilst the supermarket banks are getting to grips with trust-related issues, Virgin Money hold the honour of being Britain's most trusted bank based on a RepTrak survey of 35,000 members of the UK general public in Q1 2017 by the Reputation Institute (Virgin Money, 2017).

Not all Virgin diversifications have been successful. There was a series of failures in the mid-1990s, including Virgin Brides, Virgin Cola and Virgin Cosmetics; however, none of the failures caused systemic problems for the other brands in the Virgin stable.

Virgin Money announced its 2017 half-year results with every metric pointing to positive progress.

Underlying profits before tax were up 26 per cent to £128.6m (£101.8m in H1 2016):

- deposits up 5 per cent to £29.6bn;

- mortgages up 7 per cent to £31.8bn;

- credit cards up 13 per cent to £2.8bn;

- cost to income improved to 53.9 from 58.8 per cent.

Virgin Money's own customers have provided a ringing endorsement of the bank by providing them with a Net Promotor Score of +39.

Questions

1 How would you describe the rise of Virgin Money? What opportunities did Virgin Money capitalize upon and what aspects of the parent organization have helped Virgin Money establish itself as a major player in the UK financial services marketplace?

2 Trust is a valuable commodity in financial services; what lessons could your bank learn from Virgin Money?

3 Apply the aspects of Virgin Money's journey to that of your bank – what comparisons and differences can you identify?

The current position

The new challenger brand banks, such as Virgin and Metro are now well-established players within the UK retail financial marketplace. They have capitalized on the disruption caused by the financial crisis of 2008 and have been able to grow their respective branch networks at a time when the traditional banks have been aggressively closing their branches. Challenger brand banks are enjoying positive feedback and trust from their customers; meanwhile, the traditional banks are still trying to recover from a dramatic loss of customer trust following misdemeanours of the past. Customers will not forget the part they played in the financial crisis along with accusations of mis-selling and greed associated with bankers' bonuses.

Metro Bank

Metro Bank PLC is a retail bank operating in the UK, founded by Vernon Hill in 2010. At its launch Metro Bank was the first new high street bank to launch in the UK in over 150 years.

Changing the way Britain banks...

Metro Bank believes it has created a different kind of high street bank. A bank with stores, not branches, that are open when it suits its customers, seven days a week. A bank that offers drive-through banking. A bank where customers can walk in without an appointment and walk out with a working account, debit card and all. Metro Bank prides itself on telling customers, in simple terms, precisely what they're going to get. A bank that is intent on putting customers first. Children are always welcome at Metro Bank too. The provision of 'Magic Money Machines' combined with helping children in schools through financial education via Metro Bank's Money Zone programme demonstrates the bank's commitment to the next generation.

It is not just about human customers; Metro Bank loves dogs too (perhaps unsurprisingly, as Vernon Hill's Yorkshire Terrier Duffy is always by his side, whether it's at Metro's head office in Holborn or in his apartment overlooking Hyde Park). All dogs are welcome in all Metro Bank stores, with fresh water bowls and biscuits provided.

Metro Bank goes one step further to help customers with their pets. If they rehome a dog or cat from Battersea Dogs and Cats Home and have £100 or more in their account, Metro Bank will help with the rehoming costs of up to £105 for a dog or £65 for a cat.

Metro Bank believes that these innovative steps will help to turn customers into fans.

In a reversal of traditional retail banking trends, Metro Bank aims to grow the number of branches it has to 100 by 2020. Metro Bank is also growing its mortgage book after acquiring Cerberus for almost £600m. As a result, Metro Bank has increased its mortgage book by 15 per cent and aims to grow profits over the next three years (Curry, 2017).

ACTIVITY 5.3

- In a saturated market, how can the new challenger brand banks cut a market niche that delivers significant value for customers and shareholders?

- How will the challenger brand banks develop their customer proposition? Will they go towards the traditional retail bank model or will they move towards the fintech segment?

- How can leadership qualities and innovation lead to sustainable competitive advantage?

Threat and impact

As with the traditional banks, the challenger brand banks will have to be aware of the impending threat from fintechs (which we will go on to consider now) and the implications of **Open Banking**, but the brand banks are established brands and they have deepened their relationships with their customers over time. Challenger brand banks will have a major say in how the retail banking landscape shapes up in the very near future.

Open Banking   Enables customers to securely share their financial data with other financial organizations, making it easier to transfer money between different accounts and simpler for customers to shop around and buy the best product offerings. Open Banking will lead to bespoke banking experiences, specific to customer needs.

ACTIVITY 5.4

- Customers of challenger brand banks have high degrees of loyalty and trust with their banks – what insight does this give you as to how the traditional banks should go about rebuilding trust with customers?

- Evaluate the importance of partnerships, joint ventures and strategic alliances as ways of establishing a retail bank. What are the pros and cons of such business arrangements?

- What options and actions should the new challenger brand banks consider and take to ensure they are at the vanguard of the Open Banking era?

Fintechs

The emergence of this new group of potential entrants to the retail and business banking financial marketplace has evolved rapidly over the last five or so years, yet the challenge they face of breaking through successfully is formidable. PwC describes 'fintechs' as:

> The evolving intersection of financial services and technology. New fintech names emerging include Monzo, Atom and Starling. The term can refer to start-ups, technology companies or even legacy providers. The lines are blurring, and it's getting harder to know where technology ends and financial services begin (PwC, 2016).

The inference here is that the rapid growth in fintechs is already creating obscurity and with the pace of development appearing to be relentless, the future landscape for retail banking is going to change.

The market conditions

By the beginning of the 21st century, mobile technology was making an ever-increasing impact upon customers and society, with the rapid development of intuitive apps that made customers' lives much simpler through the convenience of their handheld device. Governments both domestically and in Europe could see the potential for the new digital age and moved to create legislation that would lead to a common approach for the payments industry. This led to new policies to underpin Open Banking and open

Application Programming Interfaces (APIs) via **Payment Services Directive 2**. PSD2 is covered in more depth in Chapter 9 on regulation and legislation. At the beginning of the 21st century, even new digital or **Crypto-currencies** in the form of **Bitcoin** and **Blockchain** have emerged – challenging the very form of money itself.

Application Programming Interfaces (APIs)   A set of protocols for building software applications. An API specifies how software components should interact. APIs are the foundation blocks that make Open Banking possible.

Payment Services Directive (PSD)   Originally published in 2007, PSD was the first European law to affect sterling payments. PSD2 came into force on 13 January 2018. It is legislation that helps member states move towards a single, digital market in Europe.

Crypto-currency   A digital currency that uses cryptography for security, making it difficult to counterfeit. Crypto-currency is not owned or controlled by any central authority, which means it is immune from government and central bank control.

Bitcoin   A specific type of crypto-currency that uses encryption techniques to create and regulate the units of currency and to validate the transfer of funds.

Blockchain   The digital ledger or accountancy book within which all transactions made in bitcoin or other crypto-currencies are recorded chronologically and publicly.

REGULATION

To keep yourself up to date with changes to PSD2 and Open Banking use the following links:
    Payment Services Directive 2 – https://www.fca.org.uk/firms/revised-payment-services-directive-psd2
    Open Banking – https://www.openbanking.org.uk/about-us/

The evolution

The fintechs join the retail financial marketplace at a time when several key changes have been happening. The last five years have seen the emergence of new, trendy names appearing on the landscape – Atom, Mondo/Monzo, Starling and Nutmeg to name but a few.

From a customer perspective, the existing marketplace is confusing, unclear and arguably customers remain confused as to how banks charge for their banking services and what quality of service actually means. Most customers lack the ability to have visibility across the wider financial sector and the financial institutions have not helped them. The ability to transfer bank accounts has never been easier, yet customers' desire and motivation to do so remains low – many decide just to make do with what they have, believing 'there's not much between them all anyway'. A cash card is a cash card – as long as I can get my money from a hole in the wall and all my payments get made on time, then what's the real difference other than a brand mark? Customers are also concerned about receiving the same facilities as they currently enjoy – there is a fear that some services such as provision of overdrafts may not be available from a new provider. This leads to customer apathy, with the perception of all banks being the same. Further, there is a perceived 'hassle factor' in switching current accounts from one financial provider to another. Customers worry about successfully transferring regular payment instructions or that their salary might not arrive into the new account. Even with the introduction in 2013 of the Current Account Switching Service (CASS), which guarantees the transfer process for more than 40 banks and building societies, it is still not widely known about or indeed trusted by customers. Only 3 per cent of personal customers and 4 per cent of business customers switch to a different bank in any year (CMA, 2016a).

As the marketplace has become more digitized, the need for face-to-face interaction has been lost and the demise of the retail branch network has accelerated. The branch-based competitive edge that the traditional banks have enjoyed has been rapidly eroded. Further, the historic IT infrastructure required to run a bank in the 21st century has been replaced with **cloud**-based capabilities.

> **Cloud**   Resources that are retrieved from the internet through web-based tools. There is no physical or direct connection to computer servers.

From a business banking perspective, consumer apathy is even more pronounced. The Competition & Markets Authority (CMA) reported that over half of start-up businesses open their current account at the same bank as their personal account. The report adds that '90% of small businesses get their business loans from their main bank, with little or no shopping around for other lenders' (CMA, 2016b).

The current position

Following the banking crisis of 2008, there was an eagerness to encourage new banks to the market. Metro Bank was one of the first, but it wasn't easy for them. It took them two years to get their original **bank licence** approved in 2010. Aware of the impact this was having upon potential new banks coming to market, the Prudential Regulatory Authority changed the regulatory barriers to obtaining a bank licence in 2013 (Regulation is covered in more detail in Chapter 9). By relaxing the conditions (including a lower level of capital requirements) it was hoped that this would stimulate the proliferation of new competition. Whilst the new process made it far easier than before, it is still not easy for just anyone to apply for and get a banking licence to set up a bank. That said, a year later, three formal UK banking licence applications had been received, with 26 further applications in the pipeline.

> **Bank licence**   A legal requirement for any financial institution that wants to conduct a banking business. The Prudential Regulation Authority and Financial Conduct Authority are keen to assist applicants to help reliable new banks enter the market.

Traditional retail banks and challenger brand banks account for the majority of personal and business customers – the smaller fintechs, such as Monzo, Starling, N25 and Nutmeg have yet to become household brand names and whilst the traditional banks have suffered adverse publicity due to IT failures and with their ethics and trust being called in to question by the public, yet they appear to be more trusted when it comes to management of personal information. In a KPMG global survey of almost 7,000 customers in 24 countries (including 500 UK participants) it was apparent that UK respondents trust organizations they engage with for life's most important matters such as health and wealth. Further, they least trust interaction with social media and gaming organizations (Technative, 2016). The underlying concerns relate to cyber security, what they would do with personal information and a guarantee that their information would not be shared with third parties. Legacy concerns in relation to large databases in the late 20th century being sold on to direct 'junk' unsolicited mail providers remain strong in the memory. The research found that approximately 60 per cent of people in the UK are seriously concerned about the way companies handle and use their personal information, and over a third feel they have no control over it at all. A powerful statistic was that four out of five respondents stated that control of their privacy is far more important than the potential convenience gained from sharing personal data. An alternative take on the research was the 'creepy vs cool' perception of managing data. Eighty-five per cent of participants found personalized billboards based on previous purchase patterns creepy. Similarly, 67 per cent said apps that access personal data are also creepy. However, two-thirds of respondents were happy to share their energy usage via a smart meter and four out of five would be happy to have tracking devices in their cars monitored by the emergency services. When it comes to relating this to fintechs, the delicate balancing act of being close to the line or crossing the line is extremely important when considering use of customer information (Thompson, 2017).

With half of all UK fintechs expecting their revenues to more than double in the next 12 months, uncertainty still swirls around customer adoption of the new entrants' propositions (Strzalek, 2017).

Atom, Starling, and Monzo have emerged as the market leaders and they come to the sector with innovative products, dynamic management teams and an agile approach to delivery of financial services. A brief background of each is provided below.

Atom bank is headed up by Anthony Thomson (founder of Metro Bank) and Mark Mullen (former CEO of First Direct). Atom gained its UK banking licence in June 2015 and in November 2015 BBVA from Spain purchased a 29.5 per cent stake for £45m (Financial Times, 2015). In April 2016, Atom introduced a one-year savings product and secured lending for SME firms. A residential product followed at the end of 2016, which creatively enabled the customer to monitor the approvals process via their mobile app. Atom has suspended the launch of its current account citing concerns about the practical implications that new regulation such as PSD2, Open Banking and data protection may have upon adoption rates of the new product.

Starling was founded by Anne Boden (previously COO at Allied Irish Bank) in June 2014. In January 2016, private investor Harold McPike invested $70m. In July 2016 Starling was granted a UK banking licence. Starling is one of the most progressive new entrants, creating 'Marketplace' – essentially a new ecosystem of financial products accessible via Starling's app. Fintech partners' products will be available via Starling's marketplace using its Open Banking and PSD2-compliant APIs (Greenland, 2017).

Monzo was established by the co-founder of Starling, receiving a restricted bank licence in August 2016 from the PRA and FCA. This meant that Monzo could put out products whilst it sought to prove to the regulators that it could operate as a fully functioning bank. Monzo used crowd funding via Crowdcube to raise £2.5m, attracting 6,500 investors, taking its total funding to €35m. Monzo's initial bank licence restrictions were lifted in April 2017. Monzo prioritized bringing its current account service to market for its 250,000 customers by the end of 2017 and deferred the amount of time on developing its public APIs (Finextra, 2017).

Some of the lesser-known new fintech entrants have managed to find and carve out a specific niche in the crowded financial marketplace. A few examples of these innovative fintechs are briefly described below.

Triodos is an ethical provider of online and mobile current accounts. Even Triodos bank cards are made from 'natural' plastic (Jones, 2017b). **Iam Bank** has focused its attention on the Millennial segment, aiming to provide customers with low-cost savings, pensions and investment products. Iam is unusual in that as a modern-day fintech, it sees the potential need for branches to form part of its future operating model. The acquisition of a small retail bank network will lead to Iam Bank being able to apply for its bank licence (Peyton, 2017).

Munneypot has partnered with YouDrive to provide low-cost financial advice and services. The intention is to roll out creative products combined with informative content to help educate customers about financial products and services. The WhatsApp-style interactive service helps customers make savings decisions (Wealthadviser, 2017).

But not all fintechs have been successful. **Tandem Bank** (recently renamed as Tandem Money) has recently withdrawn its savings account offer, due to having to surrender its banking licence (Financial Times, 2017). This was predicated through the withdrawal of a £29m investment pledge from Sanpower, which meant Tandem was unable to meet its regulatory capital requirements. Consequently, Tandem has reduced its headcount from 110 to 80.

Fintechs may have to choose what role they want to play in the future, perhaps as enablers – forming a strategic alliance or partnership with a traditional bank to work together to develop innovative products and services – or they may want to adopt a more independent, disruptive stance whereby they take the traditional banks on in their heartlands.

ACTIVITY 5.5

- Some commentators suggest that not all fintechs will survive. How best should fintechs protect themselves in the highly competitive financial services marketplace?

- Rationalize both the strengths and weaknesses of fintechs and elaborate upon the opportunities and threats that they face within the current environment.

- Reflect upon the lessons of the past and consider how these insights can be used to help predict the best way forward for fintechs in the future.

- Do you think fintechs are a serious threat to your bank? What defensive strategies would you put in place to help your bank to counter the threat posed by the new entrants?

Threat and impact

Fintechs are growing, and they are causing disruption in niche segments, but have yet to become truly influential and profitable. What they lack in physical high street presence they make up for in modern operating systems, designing their app-based offerings around the needs of the customer and therefore keep costs low and make scalability possible. The main challenge is to attract new customers and to build trust and confidence in the proposition.

This is where the fintechs lag behind. If a gap analysis was done, it would identify that what fintechs lack, Brand banks have and that the perfect partnership would be for fintechs to join forces with brand banks. The brand banks, however, are known for their creative flair and innovative thinking, along with their ability to adapt to the market, so perhaps they will hold court, develop their own proposition and only if needs be join forces with a fintech. Either way, the brand banks will be an interesting segment to watch over the next few years. They are very powerful businesses and have the ability to capitalize upon the successful customer propositions they have built thus far.

Cyber security remains a global concern, an example of which was the ransomware attack on the National Health Service in May 2017 (Bodkin *et al*, 2017). As fintechs look to the opportunity of customer acquisition, so too will the cyber criminals see the potential of new opportunities to commit crime. Rather than target the specific customer files, the cyber criminals may try to disrupt the APIs themselves and endeavour to interfere with the customer interface. Customers will be anxious about opening up their financial information to organizations whose quality and robustness of their IT defence protection systems is unknown. The Hiscox Cyber Readiness Report 2017 stated that almost two-thirds of firms (in the United States, UK and Germany) had experienced an attack in the last two years and that a similar percentage of organizations' cyber security budgets are set to increase by a minimum of 5 per cent over the next year. There is, however, a sobering apathy in the UK, with a third of UK businesses stating that they have changed nothing after experiencing a cyber security incident in the preceding year (Hiscox, 2017).

Fintechs lie in wait to take advantage of Open Banking; however, they will not get a free run at the market and they will need to be able to overcome consumer fears in relation to data security. PwC research reveals that whilst a quarter of financial services companies have yet to interact with new market entrants, almost a third are involved in a partnership with a fintech. It may well be that the other financial institutions are simply keeping a close eye on the evolving marketplace and will look to acquire a fintech firm at a future time. Irrespective of this, the path to the future remains uncertain, with concerns relating to IT security, potential regulatory changes and conflicting business operating models all being prevalent factors. One thing is certain; change is coming and it is coming fast. The incumbent banks need to have a strategy to take advantage of the new banking world, as failure to do so will see them being left behind. Some are already entering into collaborative partnerships, such as RBS with Iwoca, to develop peer-to-peer lending propositions. Whilst undoubtedly the creation of APIs and Open Banking will make things quicker, simpler and more convenient for customers, the ultimate success of Open Banking will be determined by customers, as will the subsequent extent of the disruption Open Banking will have on the traditional banks. But the threat might not be from the low-brand-value fintechs, but rather from the seemingly latent, potential banking brand giants such as Amazon, Google and Facebook, who as yet have to really show their hands.

ACTIVITY 5.6

- Why has the government relaxed its barriers to entry conditions so that new fintechs can obtain a bank licence more easily?

- Do you think fintechs will take over the future of retail banking or will the traditional banks prevail? Explain your answer.

- Cyber security is a major concern. How best should your bank prepare for such events happening to them?

- How should the traditional banks respond to the threat of fintechs and the arrival of Open Banking?

- Is your bank ready for Open Banking? Do you know what strategic path your organization will follow? What approach would you recommend?

Non-traditional substitute banks

Many large brands such as Apple, Google, Facebook, Amazon and PayPal are dabbling in payments and fringe retail banking activities, but as yet none have gone all-in to create their own retail bank. There is a proliferation of joint ventures and partnerships as they test the marketplace, jockeying for position, learning and developing concepts and understanding what customers want.

PayPal is introducing 'Business in a Box', which draws together a range of financial services and tools for new small business set-ups. Services include accountancy packages, inventory, financial management and setting up an online shop front for digital sales (Perez, 2017a).

Though not a directly aggressive move by Amazon into financial services, American Express has teamed up with the retail giant, so that AmEx's US customers can now use Alexa to check account balances and transactions via simple voice commands. Amazon has also developed its own Amazon Pay service in France, Italy and Spain, enabling customers to pay for goods and services at participating third-party merchant websites (Rao, 2017).

Not to be outdone, Google's Android Pay has established many partnerships with banks throughout the world. Android Pay is now available as an integrated payment solution within mobile banking apps provided by banks around the globe, including Bank of America and Bank of New Zealand. This is the first time Android Pay has been available within mobile banking apps (Perez, 2017b).

In a limited marketplace in the United States, Facebook Messenger is testing the introduction of a powerful artificial intelligence personal assistant, known as 'M', similar to Apple's Siri and Microsoft's Cortana, but with the enhanced ability to interpret future requirements and make recommendations proactively (Fingas, 2015). If during a conversation, payments are discussed, eg 'you still owe me $20...' M will pop up and recommend that the parties use Messenger's payments service.

ACTIVITY 5.7

- Substitute banks are the greatest threat to the traditional retail banks. How and why might this be the case?

- Identify key players that are yet to fully embrace retail banking. What unique values and qualities do they have that make you consider them to be a viable threat to the recognized incumbents within the UK financial services sector?

- What lessons do you think your bank could learn from innovative organizations such as Google, Amazon and Apple?

Chapter summary

- There has been a vast array of new entrants over the last 30 years.

- Supermarket banks and challenger brand banks have become viable competitors in their own right.

- Cyber security is the number one threat to all retail financial organizations in the 21st century.

- A large number of new, dynamic, innovative fintech companies are emerging and the regulatory barriers to becoming a bank are reducing; the threat to the traditional banks has never been greater.

- Not all fintechs will succeed; indeed many will fail.

- Just as with the creation of the supermarket banks, partnerships will be struck with fintechs to take their products and services to the mass market.

- Sharing of information and intelligence will happen to create new customer propositions.

- Non-traditional alternative substitutes to banks are sleeping giants. Organizations such as Google and Amazon have yet to fully engage with banking and if they do, their influence on the future model of retail banking will undoubtedly be significant.

- The future of retail banking may be uncertain, but it is also very exciting. One thing is certain – it will all change one way or another within the next five to ten years.

Objective check

1 What are the drivers that gave rise to the evolution of supermarket banks, challenger brand banks, fintechs and substitute banks?

2 List the differences between the retail banking propositions offered by supermarket banks, challenger brand banks, fintechs and substitute banks.

3 What are the threats posed to traditional retail banks by supermarket banks, challenger brand banks, fintechs and substitute banks?

4 What are the opportunities and challenges that lie ahead for supermarket banks, challenger brand banks, fintechs and substitute banks?

Further reading

Barclays (nd) Barclays essentials – banking while you shop [online] www.barclays.co.uk/Helpsupport/BarclaysEssentialsdoyourbankinginAsda/ P1242673687193 [Accessed 21 August 2017]

Boyce, L (2014) Get ready for a new bank explosion, *This is Money*, 18 April [online]http://www.thisismoney.co.uk/money/saving/article-2606119/ FCA-reveals-29-firms-lodged-banking-licence-applications.html [Accessed 23 August 2017]

Chartered Banker (2014) American Express – big opportunities from big data, April, p32

CMA (2015) Retail banking market investigation – Tesco Bank case study, 21 May [online] https://assets.publishing.service.gov.uk/ media/555dc4e2ed915d7ae200000b/Tesco_Case_Study.pdf [Accessed 15 August 2017]

Current Account Switching Service [online] https://www.currentaccountswitch. co.uk/Pages/Home.aspx [Accessed 18 August 2017]

Denton, J (2014) Is the Virgin money float a good opportunity to buy a 'challenger' bank? What the City experts say..., *This is Money*, 15 November [online] http://www.thisismoney.co.uk/money/investing/article-2833239/Is-Virgin-Money-float-good-opportunity-buy-challenger-bank.html#ixzz4qWYWyiu7 [Accessed 20 August 2017]

The Economist (2009) Scientific management, 9 February [online] http://www.economist.com/node/13092819 [Accessed 20 August 2017]

The Economist (2012) The third Industrial Revolution, 21 April [online] http://www.economist.com/node/21553017/ [Accessed 20 August 2017]

FCA (2015) Revised Payment Services Directive 2 (PSD2) [online] https://www.fca.org.uk/firms/revised-payment-services-directive-psd2 [Accessed 5 January 2018]

KPMG (2017) Crossing the line: Staying on the right side of consumer privacy 2017 [online] https://assets.kpmg.com/content/dam/kpmg/xx/pdf/2016/11/crossing-the-line.pdf [Accessed 20 August 2017]

Martin, B (2017) Brussels start probe of Royal Bank of Scotland plan to abandon W&G sale, *The Telegraph*, 4 April [online] www.telegraph.co.uk/business/2017/04/04/brussels-starts-probe-royal-bank-scotland-plan-abandon-wg-sale/ [Accessed 20 August 2017]

Open Banking (nd) About us [online] https://www.openbanking.org.uk/about-us/ [Accessed 5 January 2018]

References

Arthur, C (2016) Tesco cyber-raid raises serious questions over UK banks' security, *The Guardian*, 12 November [online] https://www.theguardian.com/business/2016/nov/12/tesco-cyber-theft-serious-questions-bank-security [Accessed 20 August 2016]

Atkins, S (2016) Tesco launches own mobile payment app: PayQwiq, *Contactless Intelligence*, 1 April [online] https://contactlessintelligence.com/2016/04/01/tesco-launches-own-mobile-payment-app-payqwiq/ [Accessed 9 November 2017]

BBC News (2013a) Barclays to move four bank branches to Asda, 8 November [online] www.bbc.co.uk/news/business-24853732 [Accessed 20 August 2017]

BBC News (2013b) Horsemeat scandal: Tesco reveals 60% content in dish, 11 February [online] www.bbc.co.uk/news/uk-21418342 [Accessed 21 August 2017]

Bodkin *et al* (2017) Government under pressure after NHS crippled in global cyber attack as weekend of chaos looms, *The Telegraph*, 13 May [online] http://www.telegraph.co.uk/news/2017/05/12/nhs-hit-major-cyber-attack-hackers-demanding-ransom/ [Accessed 20 August 2017]

CMA (2016a) Competition & Markets Authority: Making banks work harder for you, 9 August [online] https://www.gov.uk/government/uploads/system/uploads/attachment_data/file/544942/overview-of-the-banking-retail-market.pdf [Accessed 3 December 2017]

CMA (2016b) CMA wants banks to work harder for their customers, 17 May [online] https://www.gov.uk/government/news/cma-wants-banks-to-work-harder-for-their-customers [Accessed 8 December 2017]

Cope, N (1999) Retailing: M&S will accept credit cards in bid to boost sales, *The Independent*, 3 November [online] http://www.independent.co.uk/news/retailing-ms-will-accept-credit-cards-in-bid-to-boost-sales-1122125.html [Accessed 9 November 2017]

Curry, R (2017) Metro Bank buys £600m UK mortgage portfolio, *The Telegraph*, 2 June [online] http://www.telegraph.co.uk/business/2017/06/02/metro-bank-buys-600m-uk-mortgage-portfolio/ [Accessed 10 November 2017]

Financial Times (2015) Spanish lender BBVA enters UK with Atom Deal, 23 November [online] https://www.ft.com/content/b71ad596-91f3-11e5-94e6-c5413829caa5 [Accessed 11 November 2017]

Financial Times (2017) UK Bank Tandem loses licence after funding blow, 20 March [online] https://www.ft.com/content/b1499004-0d7f-11e7-b030-768954394623 [Accessed 21 November 2017]

Finextra (2017) Monzo puts API development on the back burner, 12 May [online] https://www.finextra.com/newsarticle/30561/monzo-puts-api-development-on-the-back-burner [Accessed 15 November 2017]

Fingas, J (2015) Facebook 'M' makes Messenger your personal assistant, *Engadget*, 26 August [online] https://www.engadget.com/2015/08/26/facebook-messenger-m-assistant/[Accessed 25 November 2017]

Gadhia, J (2015) Innovation and product development, *Virgin Money*, 10 November [online] http://my.virginmoney.com/2015/11/10/innovation-and-product-development/ [Accessed 10 November 2015]

Greenland, M (2017) Starling Bank's Marketplace goes live, *Specialist Banking*, 14 September [online] http://specialistbanking.co.uk/starling-banks-marketplace-goes-live/ [Accessed 15 November 2017]

Hiscox Cyber Readiness Report [online] https://www.hiscox.co.uk/cyber-readiness-report/ [Accessed 17 August 2017]

Jones, R (2017a) Asda money launches loans offering with Freedom, *Financial Reporter*, 16 August [online] http://www.financialreporter.co.uk/specialist-lending/asda-money-launches-loans-offering-with-freedom-finance.html [Accessed 20 August 2017]

Jones, R (2017b) Is Triodos the ethical bank that could replace the Co-op? *The Guardian*, 29 April [online] https://www.theguardian.com/money/2017/apr/29/triodos-ethical-bank-replace-co-op-bank [Accessed 15 November 2017]

Money Supermarket (2012) Study reveals consumer attitudes towards 'super-market banks' [online] https://www.moneysupermarket.com/press-releases/study-reveals-consumer-attitudes-towards-supermarket-banks/ [Accessed 9 November 2017]

Neville, S (2013) Sainsbury's takes full control of bank, *The Guardian*, 8 May [online] https://www.theguardian.com/business/2013/may/08/sainsburys-bank-stake-lloyds[Accessed 9 November 2017]

Perez, S (2017a) PayPal launches a small biz toolset, 'Business in a Box,' with WooCommerce & Xero, *Techcrunch*, 1 May [online] https://techcrunch.com/2017/05/01/paypal-launches-a-small-biz-toolset-business-in-a-box-with-woocommerce-xero/ [Accessed 19 November 2017]

Perez (2017b) Android Pay now works in Bank of America, USAA, Discover & other mobile banking apps, *Techcrunch*, 12 April [online] https://techcrunch.com/2017/04/12/android-pay-now-works-in-bank-of-america-usaa-discover-other-mobile-banking-apps/ [Accessed 24 November 2017]

Peyton, A (2017) Challenger Iam Bank to launch in UK, *Banking Tech*, 2 May [online] http://www.bankingtech.com/2017/05/challenger-iam-bank-to-launch-in-uk/ [Accessed 20 November 2017]

Pratley, N (2017) Tesco has settled with the SFO, but it faces more headaches ahead, *The Guardian*, 28 March [online] https://www.theguardian.com/business/2017/mar/28/tesco-sfo-accounting-scandal-shareholders-booker [Accessed 20 August 2017]

PwC (2016) What is a finTech? April [online] https://www.pwc.com/us/en/financial-services/publications/viewpoints/assets/pwc-fsi-what-is-fintech.pdf [Accessed 18 August 2017]

Rao, L (2017) American Express debuts its first Amazon Alexa skill, *Fortune*, 11 May [online] http://fortune.com/2017/05/11/american-express-alexa-skill/ [Accessed 20 November 2017]

Salmon, J (2014) Traditional bank branch is dead, insists Virgin Money boss Jayne-Anne Gadhia, *This is Money*, 5 March [online] http://www.thisismoney.co.uk/money/news/article-2573283/Traditional-bank-branch-dead-insists-Virgin-Money-boss.html [Accessed 10 November 2017]

Silverman, R and Philipson, A (2013) Tesco beefburgers found to contain 29% horse meat, *The Telegraph*, 15 January [online] www.telegraph.co.uk/news/uknews/9804632/Tesco-beef-burgers-found-to-contain-29-horse-meat.html [Accessed 20 August 2017]

Stevens, M (2015) Banks 'most trusted' on money matters, *Fstech*, 13 July [online] http://www.fstech.co.uk/fst/Bank_Trust_MoneySuperMarket_Survey.php [Accessed 9 November 2017]

Strzalek, A (2017) UK FinTechs expect revenue growth to double, *Fstech*, 7 September [online] http://www.fstech.co.uk/fst/UK_FinTechs_Expect_Revenue_Growth_To_Double.php [Accessed 11 November 2017]

Technative (2016) Brits trust banks more than social media companies when it comes to personal data, 6 November [online] https://www.technative.io/brits-trust-banks-more-than-social-media-companies-when-it-comes-to-personal-data/ [Accessed 20 August 2017]

Thompson, M (2017) Data, privacy and crossing the line, *KPMG*, 2 February [online] https://home.kpmg.com/uk/en/home/insights/2017/02/data-privacy-and-crossing-the-lines.html [Accessed 20 August 2017]

Treanor, J (2016) Tesco bank cyber-thieves stole £2.5m from 9,000 people, *The Guardian*, 8 November [online] https://www.theguardian.com/business/2016/nov/08/tesco-bank-cyber-thieves-25m [Accessed 20 August 2016]

Virgin Money (2017) Results for the half-year to 30 June 2017, 25 July [online] https://uk.virginmoney.com/virgin/news-centre/press-releases/2017/virgin-money-group-results-for-the-half-year-to-30-june-2017.jsp [Accessed 10 November 2017]

Wealthadviser (2017) Munnypot partners with YouDrive, 13 April [online] https://www.wealthadviser.co/2017/04/13/250671/munnypot-partners-youdrive [Accessed 20 November 2017]

Williams-Grut, O (2017) Tesco is paying £235m to settle two investigations in to its accounting black hole, *Business Insider*, 28 March [online] uk.businessinsider.com/tesco-settles-fca-sfo-dpa-2014-accounting-scandal-2017-3 [Accessed 20 August 2017]

Winterman, D (2013) Tesco: how one supermarket came to dominate, *BBC News*, 9 September [online] www.bbc.co.uk/news/magazine-23988795 [Accessed 20 August 2017]

06

Distribution of retail banking services via a range of customer channels

INTRODUCTION

By the end of this chapter you will have a comprehensive insight into and understanding of retail branches, call centres and digital channels as well as an overview of some of the emerging channels such as mobile, bots, video conferencing and robo-advisers. Each channel review section will start with considerations from a retail banking perspective, followed by a customer-centric usage and impact analysis and will conclude with most recent events with a view to the future prospects for the respective channels.

LEARNING OBJECTIVES

By the end of this chapter you will be able to:

- analyse the customer channels and how they are deployed by branches strategically;
- explain the suitability of channels offered from a banking perspective;

- explain the suitability and usability of channels offered from a customer point of view;
- evaluate the consistency of service offered through each channel and the challenges on banks in achieving this goal.

Branches

Banking perspective

The number of UK banks has reduced to just six in 2010 from 32 in 1960. The financial crisis in 2008 caused a concentrated period of consolidation that led to the six largest banking groups in the UK holding a market share of 89 per cent of current accounts (PwC, 2017). This consolidation combined with various other factors such as the emergence of new channels has caused the number of branches in the UK to steadily decline for almost 30 years. There were 20,583 UK branches in 1988 but only 8,837 in 2012 – a reduction of 57 per cent (Edmonds, 2018). A further 222 branches closed during 2013, followed by another 500 closures in 2014 and 681 in 2015.

As a way to manage bank closures sensitively, UK retail banks entered into an original agreement with the government in March 2015. The arrangement set out a number of key principles, including a pre-closure assessment, completion of an impact assessment and ensuring continued provision of alternative ways to bank, and a pledge to engage with local communities ahead of branch closures. The most recent derivative of the accord includes a number of enhancements as recommended by Professor Griggs (UK Finance, 2017):

1 Banks, where possible, will engage with customers as soon as possible after they have made the decision to close a branch and not wait until 12 weeks before, which will be the minimum standard not the norm.

2 Banks will engage more directly with their older and/or more vulnerable customers when a branch closes to help them explore alternative ways to bank which are available to them.

3 Banks will ensure that skilled personnel are available to help customers who continue to require assistance.

4 For each branch closure banks will provide an impact assessment that will be split into two distinct parts:

a) the reasons for closure being available to customers at least 12 weeks in advance of the closure of the branch;

b) following public consultation, clarify what issues were raised and what the bank has done to address them.

The new version of the standard applies in full to all bank branch closures announced after 1 May 2017, and to any future communications regarding closures previously announced but actually closing after 1 August 2017. Whilst not putting a stop to bank closures the accord endeavours to do the right thing by customers and to support them with the transitional move from traditional branch-based banking to new alternative ways of managing their finances.

Customers, demographics and usage of the branch channel

Branches have been the traditional home for customers of all demographic groups, enabling them to conduct their financial business for decades, if not centuries, in communities, towns and cities throughout the country. Only in the last three decades or so have we seen the emergence of new retail banking channels that have influenced the decline in traditional branch usage, but this does not necessarily mean the complete and utter demise of the branch in its entirety. Whilst swathes of customers have adopted new technology to service their modern-day transactional financial needs, branches still perform essential transactional services for elderly citizens in communities and provide a pivotal role in the provision of advice, products and services for more complex financial needs and requirements such as home buying and bereavement services. Customer branch-based transaction data analysis shows the dramatic, yet not surprising decline in the transactions levels. During 2016, 278 million transactions were processed through branches, down from 476 million transactions five years earlier in 2011 – a reduction of 32 per cent. RBS reported a 43 per cent reduction in branch transactions since 2010 (BBA, 2016a). Whilst customers are finding new ways to conduct the transactional aspects of their banking needs and the number of branches continues to fall, the landscape of branch-based banking will not be wiped out altogether.

Customer action groups have long tried to protect customers from extensive branch closures in the UK, particularly to preserve the 'last bank in town'; however, the upswell in use of alternative channels has led to a tsunami of branch closures which ultimately led to the Campaign for Community Banking Services (CCBS) effectively throwing in the towel in the summer of 2016, after 546 more branches closed in the first half of 2016.

CCBS stated, 'Branches are being hit by closures and we don't want people to think they can stop it... There is no hope of changing anything' (Daily Mail, 2016). After 17 years of leading the campaign against branch closures, CCBS closed down.

The environment is changing, evolving and reshaping. Branches still have a role to play in the future of retail banking in the UK; their precise context and role within the **omni-channel** mix needs to be established but the early shoots of the repositioning can be seen from the activity that is currently happening across the industry. We will discuss this further in the next section.

> **Omni-channel**   A seamless approach to customer experience that integrates different methods of interaction (eg branch, call centre, online and mobile).

Analysis and examples of current and future branch strategy of banks

Retail banks are comprehensively reviewing their branch networks to ensure they are fit for purpose for the 21st century. Whilst the number of transactions in the banks' high street branches may have fallen sharply, many customers still want to visit their branch to help them manage those bigger moments in life, such as buying a house or assessing their longer-term financial planning options. Retail banks are gearing up for the future, removing obsolete cashier counters and introducing more meeting space, technology advice bars and private interview rooms, some kitted out with new video conference technology to help connect and meet the needs of all demographic groups of customers. Whilst the media headlines emphasize the extensive programmes of branch closures, seldom do they tell of the reconfiguration and major investment programmes that are underway for the branches that remain. Nationwide announced in 2016 that over the next five years it would invest £500m in its branch upgrade programme (Finextra, 2016).

Metro Bank had 44 branches in 2016 and aims to increase its branch numbers to 100 by 2020 (Williams-Grut, 2016a) thus creating 2,500 additional jobs. Metro continues to invest in branches in numerous ways, from innovative state-of-the-art technologies such as **teller cash recycling machines** to support branch cashiers, to the instant provision of debit cards via Magtek ExpressCard 1000 and in-branch cheque book printing via Checkprint. Metro Bank has also deployed new drive-through branch formats to enable people to bank from the comfort of their own car. The first drive-through opened in Slough in 2013 followed by a second in Southall, London.

> **Teller cash recycling machine (TCR)** Provides a safe and secure repository for cash in an open branch environment. The TCR counts and verifies all bank notes received and issued, thus saving teller cashier time and eradicating any potential human errors in cash management.

Nationwide has introduced Cisco video conference booths into 60 of its branches. The in-store facility enables customers to meet mortgage advisers via video link, who can provide a full end-to-end compliant mortgage service. Nationwide completed a retail branch Wi-Fi technology upgrade programme for all 700 of its branches in March 2016, and aims to invest £500m in a five-year programme to transform and modernize its branches by 2020 (Finextra, 2016).

Lloyds was forced to sell 600 branches to comply with EU competition rules, and 631 branches were rebranded as TSB. The remaining 1,300 branches became Lloyds Bank branches. Yet Lloyds continued to invest in its branch network, opening a digital-focused flagship branch in Manchester in 2017 (Lloyds Banking Group, 2017). The 21st-century branch combines face-to-face expertise with state-of-the-art technology. The seven-days-a-week store features a digital zone to help educate customers new to internet banking, offering educational support as well as demonstrations – very similar in approach to Apple's in-store Genius Bar. Other technological enhancements include a new deposit facility for valuable possessions, which incorporates the latest biometric fingerprint technology to allow customers to access the store and retrieve their items. Lloyds has also been busy at the other end of the branch spectrum by introducing micro-branches. These outlets will be manned by two members of staff and all traditional cashier counters will be removed. Staff will be armed with tablets and will be able to help customers to use branch-based automation such as pay-in machines (Jones, 2017).

After acquiring Northern Rock's branches in 2011, Virgin has rationalized the network and now has 70 Virgin Money stores across the UK. The Virgin branch strategy is about being different. The complementary Virgin Lounges, which provide refreshments and a relaxing space for customers to use Wi-Fi and iPads, are strategically located in seven primary locations across the UK (Virgin, 2017).

Barclays has invested £1bn in retail technology and branch refurbishment since 2010. It has reconfigured some of its under-utilized retail branch space to support customers and staff to use Barclays apps and has used dormant branch space to create Eagle Labs with 3,000 staff, known as 'Digital Eagles' (Barclays, 2017) on hand to support customers and non-customers alike. Nearly 47 per cent of the British population have never taken steps to improve their digital skills (Chartered Banker, 2016a). The Labs have a variety of technologies available, including 3D printers to help businesses and entrepreneurs to develop manufacturing prototypes. In a joint venture with BT, Barclays now has free Wi-Fi in 1,500 branches. In a strange quirk of fate, Barclays' London-based branches are trialling the provision of an Amazon delivery locker service.

Investment continues within branch networks, with Bank of Ireland planning to invest €10m in 2017 by upgrading retail and business banking facilities – adding a further 90 external deposit and withdrawal ATMs (Hancock, 2017).

In 1871, bank holidays were introduced to give staff time off work, a practice that was soon adopted by many other businesses. In 2015, RBS became the first bank to break with the tradition by opening many of its branches on the public holidays – a very clear statement that some, if not all branches remain an important part of the retail banking model in the 21st century.

ACTIVITY 6.1

- Explain why retail banks have closed so many branches in the last decade.

- Why do branches still play an integral part in a retail bank's distribution strategy?

- Excess retail branch space needs to be put to better use. Provide examples of innovative practices being deployed by retail banks.

- Branch numbers have fallen, yet the number of bank licences has risen. Explain.

- Evaluate the implications that branch closures have upon various customer groups within society.

- Within your own organization, what has the recent approach been to retail branch strategy? How suitable is your branch network for meeting the future needs of customers?

ATM

Banking perspective

The first ATM was introduced to the public at Barclays' Enfield branch on 27th June 1967 courtesy of inventor John Shepherd-Barron (Chartered Banker, 2017a). The underlying reasons for creating the ATM were to relieve branch congestion, prevent banks having to increase their opening hours, and reduce rising labour costs (Chartered Banker, 2016b). Since the early days of merely dispensing cash, the ATM has evolved to provide a myriad of further services. From the 1970s to the 2000s, ATMs could be used for cash withdrawals, account balance information, printed receipts and, in some cases, an envelope-based cash deposit service. From the year 2000 to 2010, the ATM developed even further. Additional services included mobile phone top-ups, ticketing, payment to utility companies and money transfers. From 2010 to the present day, the ATM has become an integral part of banks' omni-channel strategy – targeted marketing and advertising delivered on-screen to specific customers, along with local information services. The core functionality has been further improved to provide multi-media ATMs, with rapid cash dispensing capability. Some UK ATMs can now accept cheques (and produce a digitized image of the cheque as a receipt) and bulk cash-based deposits. UK ATMs can also operate on a contactless basis, ie there is no need for a physical card and PIN to be entered to gain access to ATM services.

In 1998 there were 25,000 ATMs in the UK, with almost 20,000 of those located at branch locations. Twenty years on there are closer to 70,000 machines, which in 2016 dispensed £175bn (Chartered Banker, 2017a).

Paradoxically, however, only a few of the retail bank ATM-oriented businesses actually make a profit from their ATM networks. This is acutely felt by banks that have both large debit card portfolios and large ATM-installed estates – namely the traditional retail banks in the UK. This is due to the phenomenon of negative economic performance that is created by the interchange or reciprocity fees that are unseen by customers, but are costs borne by retail banks. Interchange fees are broadly calculated by dividing the cost of running the free-to-use LINK network by the number of transactions from the debit card provider. For many of the major UK retail banks, this means that the ATM component of their combined business forms a loss-leading element. The retail banks are calling for a reduction in the ATM reciprocity charge from 25p to 20p per transaction. In simplistic terms, this would see the value of reciprocity charges fall by 20 per cent in one fell swoop. Combining this with a reducing number of ATM transactions due to the growth of contactless payments, pressure is being placed upon the LINK network that oversees the UK ATM network. The remodelling and potential demise of some parts of the ATM network comes into stark perspective. The ATM Industry Association, has calculated that at least 10,000 free-to-use cash machines could be at risk from the changes in the ATM marketplace (Treanor, 2017).

Growth in the number of ATMs fell by 6 per cent across Europe between 2010 and 2016. The main reason for this can be attributed to the consolidation in the number of retail banks across Europe and to the rapid growth of electronic point of sale withdrawal and transactions. Low-value simple contactless payments are replacing the need for people to hold cash for traditional everyday cash payments (Accenture, 2016). All other global markets grew, with Central Asia growing at 37.2 per cent.

All aspects of the ATM infrastructure are controlled by the retail banks and accordingly they can influence the location, the customer experience and the security of the ATM transactions. This compares more favourably than the third-party reliance of fintechs for provision of their transactional services.

Customers, demographics and usage of the ATM channel

ATMs remain a central channel touchpoint for customers and form an integral part of banks' multi-channel or omni-channel experience. The ATM has evolved to be a channel that sits in harmony with branch, mobile and internet, yet the digital transaction and contactless card payment market is maturing at great pace and pressurizing the future need for cash as a transaction medium.

The ATM channel is recognized around the world, is well established and, perhaps most important of all, is trusted by customers. The network of ATMs is mature, with deployment of machines covering almost every corner of the developed world. Not only does this give the retail banks physical presence, it reinforces its brand representation.

ATMs provide services to all sections of society and are particularly attractive as a service option for customers who have the most simple and basic of transactional requirements. As of 2010 there were nearly 8.5 million basic bank accounts under management by 16 banks across Britain, all of them allowing free access to any ATM by any cardholding customer. But the first signs that UK retail banks were reappraising their position came in 2011 and whilst positioned as a way to reduce reciprocity charges, it was the most basic of bank account holders that suffered from the changes. Both Royal Bank of Scotland and Lloyds TSB advised basic account holders that they would no longer be permitted to use ATMs operated by an independent bank or third party, though both Lloyds and RBS state that their cardholders can still access their own respective ATM networks. The action would remove the reciprocity fees that LINK would charge for the million or so basic bank account holders that had previously enjoyed free access to the entire network of ATMs.

Yet the cost-cutting savings are only a small part of the story. The bigger story is the social impact of restricting access to a network of fewer ATMs to a group of customers that has traditionally originated from the financially excluded segment. By withdrawing such large numbers of potentially financially challenged customers from the LINK network of ATMs, the LINK machines located in the very communities where they were designed to drive financial inclusion would now be vulnerable and at threat of closure if no longer deemed to be economically viable. 'Issuers removing all LINK access for basic bank accounts and/or leaving LINK could risk closing or turning fee paying approximately 4,000 ATMs nationally' (Cluckey, 2012).

Whilst cash remains important within society and customers require a single touchpoint, the future for smart ATMs looks entirely plausible. ATM innovators need to listen to feedback from customers and react to the social needs of the public. Examples of where financial institutions have reacted and adapted their ATM functionality (in response to feedback from customers) include the introduction of ATMs issuing stamps in the United States. In Russia, customers can access the internet via ATMs. The proliferation of customer-centric value-adding activities via ATMs means that retail banks can no longer view the ATM as a cost-reduction channel, but instead as a valuable source of income generation. Whilst internet and mobile banking has undoubtedly influenced and reshaped the retail banking landscape, branch banking and ATMs are still fundamental components of customers' relationship with retail banks.

In a similar way to the rise of the ATMs (in response to customer demand and social desire to simplify and automate cash-based branch transactions in the late 1960s), technology has moved on and now represents a threat to the existence of ATM channels. Digital, mobile and contactless technology has led to a modern-day phenomenon that has changed customer behaviour and generated a new social desire for simple, non-cash-based transactions. According to the UK Card Association, 325 million purchases were made using contactless in the month of November 2016 alone (Chartered Banker, 2017b). Whilst the creation of the ATM itself did not directly cause the closure of branches, it undoubtedly had a part to play in the reduced need for cashier counter-based services that traditional branches provide. Merchants National Bank in Iowa, the United States, was the first bank to introduce a teller-less branch which provided a 24/7 service – this was the start of self-service banking (Chartered Banker, 2016c).

Contactless payments will have a direct impact on the need for cash for simple day-to-day payments and consequently the need for ATMs. When considering the wider pressures on the LINK ATM network, the future growth curve of the ATM industry in the UK will come under challenge. In the UK, we may well be on the cusp of an ATM rationalization and consolidation programme, potentially replicating the branch closure programme that we have observed in the last decade or so.

Analysis and examples of current and future ATM strategy of banks

ATMs remain an essential component for the provision of low-cost financial services to ensure financial inclusion within the UK and abroad. In the UK, investment continues to be made in ATM infrastructure. Nationwide completed an upgrade of its 1,360 ATMs to Windows 7 software in 2016, which not only provides a better customer experience but offers a more secure operating platform and enables support to be provided remotely (Adams, 2016). In November 2016 Barclays introduced the next generation of ATMs that enable Android users to make withdrawals with a tap of their device. This functionality is currently only available for Barclays customers (Brignall, 2016). HSBC, in conjunction with the Royal National Institute of Blind People, has introduced 1,500 talking ATMs across the UK, enabling customers who are visually impaired to hear spoken instructions (Smith, 2017). Turning to Europe, Idea Bank in Poland introduced a new form of mobile banking by investing in a fleet of BMW i3 cars with ATMs fitted inside, so that the bank can take its cash machines to its customers. The service has proven to be very popular with business customers, who can request a visit via an app so that they can pay in cash and cheques (Autoweek, 2015).

ACTIVITY 6.2

- If cash is being replaced by contactless transactions, why are retail banks investing in their ATM networks?

- Explain the financial pressures that the major retail banks/debit card providers face in relation to the ATM interchange/reciprocity charges and how this might threaten the very existence of the ATM network.

- Why do ATMs still have a part to play in the retail banking distribution mix?

- What are the strengths and weaknesses of having an ATM distribution channel?

- What is your bank's approach to ATM strategy? Does your bank invest in new branch-based ATMs and/or remote free-standing ATMs? Does your organization trial new, enhanced-functionality ATMs? What services do these new ATMs provide?

- Reflect upon customers – how should ATMs be better aligned to serve the differing needs of segments of customers?

- How can ATMs reinvent themselves to deliver customer value in an increasingly cash-free society?

Call centres

Banking perspective

Whilst Girobank was first to launch telephone banking services in the early 1980s, the first major call centre-centric financial services-oriented business to emerge was Direct Line who, in 1985, built its entire general insurance operating model around call centre operations. First Direct launched the world's first telephone-only bank shortly afterwards in 1989. This enabled customers to talk to a member of staff 24 hours a day, 365 days a year. Once again emerging technology was the catalyst for creating this evolutionary channel in retail banking. Automatic Call Distributor (ACD) technology enabled incoming calls to be filtered and directed to the most appropriate call handler (based upon advanced algorithms which could route calls based on call handler skills, time call handlers have been waiting, etc). The

ACD system essentially automated the role of a telephone operator and removed the need for a further hand-off. All the pre-assessment work was done before the call was even connected to the call handler who would ultimately speak with the customer.

One of the major exponents of ACD technology was US firm Aspect, who entered the UK market in the late 1980s at a time when deregulation in the British telecommunications industry led to a reduction in telephony servicing costs. This explosive combination of new technology combined with deregulation created the perfect conditions for the creation of the UK's first direct bank (ie one without any branches) – First Direct in 1989. This set the tone for all other UK retail banks to actively grow their respective domestic customer service call centre operations in the next decade.

By the mid to late 1990s the internet began to grow rapidly, with websites increasingly becoming the primary reference point for customers gathering information about financial products and services. As retail banks sought to further reduce costs, many but not all chose to relocate their call centre operations offshore. As discussed in the previous chapter, as a result of consumer pressure, many banks have reversed their original decision and have relocated their call centre operations back in the UK. We will look at this in more depth in the Lloyds TSB case study later in this chapter. Call centres in the UK have further retrenched to become centres of expertise for resolving customer enquiries and managing complaints.

Retail banks have evolved their call centre operations to move from handling reactive inbound calls to a more proactive stance through making outbound sales calls. Using predictive diallers, they could use complex customer algorithms to identify customer segments to sell specific products to customers over the telephone. The call centre model had morphed from a low-cost, alternative-to-branch channel to meet customer servicing requirements into a profit-generating machine by contacting outbound sales leads from an automated dialler that would connect potential prospects to the waiting sales advisers.

Even with the emergence of digital banking, there is still a place for a telephone banking proposition. Sometimes customers simply cannot find what they are looking for and the telephony channel offers a more agile solution than the digital platform (Chartered Banker, 2015).

Market conditions enabled the growth and development of the UK retail bank call centre, not only by encouraging customers to complete simple enquiries from the comfort of their own home at a time suitable to them; it started a process of migration of customer activity from traditional branch-based behaviour to alternative, lower-cost service channels. The primary objective of reducing day-to-day enquiries from branch to telephony led to cost reductions for retail banks. From humble beginnings, the call centre then developed into a major source of revenue generation. Organizations such as Bank of Scotland (which did not originally have a branch network in England), under the Banking Direct sub-brand, could utilize the outbound call functionality to sell mortgages, personal loans and private banking services to customers in England and Wales.

The life of the call centre has been curtailed by the evolution of internet banking and the emergence of smartphone technologies. Digital/online banking enables customers to now perform all the same routine tasks via their smartphone or tablet rather than having to make a telephone call to a call centre. No longer is there the need for any human intervention for routine enquiries. Product enquiries and applying for new accounts can all be completed online, thus negating the need for human intervention via call centres. Customers have become increasingly resistant to unsolicited calls – the PPI effect, where personal time infringements via the telephone at home only cause resentment and an animosity towards the caller, has led to a cessation of outbound calls by banks.

Customers, demographics and usage of the call centre channel

Customer surveys had shown that people wanted speed, convenience and service from their bank – branches alone could not satisfy the demands that customers had. Branch opening hours were typically restricted from 9 am to 5 pm Monday to Friday, which meant many customers found themselves effectively excluded from being able to visit a branch, thus making it challenging for them to do their finances during this period due to work commitments. The underlying premise of the call centre model was that customers could contact their bank 24/7/365 to complement the core weekday hours offered by the branch networks and to provide a positive alternative to waiting in queues within branches, particularly at peak times, to handle simple, routine enquiries. Initially customers could perform a variety of straightforward tasks via telephone banking – balance enquiries, ordering a bank statement, amending a standing order, checking previous transactions, stopping cheques, transferring money and paying their bills. Arguably the strategy was bank-led and customers were encouraged and directed by branch staff (who were promoted and incentivized) to extol the virtues of telephone banking to customers as the cost to serve customers (from a bank perspective) was far cheaper via a centralized call centre model, rather than having to provide account management staff in all of their branches. In many ways customers were pushed towards telephone banking rather than being naturally drawn to a new service proposition.

Analysis and examples of current and future call centre strategy of banks

In the beginning, customers did not seem to miss their local branch. Following its launch in the late 1980s, First Direct handled around 2,000 calls from customers per day and by the end of the first year of business, 100,000 customers had joined First Direct. In time, all major banks offered telephone banking as an alternative and complementary way for customers to service their banking requirements. Only in recent years, with the advent of internet and mobile banking, has the use of telephone banking started to tail off. Since mobile banking apps have become available, there has been a steady decline in the number of people using telephone banking services. YouGov polling from June 2014 for the BBA shows that less than 10 per cent of customers use telephone banking at least once a month.

In August 2016, Barclays introduced voice biometric technology thus removing the need for customers to go through the traditional process of providing answers to a series of questions to get access to their account information over the telephone (Information Age, 2016).

Abbey operated two call centres in Bangalore and Pune from 2003; however, following adverse customer feedback, Santander reversed the decision and returned the 1.5 million calls to centres in Glasgow, Leicester and Liverpool. The decision created 500 new jobs in the UK (Independent, 2011).

CASE STUDY
Lloyds TSB call centres and branch calls
(Treanor, 2007)

In the mid-1990s retail banks in the UK were opening call centres with the promise of providing customers 24-hour access to their bank accounts. The centralization of telephony operations inevitably led to branch-destined calls being rerouted to the call centres, leaving branch staff to focus on and serve customers face to face.

Of the traditional retail banks, only Royal Bank of Scotland and NatWest continued to let customers call their branches directly.

The next step was for Lloyds to acquire a call centre in Mumbai in 2004, with 700 staff. As a direct result, Lloyds closed its Newcastle call centre with the loss of 968 jobs.

In the UK, however, customers were venting their frustration, citing language barriers as being the primary cause of their dissatisfaction with the offshore telephone operation. The Lloyds TSB in-house union, the Lloyds TSB Group Union, claimed that over 400,000 Lloyds TSB customers had signed a petition saying they were opposed to having their financial arrangements handled abroad.

In an attempt to redress the situation, Lloyds initially completed a successful pilot of 42 branches to test the return of calls-to-branch service. The remaining 2,000 branches joined the initiative from April 2007.

The bank's central call centres take 2.25 million calls a month and the bank insists that only 5 per cent of all calls need to be directed to branches.

Questions:

1 What lessons should banks take from Lloyds' offshoring experience?

2 The trade-off was cost reduction vs customer experience, with the hope customer experience would not suffer – are there any other similar tensions within your organization where customer experience may be adversely impacted in the name of cost savings?

3 Are other forms of offshoring work acceptable within retail banking? Are you aware of any successful offshoring practices that have previously been deployed?

4 Explain why it is important to listen to customer feedback before developing channel propositions. What problems might you encounter if you fail to listen to the needs of the customer?

ACTIVITY 6.3

- Explain how external conditions gave rise to the emergence of call centres in the UK.
- What benefits did the creation of call centres bring to UK retail banks?
- Explain why call centres have struggled to become a dominant channel in recent years – is there a role for call centres in the future?

- Do customers still need call centres in the 21st century? Can you identify any specific segments of customers that would be more attracted to conduct their financial business over the telephone rather than in branches or via mobile app?

- How do call centres fit with the current operating model of your bank? Has the role of the call centre changed in recent years? If so, how?

Online digital banking

Banking perspective

The expressions 'online' and 'e-commerce' emerged in the 1980s and originally related to the use of a terminal, keyboard and TV (or monitor) to access the banking system using a standard telephone line. The forerunner to online digital banking that we know today was established in the UK in 1983, when Bank of Scotland set up Nottingham Building Society customers on the UK's first internet banking service, known as Homelink. The system required a computer or a keyboard, connected to a television set and a telephone line. This associated software enabled customers to get 'online' to see their transactions, make bank account transfers and pay their bills. The subsequent evolution of the internet and improved broadband infrastructure over the next decade gave rise to increased speculation that 'clicks would replace bricks' and by the mid-1990s, concerns about the future of the traditional branch network were becoming commonplace, as increasing numbers of banks began to view web-based banking as a strategic imperative for their future operating model. Banks could see the potential to reduce their cost of transactions and that the internet would provide a platform for marketing products and services to both existing and new customers.

Turning to the present day, many retail banks are at the early stages of developing their digital channel lifecycle strategy, making their initial foray and tentative steps into social media, by experimenting with digital integration and dabbling with some basic and arguably blunt marketing and communication activities. In practical terms, this is when social media is used as a simple product-push platform, with little or no interaction with customers. In simplistic terms this amounts to an electronic presentation of product information, which is promoted widely to a broad, untargeted audience. Following the events of the banking crisis in 2008, banks have had to be very cautious with their investment decisions and this has had a bearing on the degree of investment made by retail banks to develop a truly integrated omni-channel proposition. Ninety per cent of European banks invested less than 0.5 per cent of their total spending on digital (Olanrewaju, 2014).

Customers, demographics and usage of the online digital banking channel

When internet banking was launched in the 1990s, the vast majority of the customer base had yet to embrace the use of computers at home for internet services, hence a far smaller proportion (compared to mobile banking) of the population were able to engage with the internet banking proposition. In the early days, the world wide web was used as a source of information and research, rather than as a transactional tool for purchasing goods and services. At the time the underlying technology was also far more limited both in terms of the costly acquisition of the computing hardware, and the unreliability of connections, with people relying on modem/telephony dial-up connections that were far slower than the broadband capability we all enjoy and take for granted today.

Whilst during the mid to late 1990s the banks were driving forward with their aspirations to deliver e-banking services, customers were still hesitant and remained reluctant to adopt the new technology. Particular concerns about the safety of their money and the security of transacting on the internet were particular barriers. It was only when wider retail businesses such as eBay and Amazon demonstrated that transacting online was safe and secure, that the barriers for retail banking online came down. In the United States, by 2000, 80 per cent of banks offered e-banking services. Customer adoption of digital banking grew slowly. Bank of America, for example, took 10 years to acquire 2 million e-banking customers. Once the calendar clicked over from December 1999 into January 2000 without any major computer system issues [that had been mooted due to the last two digits going from 99 to 00], growth in internet banking began to expand more rapidly. A year later, Bank of America grew its online customer base by 50 per cent and became the first bank to have 3 million online banking customers. By the end of 2001, 20 per cent of Bank of America's customers were online users.

Crucially too, switching to internet banking from branch or telephone banking was far more of a step change and culture shift than it is today for people moving from digital banking to mobile banking.

Rapid and recent changes in technology have enabled banks to dramatically improve the way they talk and listen to their customers. Under the traditional banking model, customers had to contact their bank via their branch, by letter or by telephone when they wanted information, but now this information can be sent to customers via SMS text message, either on a weekly or daily basis. Smarter use of customer information means that banks can gauge when customers are likely to ask for statements or balance updates, and ensure this information is proactively sent in advance. The other modern-day use of SMS is to proactively provide customers with text alerts to warn them that they need to take action to avoid charges. This type of advance notification would have been unheard of a decade ago. Banks are now among the biggest text generators in the country; Lloyds Banking Group alone sends 3.8 million SMS messages a week (BBA, 2015).

Text alerts are also used to contact customers immediately should there appear to be suspicious activity on their account. Previously if there was suspect activity a transaction would simply be blocked – potentially inconveniencing customers who were making a genuine purchase. The SMS technology has improved the banks' ability to contact customers at the point of a purchase to improve the customer experience and to safeguard their money.

Social media is also changing the way people communicate with each other – and with their banks. Twitter, Facebook and Instagram give banks a communication mechanism to share information with millions of customers – whether it's updates on service information or details of the latest product offers. It's not just banks that have latched onto the potential of social media. Customers are increasingly finding that it offers a convenient and direct way of interacting with their bank. Anecdotal evidence suggests that the social media teams can often resolve problems quickly and efficiently. Social media is a growing and is an important communications tool for banks, particularly with younger customers. But it's important to put this in context – banks receive more than 7,000 tweets a week from customers, but over the same period they pick up more than 2 million phone calls (BBA, 2015).

Analysis and examples of current and future online digital banking strategy of banks

More than 14 million mobile and internet transactions are processed each week (BBA, 2015). Whilst the ease of the mobile app means customers typically log onto mobile bank apps more frequently, they transfer significantly more money using conventional internet banking services (around £1.7bn a week is transferred using mobile banking apps by customers of major banks – compared with £6.4bn via internet banking). It seems that despite the rapid rise of mobile banking, there are still significant numbers of customers who bank online and have not yet fully embraced this mobile technology.

The next step of the online digital channel evolutionary journey will witness organizations proactively using digital channels to extend their brand, to increase customer awareness and to leverage interaction with consumers through the digital medium. This is a significant and strategically different step beyond that of merely pushing promotions out on a broad-brush basis, where there is little to no engagement with prospective customers.

At its peak, the more advanced form of digital channel usage enables banks to create value through effective, focused targeting through the use of advanced algorithms based upon a variety of data factors such as past buying patterns, account triggers and key events that would equate to a higher likelihood of a further financial product or service being needed. Value can be created for both customers and the banks where they can truly develop bespoke product offers for each of their customers based upon the valuable insights available to them.

In June 2016, Barclays introduced an online personal financial hub called 'Financial Wings' to provide customers with knowledge to make better financial decisions (Financial Capability, 2016). A month later Barclays created a derivative of the hub, specifically to help armed forces personnel – additionally providing them with a freephone number for when working away on military operations and a cloud-based filing system that enables personal and business customers to upload documents into their digital vault.

ACTIVITY 6.4

- How well developed do you believe the online digital channels are for a) the traditional retail banks, b) the supermarket banks and c) the emerging financial technology (fintech) banks?

- What lessons can be learnt from online digital services provided by organizations outside the financial sector?

- What threats exist to the online digital channel within your organization?

- The emergence of new technologies does not always mean that customers will be ready to adopt new products. Apply this principle to both failed and successful technological innovations to identify how well organizations have balanced the tension between new technology and customer needs.

- Do you believe online digital banking will have a part to play in the future channel mix of retail banking?

Mobile

Banking perspective

Mobile banking has become a unique and expanded service which has emerged as a by-product of online digital banking. Innovation in the design of smartphone technology combined with investment in 4G telephony infrastructure and high-speed broadband has led to the explosion of mobile banking adoption.

David Ebstein, Head of Digital for Financial Services at EY, comments:

> The British public is voting with its thumbs. Being mobile-enabled is a must, not a maybe, and banks that don't engage properly with mobile channels risk losing relevance in customers' lives. The next frontier of innovation will be delivering an exceptional customer experience through mobile, across products and services, and going beyond banking. The mass migration to mobile banking is an opportunity for banks to better engage with customers and regain trust customer by customer. Competition is intensifying, and successfully joining the dots between mobile, internet and branch banking could make the difference between winning and losing customers (BBA, 2015).

Existing mobile and new digital ways of interacting with banks mean that the number of customer transactions will increase in the future. Increasingly more and more people are using bank mobile apps to look after their finances. More than 40,000 banking apps were downloaded each day in 2015 – an increase of 25 per cent on the previous year. Further, 11 million log-ins to banking apps took place per day in 2015 – up 50 per cent on the year before. The average number of customer log-ins to mobile apps per month is 36 (BBA, 2016a).

Banking apps are stripped down and simplified processes that are uncluttered and enable customers to manage their finances around their day-to-day life with ease. The technology is simple and straightforward and takes the hassle factor out of banking. The process of simple banking tasks can be completed in a matter of seconds rather than minutes or hours, which would have been synonymous with using other channels such as digital banking, call centres or branches. The introduction of mobile banking apps has removed stress from the lives of customers.

Customers, demographics and usage of the mobile channel

The emergence and rapid growth of mobile banking over the last decade has transformed the way that customers look after and maintain their finances and it is now used by millions of customers on a daily basis. Due to the intuitive technology that has been created, customers have embraced the mobile channel at a phenomenal rate – much quicker than with either digital banking or telephone banking services. The underlying reason for the amazing rate of adoption can be attributed to the subtle but important differentiating factor that customers were eager to utilize their mobile device for banking – they did not need convincing or persuasion to move to an alternative channel. By the time mobile banking applications were launched there was already a mature smartphone market – which had a critical mass of people using smartphones and tablet devices. An example of this was Barclays, where 8 out of 10 consumers were already making digital transactions – be it ordering groceries, booking holidays or downloading films and music. This has paved the way for the huge growth in digital banking. Online YouGov polling for the BBA from June 2014 found that only 16 per cent of customers never use online or mobile banking.

As the number of mobile banking customers continues to grow, so will the number of new user segments. Established user requirements will be different from those of new adopters – and this is where banks can learn from the latter segment in order to attract new users. Banks can also provide value to more potential mobile banking customers by understanding what the original barriers to adoption were and why this specific segment took so long to adopt mobile banking. The insight from these customers will help banks to improve their customer experience and encourage further customers to engage with their mobile banking proposition.

Around 167,000 RBS and NatWest customers use their mobile banking app between 7 am and 8 am on their morning commute. On Friday 30 May 2014 the bank's app had 3.65 million log-ins – its busiest day so far. NatWest and RBS's mobile app has received more than 1.25 billion log-ins so far. Lloyds Banking Group's weekly app use rose from 2.1 million in 2012, to 4.7 million in 2013 and 6.6 million during 2014. More than £1.7bn was transferred a week in 2014 using mobile phones or tablets – a 40 per cent rise on the previous year. Banking apps for the group – which includes Halifax and Bank of Scotland – were been downloaded more than 7.2 million times. At peak times, the app was being used 138 times per second (BBA, 2014).

By 2017, around 22 million people in the UK were regularly using banking apps, which was a 12 per cent rise on the previous year. The rise is being attributed to ease of use and increased functionality with the banking applications. Further, an estimated 5.5 billion log-ins to banking apps took place during 2017 – a 13 per cent rise on the previous year.

In addition, millions of customers have requested to receive SMS alerts from their bank. An estimated 512 million of these text messages were sent to UK customers in 2017 – over 16 per second (UK Finance, 2018).

Analysis and examples of current and future mobile strategy of banks

Retail banks have to continue to evolve their mobile banking strategy. The key to success is matching increasing consumer demands and expectations with useful, easy-to-use tools that dovetail with the capabilities of mobile devices. As mobile becomes the most prominent interface and therefore the primary channel of engagement for customers, banks have to continuously revise and adapt their mobile banking strategy.

The generic core mobile strategy of retail banks today is to provide four main attributes of mobile functionality:

1 Basic banking functions – provision of an efficient and intuitive app-based package whereby customers can check balances, transfer money and pay their bills.

2 SMS alerts and notifications – proactive communication from banks to protect customers from breaching their overdraft facility or to notify of potential fraudulent activity.

3 Access to the bank's website to optimize opportunity for additional purchase of products and services.

4 Contactless functionality – enables customers to pay for goods and services directly via their mobile device

Whilst these offerings satisfy customers today, the current range of services will not satisfy customer demand in the future. Banks need to be able to react to changes in mobile technology, such as wearable technology like smartwatches, but equally they need to weigh up the value that the new technology may provide, otherwise investment in the solution may fail to generate sufficient return on investment.

In January 2016 HSBC trialled a new app called 'Nudge' to 500 customers over a three-month period. The bank says the service has already saved customers £85m in overdraft charges (Business Reporter, 2016). The app monitored customers' transaction activity, identifying trends and habits and sending 'nudges' to make users aware of their expenditure. Domained within the new HSBC cloud IT architecture, the app took six weeks to create.

A further customer-friendly app was introduced as another trial by HSBC in December 2016. In partnership with fintech Pariti, 'SmartSave' enables the automatic transfer of funds between main current accounts and savings accounts to ensure all funds that could earn interest in savings accounts automatically do so, thus maximizing personal customers' ability to earn interest (Lewis, 2016).

Santander have enhanced their SmartBank app further with support from Nuance, to enable payments to be made by voice-based instructions (Boyce, 2017).

In April 2017 Barclays partnered with fintech 'Donate the Change' to embed Barclaycard's bPay contactless chips into wearable devices that when used to make touch and go payments for up to £30, without the need for a card and PIN, trigger an automatic rounding donation to the charity of the wearer's choice (Strzalek, 2017).

Israel's Bank Leumi has introduced a freestanding mobile bank modelled on customer use of social media feeds. The mobile banking platform, known as 'Pepper', is designed to cope with all of customers' day-to-day banking requirements (Andreasyan, 2016).

ACTIVITY 6.5

- Consider the availability of technology and the demands of customers to explain the rapid growth of the mobile banking app phenomenon.
- What channels are under threat from the evolution of the mobile app proposition?
- How do you envisage the future development of mobile banking app technology?
- Where can future value come from and can retail banks secure regular income streams from the app-based channel?
- What mobile-based innovation have you seen in your financial institution recently?
- What mobile innovation would you like to see next within retail banking?

Bots

Banking perspective

Bots are digital virtual assistants that can answer questions and help achieve things without having to interact with another human. They are artificial intelligence computerized assistants. The most popular talking bots in the retail environment are Alexa (Amazon), Siri (Apple) and Cortana (Microsoft). They can be used to provide directions, help book flights and hotels, even order takeaway food. In a more basic form, non-talking bots have been deployed to provide prompts and timely intervention and advice. For banks this offers an alternative to traditional SMS communications for alerts and notifications. Further, the technology will enable a more accurate, tailored, segmented approach to bank communication with niche customer demographic groups.

Customers, demographics and usage of the bot channel

The days when the only way to deliver customer service was through one-to-one, face-to-face relationships via branch networks are over. Personal conversations via call centres are also under threat of being replaced with social media options that enable banks to respond to customer enquiries. The lead has been taken by organizations such as Facebook who have changed the nature of the customer engagement model with the creation of Facebook Pages. Twitter has also underpinned this form of customer engagement as a preferred way to communicate with brands across the spectrum. Tech-savvy and social media-aware customer segments have embraced this form of engagement and they have used this to create a new channel of engagement with banks. The nature of customer engagement is evolving again. The technology that enables the evolution is artificial intelligence (AI). Gartner projects that more than 85 per cent of customer interactions will be managed without a human by 2020, and chatbots are also expected to be the number one consumer application of AI over the next five years, according to TechEmergence (Business Insider, 2016). Bots may well be able to manage the majority of simple task-based enquiries in the future; however, there will be interactions which will be complex or sensitive in nature where human intervention will be more appropriate. Human professionalism and judgement will still be required to ensure decision making is executed decisively and in a fair and consistent manner.

Analysis and examples of the current and future bot strategy of banks

Bots are emerging at a rapid rate within retail banking and are being tested and evaluated in a variety of situations.

Bank of New York Mellon has introduced more than 220 bots in the past 15 months with the sole aim of driving efficiency and reducing costs (Irrera, 2017). It is estimated that fund transfer bots are already saving the bank $300,000 per annum through reducing the time it takes employees to identify and deal with data mistakes and processing payments.

Western Union and MoneyGram have both taken to Facebook Messenger and have launched bots that let US customers transfer money worldwide. This development means that MoneyGram customers can send funds to 350,000 locations worldwide and the Western Union bot can send money to more than 200 countries in 130 different currencies (Finextra, 2017a).

Wells Fargo has taken the bot model even further and has been piloting an artificial intelligence customer services agent within Facebook's Messenger system. The bot can provide account information and resolve simple problems such as password resets. Wells Fargo has been using Messenger as the primary interface for answering customers' questions (Finextra, 2017b).

RBS is currently testing a life-like avatar called Cora, who it is hoped will be able to support customers with basic queries, giving its digital banking platform a more human face (Rumney, 2018).

ACTIVITY 6.6

- What impact might bots have upon the traditional income streams that retail banks may have previously benefited from?

- Though a relatively new channel, what lessons can be learnt from other organizations and how can retail banks take advantage of these learnings?

- How proactive are the traditional retail banks in the bot environment? If not in the external customer market, are there any examples of internal use of bots?

- Evaluate which groups of customers will be most likely to adopt Bot technologies. How should banks develop their customer strategies to ensure bot technology reaches as many customers as possible?

- Are there any bots in your business? What do they do and what opportunities do you see for them in the future of retail banking?

- As our reliance on technology to deliver financial services increases, what ethical challenges does this bring to the financial sector?

- Artificial intelligence is becoming increasingly sophisticated, with machines being able to learn; who, therefore, is ultimately responsible and accountable for decision making?

- With artificial intelligence and the use of bots increasing rapidly, what might the consequences be for human professionalism and judgement within banking?

Video conferencing

Banking perspective

Video conferencing is an emerging channel, the reliability of which has improved significantly over recent years due to technologies such as high-speed, high-definition video links and the ability to scan and upload formal documentation. The premise is to enable the connection of a central team of bank experts to customers via an organization's branch locations. From a bank's perspective, the centralization of skilled advisers means that banks can gain economies of scale benefits rather than having representatives in all branch locations. This approach can include services provided by mortgage advisers, investment consultants and insurance agents.

Customers, demographics and usage of the video conference channel

Video conferencing may seem a radical step change in the provision of advice, but for the up-and-coming generation, this is nothing new and nothing to fear – they have been exposed to video conference services such as Skype and FaceTime since their early days and accordingly they do not hold any reservations about this form of communication. For other customer groups, the key to the successful introduction of video conferencing is local support and education. Banks who provide video conferencing services via their branch networks need to design their proposition in such a manner that the majority of customers have a positive experience – not simply leaving customers in an interview room with a blank screen facing them. Introductions need to be made, simple usage instructions should be provided and there needs to be the provision of on-site technical support to address any connectivity issues should they arise.

Modern video conference services, whether offered in branches or directly via mobile device, offer great potential for retail banks. Delivering video conferencing technology in a smart way can create a decisive competitive edge for banks through the creation of an ideal environment for individual advice from any location that suits the customer. Banks need to recognize, however, that different customer segments will require different degrees of support to ensure video conferencing can be successfully deployed.

Analysis and examples of current and future video conferencing strategy of banks

In December 2014, Barclays was one of the first UK banks to launch video banking to offer digital face-to-face interactions to its high-value, 'Premier' customers. Typically, these customers have complex needs and require advice and help from experts in a number of specialist fields such as trade, pensions and taxation (Jones, 2014). It has taken a while, but other retail banks have followed and momentum has now gathered as the supporting video link technologies have evolved over time. In March 2016, Lloyds launched its remote mortgage advice service, where customers can access a video link from their laptop or tablet, enabling them to have a face-to-face interview online (Lloyds Banking Group, 2016). Within three months, HSBC announced in June 2016 that it intended to launch an investment video advice service to customers (Romeo, 2016). A year later, Santander introduced a mortgage video service in 63 branches throughout the UK. Customers will be able to apply for a mortgage by using a video link from the branch – connecting them remotely to a UK mortgage adviser. Santander aims to refine the service further, enabling customers to link directly to mortgage advisers from their own home (Wright, 2017).

ACTIVITY 6.7

- What challenges are faced by retail banks when introducing a video conference channel from scratch?

- Why is video conferencing becoming increasingly popular as a retail bank channel?

- How do you think different customer segments will react to the increased use of video conferencing? What steps need to be taken to ensure customers find the experience a satisfactory one?

- Would video conferencing work in your bank? How would the concept fit within your existing branch infrastructure?

Robo-advisers

Banking perspective

Robo-advisers are designed to replace face-to-face interactions to help customers identify the most appropriate product to meet their needs. Robo-advisers are not robots; more specifically they are a set of questions and algorithms that are coded and aligned to product features and attributes. The catalyst for hard-wired (decision tree-driven) advice via an automated medium (ie customer responses to specific questions result in a specific path being followed) originates from the Retail Distribution Review in 2012 and again when the Financial Conduct Authority (FCA) published its Financial Advice Market Review (FAMR), which concluded that up to 16 million people in the UK could be trapped in a 'financial advice gap' where they need advice but can't afford it (Williams-Grut, 2016b). This is where robo-advisers have identified an opportunity in the market. Robo-advice has lowered the barriers of entry – there is no need to invest in training in human skills, rather technology can be used to ask the essential questions that are aligned to the decision tree framework to then recommend the most appropriate product within the scope of the product portfolio. On the face of it, then, nothing could go wrong – advice would always be spot on – yet commentators are concerned that 'hard wiring' or the underpinning algorithms may be incorrect and could result in an even greater level of mis-selling (Chartered Banker, 2017c).

Customers, demographics and usage of the robo-adviser channel

Robo-advisers are currently targeted towards niche customer groups and product areas such as savings, investments and mortgages. The majority of customers cannot afford the hourly fees that independent financial advisers charge; the costs of the existing service model make financial advice prohibitive to most groups of customers. Lawrence Wintermeyer, CEO of the UK's fintech industry body Innovate Finance, told Business Insider, 'The average person generally can't afford an advisor for his pension now'. He added, 'IFAs and the processes they go through really were designed for people with a lot of money. It's not that they're not important for average people but it's kind of like a sledgehammer to crack a chestnut' (Williams-Grut, 2016b). Turning attention to the pensions market specifically, Wintermeyer identifies key customer segments that would benefit from help from robo-advisers, saying, 'You find that the pensions industry is talking about solving the problem for 55-year-olds who have been in their scheme for 20 years but they forget that there's a whole generation of millennials coming up that we really should be designing newer and simpler pensions for.'

The truth of the matter is that robo-advisers do not actually provide customers with advice. The underpinning decision tree models seek binary responses and from these outcomes the model identifies the most appropriate product, usually from a limited range of options available from within a single financial institution. The questions and decision trees do not take into account long-term objectives or changes in future circumstances.

Analysis and examples of current and future robo-adviser strategy of banks

Wealth Wizards combine software with technical expertise to create a robo-adviser platform. Their most recent 'adviser' pledges to be able to give a full retirement appraisal in less than two hours. The robo-advice system is being tested by insurance company London Victoria (LV=) and promises to generate an automated advice report in less than a minute (Cash, 2017).

BNP Paribas has established a partnership with French 3D visual design companies Vectuel and RF Studio, creating a virtual reality app for retail banking customers and a 'teleportation' capsule for home buyers. The app lets French customers go through their banking transactions and through the steps of home purchase, whilst the 'teleportation' capsule is a physical pod that customers can visit to get a full 3D, 360-degree view of buildings that are under construction (Lemmon, 2017).

ACTIVITY 6.8

- Robo-advisers are a relatively new concept; what opportunities exist within retail banking for developing this channel in the future?

- How do you think customers will perceive robo-advisers? What challenges do you think retail banks need to address to make this channel work?

- How can new entrants take advantage of robo-advice?

- What ethical implications are there for banks who deploy robo-advisers?

- In your view, would you say that banks are delegating or abdicating their responsibility for managing customers' interactions through the use of robo-advisers and what implications might this have for the competitive environment?

Consistency of service provided in a multi-channel retail bank

Mobile or internet banking will not be everyone's preferred channel of choice, and customers need options for the way in which they communicate with their bank. Channel choice gives customers flexibility, but the quality of the service and the consistency of the brand feel needs to permeate all channels for this to feel seamless. Customers should be able to commence an application on the telephone, before visiting a branch or completing the form online. Omni-channel banking will be discussed in more detail in Chapter 7. Banks have to manage all channels simultaneously and they need to hold and maintain their values irrespective of which channels customers choose to engage with.

The bank of the future won't simply offer mobile or branch-based services. It is more likely to be a multi-channel business, giving customers choice on how they choose to engage, transact and meet with their bank. Banks realize that customers want choice in how they manage their finances.

CASE STUDY

Lloyds Banking Group – approach to multi-channel banking and the importance of providing consistent service throughout the channels. Interview with Nick Williams (BBA, 2016b)

Nick Williams, Consumer Digital Director for Lloyds Banking Group, says:

> The multi-channel banking experience is important to give customers choice and ease of access to services; that's why we are also investing in new technology across our branch network. This includes further investment in intelligent deposit machines to make transactions quicker, digital posters to keep customers informed, iPads to welcome and service customers in the branch more effectively, and enabling our colleagues to use our online digital service to give customers a consistent and efficient customer experience.

Lloyds are also investing in trialing video conferencing with mortgage and wealth advisers. As we have already learnt earlier in this chapter, this can give customers more flexibility to speak to these experts when and where it suits them.

> It's important that our customers can have conversations with us how they choose to and if that's Facebook or Twitter, then they should be able to get the same level of service as our more traditional channels.
>
> There is no doubt technology is giving us all greater power to manage our own finances. Now 60 per cent of our app log-ins are simply to check a balance and with instant access to transfers and payments at our fingertips this means customers are in control. If you happen to forget then our text alert service means that we can keep you more informed.
>
> Our focus on digital is customer led, our progress is aimed at making things easier for our customers to bank where they want, how they want – and technology in general life has certainly increased the demand for that, and our ability to meet it.

Questions:

1 Reflect on Nick Williams' views; is it truly possible to deliver the same levels of service across all channels?

2 Evaluate whether letting customers lead the digital agenda is a prudent approach for retail banks.

3 Apply the branch investment approach taken by Lloyds Banking group – how does this relate to your organization? Are similar investments being made in your organization?

Chapter summary

- Branch numbers in the UK have been steadily declining for almost 30 years, as customers find new, alternative ways to conduct their banking transactions and enquiries.

- Branch closures have increased in intensity since the financial crisis of 2008.

- Branches still have a role to play in the future of retail banking in the UK; it is the precise context of that role that needs to be established. Innovative use of technology aligned to the changing needs of customers will determine the future construct of retail branch design and the optimum number of branches that will be needed.

- ATMs were born from the necessity of finding automatic alternatives to queuing in branches for cash. In many ways this was one of the first steps that led to customers defecting from branches and has played a part in the closures of branches that we see today. Now in the 2010s and with the advent of contactless payments, there is less demand for cash and ATMs themselves are now under threat.

- Call centres enable routine enquiries and simple transactions to be conducted from a customer's home or work place, without the need to go into a branch. Yet the existence of call centres is now also under threat. Digital and mobile banking channels have virtually replaced the need for call centres in the 21st century.

- Digital banking and mobile/smartphone channels are the channel of choice in the 21st century for managing bank accounts and for making payments.

- Emerging channels such as bots, video conferencing and robo-advisers are still in their infancy, but the innovations demonstrate the principle of evolution and that retail banks are actively seeking out new and creative ways of engaging with their customers.

- Retail banks must ensure that they do not trade off the pursuit of cost reduction to the detriment of the customer experience.

Objective check

1 Consider each of the customer channels discussed. How are they deployed strategically by branches?

2 Again, consider each of the channels discussed. What would you need to take into account when thinking about the suitability of each channel offered from a banking perspective?

3 What would you need to consider when thinking about the suitability and usability of each channel from a customer's point of view?

4 What challenges do banks face in providing consistency of service through each channel?

Further reading

Call Centre Helper (2011) The History of the Call Centre, 19 Jan [online] https://www.callcentrehelper.com/the-history-of-the-call-centre-15085.htm [Accessed 22 September 2017]

References

Accenture (2016) ATM benchmarking study 2016 and industry report [online] https://www.accenture.com/_acnmedia/PDF-10/Accenture-Banking-ATM-Benchmarking-2016.pdf [Accessed 9 December 2017]

Adams, D (2016) Nationwide updates ATM operating system, *Fstech*, 22 March [online] http://www.fstech.co.uk/fst/Nationwide_ATM_Upgrade_Computacenter.php [Accessed 4 December 2017]

Andreasyan, T (2016) Mobile-only bank Pepper gears up for launch in Israel, *Banking Tech*, 9 November [online] http://www.bankingtech.com/2016/11/mobile-only-bank-pepper-gears-up-for-launch-in-israel/ [Accessed 5 December 2017]

Autoweek (2015) Is this BMW i3 the future of mobile banking? 4 May [online] http://autoweek.com/article/technology/bmw-i3-future-mobile-banking [Accessed 25 November 2017]

Barclays (2017) Digital Eagles [online] https://www.barclays.co.uk/digital-confidence/eagles/ [Accessed 1 December 2017]

BBA (2014) It's in your hands [online] https://www.bba.org.uk/wp-content/uploads/2014/07/BBA_TWWBN_WEB.pdf [Accessed 24 August 2018]

BBA (2015) Mobile phone apps become the UK's number one way to bank, 14 June [online] https://www.bba.org.uk/news/press-releases/mobile-phone-apps-become-the-uks-number-one-way-to-bank/#.WuV7H0xFzIU [Accessed 5 December 2017]

BBA (2016a) The way we bank now – help at hand [online] https://www.bba.org.uk/wp-content/uploads/2016/07/TWWBN3_WEB_Help-at-Hand-2016.pdf [Accessed 4 December 2017]

BBA (2016b) The way we bank now: It's in your hand https://www.bba.org.uk/landingpage/waywebanknow/Published Summer 2016 [Accessed 25 May 2018]

Boyce, L (2017) Now you can make payments by speaking into your smartphone: Santander adds voice commands to its new app, *This is Money*, 13 February [online] http://www.thisismoney.co.uk/money/saving/article-4219356/Santander-SmartBank-app-lets-pay-people-voice.html [Accessed 24 November 2017]

Brignall, M (2016) Barclays to unveil contactless cash withdrawals, *The Guardian*, 22 November [online] https://www.theguardian.com/money/2016/nov/22/barclays-unveils-contactless-cash-withdrawals [Accessed 4 December 2017]

Business Insider (2016) Why it's time your business went all in on chatbots, 8 September [online] http://www.businessinsider.com/sc/chatbots-future-customer-service-2016-9?IR=T [Accessed 7 December 2017]

Business Reporter (2016) Nudge, Nudge: HSBC app acts like financial 'personal trainer', 19 January [online] https://business-reporter.co.uk/2016/01/19/nudge-nudge-hsbc-app-acts-like-financial-personal-trainer/ [Accessed 1 December 2017]

Cash, J (2017) LV= Backs robo-advice to boost pension profits, *Money Marketing*, 13 September [online] https://www.moneymarketing.co.uk/lv-backs-robo-advice-boost-pension-profits/ [Accessed 7 December 2017]

Chartered Banker (2015) What customers want, February/March, pp20–23

Chartered Banker (2016a) Barclays launch Eagle Labs, April/May, p8

Chartered Banker (2016b) The dawn of digital banking, April/May, pp4–45

Chartered Banker (2016c) Tried and trusted, October/November, pp44–45

Chartered Banker (2017a) Reinventing the ATM, October/November 2017, pp36–38

Chartered Banker (2017b) Customer splash out with contactless, February/March, p7

Chartered Banker (2017c) The rise of hybrid advice, April/May, p42

Cluckey, S (2012) Will UK banks break the ATM LINK? *ATM Marketplace*, 10 September [online] https://www.atmmarketplace.com/articles/will-uk-banks-break-the-atm-link/ [Accessed 4 December 2017]

Daily Mail (2016) No hope of stopping bank branch closures as campaign group closes after 17 years, 23 August [online] http://www.dailymail.co.uk/money/news/article-3755453/No-hope-stopping-bank-branch-closures-campaign-group-closes-17-years.html?ITO=1490&ns_mchannel=rss&ns_campaign=1490 [Accessed 7 December 2017]

Edmonds, T (2018) Bank branch closures – briefing paper 385, 9 February, p5 http://researchbriefings.files.parliament.uk/documents/SN00385/SN00385.pdf [Accessed 7 December 2017]

Financial Capability (2016) Barclays launches Financial Wings initiative, 21 June [online] https://www.fincap.org.uk/document/V2e40ikAAOQArDiF/barclays-launches-financial-wings-initiative [Accessed 17 November 2017]

Finextra (2016) Nationwide is currently investing £500 million branch upgrade, 22 September [online] https://www.finextra.com/newsarticle/29471/nationwide-says-technology-is-great-but-sometimes-face-to-face-is-better [Accessed 3 December 2017]

Finextra (2017a) Western Union and MoneyGram unveil Facebook Messenger bots; Mastercard and Amex Pile in, 19 April [online] https://www.finextra.com/newsarticle/30445/western-union-and-moneygram-unveil-facebook-messenger-bots [Accessed 7 December 2017]

Finextra (2017b) Wells Fargo to pilot AI-based Messenger bot, 19 April [online] https://www.finextra.com/newsarticle/30447/wells-fargo-to-pilot-ai-based-messenger-bot [Accessed 8 December 2017]

Hancock, C (2017) Bank of Ireland to spend €10m on upgrading branch network, *Irish Times*, 4 May [online] https://www.irishtimes.com/business/financial-services/bank-of-ireland-to-spend-10m-on-upgrading-branch-network-1.3071312 [Accessed 3 December 2017]

Independent (2011) Santander call centres return to UK, 8 July [online] http://www.independent.co.uk/news/business/news/santander-call-centres-return-to-uk-2309107.html [Accessed 5 December 2017]

Information Age (2016) Think before you speak: Voice recognition replacing the password, 1 August [online] http://www.information-age.com/think-you-speak-voice-recognition-replacing-password-123461752/ [Accessed 5 December 2017]

Irrera, A (2017) BNY Mellon advances artificial intelligence tech across operations, *Reuters*, 10 May [online] https://www.reuters.com/article/us-bny-mellon-technology-ai/bny-mellon-advances-artificial-intelligence-tech-across-operations-idUSKBN186253 [Accessed 7 December 2017]

Jones, R (2014) Barclays rolls out face-to-face video banking, *The Guardian*, 30 November [online] https://www.theguardian.com/business/2014/nov/30/barclays-roll-out-face-to-face-video-banking [Accessed 7 December 2017]

Jones, R (2017) Has Lloyds come up with a credible shrinking bank branch? *The Guardian*, 4 November [online] https://www.theguardian.com/money/2017/nov/04/has-lloyds-come-up-with-a-credible-shrinking-bank-branch [Accessed 4 December 2017]

Lemmon, C (2017) BNP Paribas unveils vr-based banking services, *Fstech*, 31 May [online] http://www.fstech.co.uk/fst/BNP_Paribas_VR_App.php [Accessed 8 December 2017]

Lewis, R (2016) HSBC SmartSave: New micro-savings app, *Money Watch*, 5 December [online] https://money-watch.co.uk/11112/hsbc-smartsave-savings-app# [Accessed 4 December 2017]

Lloyds Banking Group (2016) Lloyds Banking Group launches mortgage advice via video at home, 22 March [online] http://www.lloydsbankinggroup.com/media/press-releases/2016-press-releases/lloyds-banking-group/lloyds-banking-group-launches-mortgage-advice-via-video-at-home/ [Accessed 7 December 2017]

Lloyds Banking Group (2017) Lloyds Bank opens state-of-the-art branch offering new banking experience, 25 September [online] http://www.lloydsbankinggroup.com/Media/Press-Releases/press-releases-2017/lloyds-bank/lloyds-bank-opens-state-of-the-art-branch-offering-new-banking-experience/ [Accessed 4 December 2017]

Olanrewaju, T (2014) The rise of the digital bank, *McKinsey*, July [online] https://www.mckinsey.com/business-functions/digital-mckinsey/our-insights/the-rise-of-the-digital-bank [Accessed 17 November 2017]

PwC (2017) Who are you calling a 'challenger'? [online] www.pwc.co.uk/challenger-banks [Accessed 2 December 2017]

Romeo, V (2016) HSBC to launch video investment advice, *Money Marketing*, 27 May [online] https://www.fundstrategy.co.uk/hsbc-to-launch-video-investment-advice/ [Accessed 7 December 2017]

Rumney, E (2018) British bank RBS hires 'digital human' Cora on probation, *Reuters* [online] https://uk.reuters.com/article/us-rbs-avatar/british-bank-rbs-hires-digital-human-cora-on-probation-idUKKCN1G523L [Accessed 29 April 2018]

Smith, R (2017) HSBC rolls out over 1,500 talking ATMs across the UK to help blind and partially sighted customers, *City Am*, 9 May [online] http://www.cityam.com/264272/hsbc-rolls-out-over-1500-talking-atms-across-uk-help-blind [Accessed 5 December 2017]

Strzalek, A (2017) Barclaycard unveils charity donation wearables, *Fstech*, 27 April [online] http://www.fstech.co.uk/fst/Barclaycard_Charity_Donation_Wearables.php [Accessed 30 November 2017]

Treanor, J (2007) Lloyds closes Indian call centres, *The Guardian* [online] https://www.theguardian.com/money/2007/mar/02/business.india [Accessed 6 December 2017]

Treanor, J (2017) Plan to shut free-to-use cash machines could lead to 'ATM deserts' in UK, *The Guardian*, 1 November [online] https://www.theguardian.com/money/2017/nov/01/free-to-use-link-cash-machines-atm-deserts-uk [Accessed 4 December 2017]

UK Finance (2017) High street banks announce new access to banking standard, 20 July [online] https://www.ukfinance.org.uk/high-street-banks-announce-new-access-to-banking-standard/ [Accessed 2 December 2017]

UK Finance (2018) The way we bank now [online] https://www.ukfinance.org.uk/wp-content/uploads/2018/05/WWBN-FINAL-Digital.pdf [Accessed 23 July 2018]

Virgin (2017) Virgin Money Lounges – banking with a difference [online] https://uk.virginmoney.com/virgin/about-lounges/ [Accessed 8 December 2017]

Williams-Grut, O (2016a) Challenger bank Metro is opening new 'stores' while big banks are closing hundreds of branches, *Business Insider,* 14 December [online] http://uk.businessinsider.com/metro-bank-chairman-vernon-hill-on-brexit-and-growth-plans-2016-12 [Accessed 2 December 2017]

Williams-Grut (2016b) The hottest new buzzword in tech is robo-advice – here's what it's all about, *Business Insider*, 18 March [online] http://uk.businessinsider.com/what-are-robo-advisors-robo-advice-2016-3 [Accessed 7 December 2017]

Wright, A (2017) Get a mortgage by video: Banking giant Santander is latest to launch online interviews for home loans, *This is Money*, 23 June [online] http://www.thisismoney.co.uk/money/mortgageshome/article-4632354/Buyers-apply-mortgage-video-Santander.html [Accessed 7 December 2017]

07

Multi-channel versus omni-channel

INTRODUCTION

The previous chapter presented an overview of the different channels and interfaces that customers can use to engage with retail banks. This chapter progresses the retail banking distribution channel discussion further to look at how retail banks can develop a **multi-channel** and/or an omni-channel strategic approach to their distribution channels. The first section of this chapter will look at multi-channel and omni-channel, covering in detail their similarities and differentiators before progressing to consider the drivers and challenges when implementing operational strategy for multi- and omni-channel propositions and how the governance of the propositions operates.

LEARNING OBJECTIVES

By the end of this chapter you will be able to:

- differentiate between the multi-channel and omni-channel banking models;
- evaluate operational strategies for multi-channel and omni-channel propositions;
- analyse how an organization can transition from a multi-channel to an omni-channel business model;

- evaluate the costs and benefits of multi-channel and omni-channel banking;
- explain what aspects of governance and regulation banks need to consider in the multi-channel and omni-channel environments;
- reflect upon what Apple, Google and Amazon have done to enhance customer experience.

Multi-channel   The provision of more than one way or channel for customers to conduct their financial business. Typically, this will be a combination of branch, ATMs, call centre, internet banking and, increasingly, mobile. Retail banks may choose to offer some or all of the channels as part of their retail banking distribution strategy.

Multi-channel

Companies that adopt two or more channels to engage with their customers typically do so by simply bolting on the additional channel(s) to their core proposition. Whilst on one hand the provision of more ways to enable customers to engage with a company or retail bank may be seen as a positive way forward, if there is a lack of interconnectivity and consistency between the channels, this may lead to customer disengagement or, worse, dissatisfaction. Additional channels may include emerging methods of communication such as social media and video conferencing.

The reality is that as the majority of the established UK retail banks started to introduce new channels, such as call centres and digital banking, they built channel-specific operating platforms that were not designed to speak to each other. In addition, each channel typically had its own governance, requiring protocols and management information that led to inconsistency in the overarching operating model. As the number of channels increased, so did the number of complicated IT systems needed to deliver and manage the new channels, both at individual and collective levels. The original belief was that customers would migrate from one channel to another; however, in practice customers were not as polarized in their views. Customers wanted to be able to engage with all channels at any time of their choosing and for different reasons. Further, customer transactions and interactions were not directly swapped on a one-for-one basis; rather customers increased the overall number of transactions they performed. For example, rather than paying a bill in a branch, customers could make a payment over the telephone and then check later via the internet to make sure that the money had left their bank account. The growth in the number of transactions and interactions has been made possible through the emergence of complementary channels.

This creates a dichotomy for the traditional banks. They either have to invest in a new IT platform and switch all their channel applications to a single operating platform that can be accessed via all channels, or they have to use smart technologies to fully integrate the existing disparate systems so that they work (or at least appear to work) together in perfect harmony. The former option is extremely costly, would take time to test and implement and carries a vast customer account transition risk. The latter carries a high degree of risk due to adapting outdated legacy mainframe systems that still exist and are less agile than some of the cloud-based applications now available that enable effective use of smartphones, tablets and laptops.

A multi-channel proposition can work extremely well – there is no need to invest in complex omni-channel technology. Arguably, if you have the most appropriate interface available, who cares if one channel knows exactly how the other channel operates? As long as they fit together and do the collective job on behalf of the brand, then the overall customer experience will be a good one.

Multi-channel banking has developed over the last few decades, initially as independent new channels evolved due to emergence of new technologies; first came ATMs, followed by call centre technologies and latterly the birth of the internet. As each of the new channels emerged, they did so as siloed business rather than being fully integrated as a single customer offering, hence the service provided by the respective channels may not be the same and may lack consistency in terms of delivery.

Meanwhile, customers have been enjoying more enhanced services from organizations such as Amazon who use customer information more effectively to better anticipate customers' needs and deliver a more cohesive customer experience, giving value to both the retail organization and their customers. Retail banks have failed to join the dots to capitalize upon the wealth of customer information they hold and deliver a consistent, full, end-to-end service irrespective of which channel a customer may use to conduct or complete a purchase.

Omni-channel

The fundamental difference between omni-channel and multi-channel is that customers are in control of the channels they wish to use. A perfect example of this is where a customer can commence the account opening process by completing an application online or via a smartphone app, then finish completing it in the branch with help from a banking adviser or via assistance from a call centre agent. The experience should be seamless and consistent irrespective of which channel customers choose to use. There should be no need to repeat information already supplied – data provided via one channel should be accessible in any other channel. To realize a true omni-channel experience, the channel-specific operating systems need to be fully integrated; if this can be achieved, then financial services can become seamlessly embedded into the lives of customers.

The term omni-channel describes the simultaneous use of two or more channels, such as being on the telephone to a call centre whilst using a mobile app. Omni-channel also alludes to the consistency between different channels that enables seamless customer interactions. Irrespective of the channel used by a customer, personal preferences saved on one channel must be available in all other channels.

Retail banks are in an unrivalled position to better understand their customers than any other sector. Banks already have a depth of knowledge and insight about their customers' activities. They know the extent of the financial products they have, their transaction patterns – where, when and what they spend their money on – and their associated demographic profiles. By interrogating this rich source of data further, banks can develop a unique and valuable understanding of their customers. As discussed in Chapter 5, this source of competitive advantage is to be challenged due to the emergence of open banking, but until customers actually choose to give other organizations the authority to access their information, the existing retail banks hold the upper hand.

Operational strategies for multi-channel versus omni-channel

The growth of multi-channel in the late 1980s and 1990s was about creating low-cost channel choices to replace more expensive traditional transactional and sales branch-based activities. The multi-channel strategy was underpinned by branch staff being targeted and incentivized to drive customers towards low-cost alternative channels which were promoted as being more appropriate for the customers' needs, yet the banks were driving channel migration activity for more self-centred reasons – to drive down costs. Call centres and internet-based operations were far more economic from a bank's perspective, so if more transacting and accounts could be opened via those channels, then there would be less need for costly branches to perform the same activities. The customer was not the central focus of delivering the multi-channel model.

Omni-channel evolved in the 2000s and is an altogether different proposition which has, in many ways, evolved from the multi-channel model. Omni-channel attempts to recover and correct the original omission of the customer from the multi-channel model. Omni-channel places the customer at the heart of the model and builds the channels around them, providing a seamless customer experience that delivers focused advice, products and services. For the banks, omni-channel is an ideal opportunity to really understand the customer, streamline operating systems and focus attention on the various demographic groups of customers that banks serve.

The new era of retail banking heralds the need for new products and new services to all be available via the convenience of digital platforms, yet that does not necessarily mean the demise of branches; rather, the solution will be provided by the omni-channel model. Both the branch-centric and multi-channel retail banking models are now confined to the retail banking of the past. The retail bank of the future will be customer-centric, focused on self-service digital technology, complemented by existing channels such as call centres and branches and emerging channels such as social media.

Successful operational deployment of omni-channel strategies requires that organizations distinguish themselves both by delivering consistency of interactions and through a rich and detailed understanding of the channel interfaces, devices and software applications that enable customer interactions. Organizations will rigorously challenge themselves to ensure that their customers receive the same experience and messages from the plethora of different channels and devices that are available. In the modern day, an organization that provides customers with an omni-channel mix of mobile app, social media and website would need to ensure that the look and feel of the software interface as well as the messages, including the language and tone across each of the touchpoints, are consistent and seamless.

In January 2017, Forrester Research summarized the extent of the customer experience challenge faced by organizations as they strive to deliver competitive advantage in the omni-channel era: 'Brands must fundamentally rethink their CX ecosystems: the web of relations among all aspects of a company – including its customers, employees, partners, and operating environment – that determines the quality of the customer experience' (Parrish, 2014). This definition helps us understand that the successful implementation of omni-channel is not simply down to the integration of operating systems, but rather organizations need to align all other facets of the operating model to ensure harmonious delivery of the omni-channel strategy.

Whilst integrating distinct digital and physical channels into a single, seamless customer experience is undoubtedly a priority, the analysis and understanding of customer preferences enables banks to tailor specific products and services to meet the needs and priorities of each individual customer. If banks are able to implement efficient, fully integrated systems, underpinned by cohesive internal governance that creates a single customer view and delivers exceptional customer experiences, then they will be able to generate a competitive advantage over their competitors (Marous, 2014). The growth in smartphone apps combined with banks having a greater understanding of their customers means that banks will be able to offer more value-added app-based services such as budgeting or financial planning via their mobile channels. Customers also use social media as a powerful source of news and information. Existing social media intermediaries such as Facebook and Twitter can be very influential channels for banks. They need to form part of the retail banking omni-channel model and accordingly have to be managed extremely carefully as part of the overall channel mix.

ACTIVITY 7.1

- Differentiate between multi-channel and omni-channel operational strategies. What is the difference from a customer's perspective?

- What value is there in creating an omni-channel approach?

- How would you describe your bank? Is it multi-channel or omni-channel or somewhere in between?

Costs of multi-channel and omni-channel banking

There are many costs to consider when providing a multi-channel and/or omni-channel customer proposition. This section looks at the costs of transactions, technology, branding and acquisition.

Transactional cost

By adding more distribution channels, banks originally believed that they would be able to substitute high-cost branch-based transactions with direct substitute low-cost alternative channel transactions. Due to the convenience provided by non-branch-based channels, it is no surprise that branch transaction volumes have been trending downwards and that online services, especially mobile banking usage, have been trending upwards. The evidence shows, however, that there has been extensive growth in the overall number of interactions and that whilst there has been a significant shift from traditional branch and call centre channels to internet and mobile, the total number of interactions has doubled in five years, effectively adding more cost to retail banks.

2010 = 1,232m interactions:

- branch 502m (41 per cent);
- telephony 85m (7 per cent);
- internet 565m (46 per cent);
- mobile 80m (6 per cent).

2015= 2,195m interactions – up 78 per cent since 2010:

- Branch 427m (19 per cent) down 75m interactions since 2010. Still a major channel, but now the third most popular channel.
- Telephony 74m (3 per cent) down 11m interactions since 2010. Telephony is firmly the least-used channel.
- Internet 705m (32 per cent) up 140m interactions since 2010. Still growing in consumer usage.
- Mobile 895m (41 per cent) up 815m interactions since 2010. Now the dominant channel.

Projections for 2020 = 3,201m interactions – up 49 per cent since 2015:

- Branch 268m (8 per cent) down 159m interactions since 2015. No longer a major channel for current account interactions, with less than 10 per cent predicted to happen in branches.
- Telephony 64m (2 per cent) down 10m interactions since 2015. Telephony is falling further behind.
- Internet 528m (17 per cent) up 140m interactions since 2010. Growth remains steady and constant.
- Mobile 2,341m (73 per cent) up 815m interactions since 2010. The undisputed dominant channel.

The scale of change in channel usage is evidenced by the current account interaction data above which originates from BBA (produced by CACI) in 2015 (BBA, 2015).

Cost of technology

Legacy operating systems are notoriously awkward to adapt to cater for new channel demands, so inevitably every new channel that emerges requires a new operating platform to be built both at the point of contact for the staff interacting with customers and at the back end for data storage and extraction of management information. Telephony call centres are a perfect example of this, where the telephone systems (as described in the previous chapter) rely upon specific hardware and software for the calls to be received and routed to the most appropriate member of staff. In addition, all the management information such as average call handling time and abandonment rates are channel-specific metrics that simply would not have existed in any previous system owned by a retail bank but are essential to effective management of telephony operations. The costs associated with hardware infrastructure and software represents a significant capital investment for banks and that is before considering how to integrate the new channel systems with the existing channel technology, hence why the multi-channel approach evolved and omni-channel was deferred.

Costs of branding and communication

The introduction of a new channel, whether part of a multi-channel or omni-channel strategy, involves significant investment from a marketing perspective in order to successfully promote the new channel to both new and existing customers. The new channel may likely have a sub-brand name such as Bank of Scotland's launch of 'Phoneline' in the late 1980s, which heralded the bank's creation of call centres for the mass market to help service their current account customers' needs 24 hours a day, 7 days a week. The Phoneline brand was heavily marketed in all aspects of the media and was underpinned with extensive branch training to ensure all branch-based staff could promote the services of the new call centre operation.

Acquisition costs

In the omni-channel environment, organizations may choose to build on the range of existing platforms they already have, build from scratch, or acquire a competitor that has already established its business on an omni-channel platform that has already been proven to work. Either way, costs are involved. Costs of acquisition and subsequent investment in technologies are showcased in the BBVA case study below.

CASE STUDY
BBVA

In 2014, Spanish bank, BBVA, acquired a US online banking platform called Simple for US $117m. In March 2014, BBVA announced the creation of a brand-new digital banking division, with the aim to turn BBVA, Spain's second-largest bank, into 'the first bank in the world to transform into a pure digital house' (INSEAD, 2017).

BBVA's aim was to deliver a consistent customer experience for all products, services and marketing across all channels and devices. To achieve this, BBVA had to deliver and combine two distinct activities. First BBVA had to better utilize the extensive amounts of customer information that it held. If it could use this information proactively, it could generate a significant competitive advantage, not least against the emerging fintech organizations. Second, BBVA had to invest heavily in its legacy technology platforms to create a new global technology infrastructure that would be capable of delivering the consistent, seamless omni-channel proposition. In each of the last two years of the process, BBVA invested around €850m per year in its new IT platform.

Questions

1 Do you believe that BBVA will reap a significant return on its investment? Explain your answer.

2 Where does your bank stand on investment into legacy technology platforms? Why do you think some CEOs of major retail banks have failed to make significant investments in the underlying technology of banking systems?

3 How should traditional banks approach transitioning from bespoke, legacy, siloed, multi-channel systems to a single, more agile omni-channel, single-governed operating environment?

Benefits of omni-channel banking

Customers are already experiencing very personalized marketing experiences from retail organizations such as Amazon – irrespective of how the customer engages with them. If done right, the customer experience is sublime. It feels comforting, smooth, seamless, flawless. But this is only feasible through truly understanding the end-to-end customer experience journeys and how the web of channels has to interact to underpin the customer experience. Complex algorithms underlie the identification of the appropriate product and enable the appropriate timing and presentation of the product to the customer irrespective of the channel they choose to purchase from. Retail banks have to develop the same thinking – to design their processes and products around the customer and to ensure through omni-channel banking that customers will have a consistent experience, whether they choose to bank via a mobile device, by telephone or visiting a branch. If retail banks fail to invest in the creation of omni-channel banking, there are plenty of other institutions that have already invested in their infrastructure and are unbridled by legacy systems and archaic cultures, who would relish the opportunity to move into the financial services marketplace.

Customers are ready, and so is the technology. Retail banks need to invest in enabling this new approach to avoid potential disintermediation and to retain their competitive position.

Retail banks will, however, need to exert caution. New regulation in the form of the General Data Protection Regulation (GDPR) replaced the Data Protection Act 1998 on 25 May 2018, which means that banks have to be extremely wary as to how they use customers' data to tailor and enable accurate product promotion and generate competitive advantage. In the list below, the first bullet point is of particular interest in that use of the information provided by customers should be 'limited to what is necessary in relation to the purposes for which they are processed'. In other words, if you provide information in relation to transactions, banks should not abuse this knowledge or data for an alternative reason and only use it as 'necessary', which may infer not using it for marketing purposes.

Article 5 of the GDPR requires that personal data shall be (GDPR, 2018):

- Processed lawfully, fairly and in a transparent manner in relation to individuals; collected for specified, explicit and legitimate purposes and not further processed in a manner that is incompatible with those purposes; further processing for archiving purposes in the public interest, scientific or historical research purposes or statistical purposes shall not be considered to be incompatible with the initial purposes; adequate, relevant and limited to what is necessary in relation to the purposes for which they are processed.

- Accurate and, where necessary, kept up to date; every reasonable step must be taken to ensure that personal data that are inaccurate, having regard to the purposes for which they are processed, are erased or rectified without delay.

- Kept in a form which permits identification of data subjects for no longer than is necessary for the purposes for which the personal data are processed; personal data may be stored for longer periods insofar as the personal data will be processed solely for archiving purposes in the public interest, scientific or historical research purposes or statistical purposes subject to implementation of the appropriate technical and organizational measures required by the GDPR in order to safeguard the rights and freedoms of individuals.

- Processed in a manner that ensures appropriate security of the personal data, including protection against unauthorized or unlawful processing and against accidental loss, destruction or damage, using appropriate technical or organizational measures.

REGULATION

For updates on General Data Protection (GDPR) regulation, check here:
https://www.eugdpr.org/key-changes.html

Governance of multi-channel and omni-channel propositions

The historic channel silo approach to retail bank channels (under the multi-channel framework) with its bespoke operating systems that failed to communicate with each other, is no longer a viable or indeed sustainable proposition in the 21st century.

As mentioned earlier in this chapter, the original siloed approach to multi-channel propositions led to new governance, protocols, reporting and management information being produced for each of the new channels as they emerged. For each new channel, governance and technology were essentially added on as a new vertical to the existing organization. At the time there lacked an integrated, cohesive and single horizontal view to governing and managing across the combined business entity.

Channel-specific governance led to a disparity and indeed facilitated internal competition between the channels, hence the service provided by the respective channels differed and was inconsistently delivered to customers. This approach led to strange behaviours being exhibited within organizations' distribution channel teams and ultimately led to conflict in operational strategies as channels competed internally for market share to become the dominant channel. This approach was completely at odds with what customers wanted. There was a disconnect between what the banks thought they should be doing and what customers were looking for. When banks realized this, omni-channel strategy and a common approach to customer-centric reporting, technology platforms and governance were born – putting the customer at the heart of what retail banks do.

Omni-channel banking offers customers access to a variety of channels but with more consistency, having the same governance arrangements, potentially built on a common, single technology platform, with reports and management information available from all channels to enable an overarching customer-centric retail bank perspective to be analysed.

Transitioning from multi-channel to omni-channel

If it is not practical or feasible for existing retail banks to simply wipe their technology slate clean and start again with a new, single, customer-centric, omni-channel operating platform, then the only alternative is for retail banks to create the illusion of a single, all-encompassing system that will enable the harmonious interaction between customer and banks – irrespective of how the customer wishes to engage with the bank. This can be achieved through the introduction of smart bridge or middleware technologies that can join up the distinct channels to give an omni-channel feel.

Banks are in the unique and enviable position whereby they have the opportunity to capitalize on the power of extensive knowledge and insight to the lives, priorities and interests of their customers. For many years, information, in particular transactional data, has simply been processed and recorded but never really interrogated to create a valuable customer proposition. Only in recent times has the true value of customer data been understood, but we have to caution against any infringement of GDPR. New players are adopting different approaches to move into the data market-place. Apple Pay does not record what customers have spent their money on, nor does it keep information on the transactions, but it does take a tiny margin on every transaction. Conversely, Google adopts an almost polar opposite approach – Android Pay does not take a margin per transaction, it wants something else. Within the terms and conditions Android Pay states that it will collect information about transactions, the time and date the transactions happened, the location and description, even any photos associated with the transaction. The traditional financial margin model is being replaced with a new source of income generation – data. Customer data, in particular transactional data, is one of the richest forms of insight about customers. Banks have been slow to realize the wealth of information they have in their possession and have failed to see the true value of the data they hold. Yet we can already see signs of the social media giants using complex algorithms to present targeted adverts to individuals.

It is imperative that the banks take the opportunity to utilize their data to create bespoke offerings to meet the needs and priorities of each and every individual customer. The banks that can capitalize on their extensive customer data information pool and can combine it with smart marketing tools will generate an edge over the competition. Banks can take advantage of the omni-channel approach to get a better understanding of their customers. Banks can already see customers' product use, their transaction patterns and demographic profiles. By combining channel usage, banks and marketers can develop an even more detailed profile of their customers. Understanding not only what the customer looks like, but also how they conduct their banking, can enable an even more improved product offering via their preferred channel. Omni-channel will be a primary mechanism to deliver bottom-line profits and provide banks with a viable proposition to attract and retain customers as well as making them more profitable. But banks cannot delay – as discussed in Chapter 5, the emergence of PSD2 and open banking may well lead to the loss of any data-based competitive advantage that has historically been the sole domain of the traditional banks. Changes in regulations mean that these barriers are coming down and only time will tell if the traditional retail banks have failed to capitalize on the wealth of information upon which they have been sitting for many years.

Omni-channel – the US perspective

Based upon a US Retail Banking Study compiled by Gallup in 2014, three main themes emerged (Hughes, 2014):

1 Three main channels account for the majority of US customer banking needs. Unsurprisingly perhaps, branch, ATM and online are the dominant components of the multi-channel mix in the United States. Almost half (46 per cent) of US retail banking customers surveyed had used all three of these channels in the previous six months. As discussed in Chapter 4, from an economic perspective, whilst it may cost a bank more to serve customers via the three-channel model compared to digital- or telephony-only organizations, it was observed that these customers keep an average of 4 per cent more of their deposits with their primary bank and generate an estimated $155 more in profit per year to their primary bank than people who don't use all three of these channels.

2 Mobile banking usage is increasing, but it is adding to, not replacing, other channels. Among the largest US banks that Gallup studied in both 2012 and 2013, heavy users (at least once per week) of mobile banking increased by 11 per cent (more than in any other channel). Not surprisingly, 57 per cent of Millennials/Gen Y customers have gone mobile for their banking. That percentage falls to 37 per cent for Gen X customers, 16 per cent for baby boomers, and less than 10 per cent for seniors.

The increased mobile usage has not led to a direct correlation with customers' use of other channels. The Gallup research shows that customers who use mobile banking also use other channels more frequently than the average customer. Among mobile banking users:

- 79 per cent have also used a branch in the last six months;
- 84 per cent have gone to an ATM;

- 95 per cent have used online banking;
- 58 per cent have spoken to a call centre agent;
- 15 per cent have contacted their bank via Twitter;
- 19 per cent have contacted their bank via Facebook (compared to only 1 and 2 per cent for Twitter and Facebook respectively among non-mobile users).

3 Social media customers are valuable. Slightly less than 9 per cent of customers contacted their bank directly via Facebook or Twitter during the six months of the Gallup study, and roughly half of those have done both. These socially engaged customers are both younger (91 per cent are either Gen X or Gen Y) and more affluent. These customers also are more engaged with their bank and hold much more positive feelings towards their bank than the typical customer.

Whilst increasing numbers of customers are moving to digital channels to conduct their day-to-day banking needs, they are not abandoning traditional channels at the same pace. The Gallup research found that, even among those who visited a branch less than once a month, 80 per cent chose to initiate their account opening in a branch and only 8 per cent started by opening their account online. When customers did open their account online, they were far less satisfied with the account-opening experience (by nearly 20 percentage points) than were those who opened their account in a branch.

Limitations of omni-channel

Undoubtedly the omni-channel proposition is an extremely powerful way of delivering customers with much-improved experiences. The problems arise when the needs of the customer are non-standard and fall outside the omni-channel framework. This can happen when something has gone wrong or when the customer has cause for concern. Breaking through the standard interfaces of call centre IVR or being pushed a product when using the internet or mobile app, all adds to the heightened tension that customers feel during a period of service failure. Where the customer need or requirement does not follow the standard process rails, it means that there is inevitably a disconnect between what the customer needs and the service provided by the retail bank. One of the main problems is that the member of staff dealing with a non-standard enquiry needs to access a single view of the customer to enable them to readily resolve any issue – they need a live, real-time perspective of what action the customer has taken, the channels used and the process they have followed. In its most basic form, if a customer is looking at a front-end system or app, and the member of staff is looking at a back-office system, then there is an inevitable disconnect between the two information systems.

The majority of traditional bank systems were developed solely for the use of bank staff. As we now know, the move from branch banking to mobile and digital banking has commenced and will continue to develop at pace in the years ahead, but the legacy bank systems have not evolved at the same rate as customers are adopting the modern channels. This means that banks have been attempting to deploy customer-facing banking systems that were traditionally designed to be back-end, employee-based systems.

The solution to this problem is to provide a single user interface which joins together the disparate systems that retail banks have so that both staff and customer have a common information source that is transparent to all parties. There is no need for banks' legacy systems to be discarded, but there is a pressing need to ensure that an appropriate middleware technology is used to bring the IT strands together to create a single user application.

ACTIVITY 7.2

- Consider retail organizations within the financial sector. Identify one that follows the multi-channel model and another from the same sector that follows omni-channel. What do you perceive to be the difference in the customer experiences within the respective businesses?

- From a retail banking perspective, what are the advantages and disadvantages of investing in the delivery of an omni-channel strategy? What alternative strategies could a retail bank deploy instead of investing in an omni-channel strategy?

- How does omni-channel banking create competitive advantage for retail banks? Is it a sustainable competitive advantage?

- What can retail banks do to protect their competitive advantage? What threats exist to retail banks' omni-channel competitive advantage?

Chapter summary

- Multi-channels have grown over time to incorporate a range of customer interfaces that have operated independently and in some cases have been bolted on over time.

- Omni-channel is an all-encompassing, customer-centric approach to developing a variety of interfaces that feel almost seamless to the customer.

- Channel transaction usage his shifted from branches and telephony in 2010 to mobile and internet in 2015, with the pendulum set to swing even further in favour of mobile by 2020.

- Since the implementation of GDPR in May 2018, retail banks need to exert caution when using customers' data for the purposes of marketing activities.

- Multi-channel propositions had their own individual channel governance which led to conflict between channels. Omni-channel governance takes a broader, more integrated view of the customer proposition and of the entire retail bank.

- Transitioning from multi-channel to omni-channel comes at a substantial cost to the traditional retail banks, but it is an investment in the future.

- Whilst mobile banking transactions are growing at a phenomenal rate, many of the transactions are new, additional transactions that have arisen from the convenience of the technology.

- Social media channels (in the United States) have yet to become a major channel for direct engagement with retail banks.

- The principles of the omni-channel model can come under pressure when non-standard customer interactions need to be serviced.

Objective check

1 What is the difference between the multi-channel and omni-channel banking models?

2 What operational strategies do you need to consider for multi-channel and omni-channel propositions?

3 How can an organization transition from a multi-channel to an omni-channel business model? Where is your organization on the journey from multi-channel to omni-channel banking?

4 What are the costs and benefits of multi-channel and omni-channel banking?

5 What aspects of governance and regulation do banks need to consider in the multi-channel and omni-channel environments? What difference and commonalities exist?

6 What have Apple, Google and Amazon done to enhance customer experience in the data-centric world within which we live?

References

BBA (2015) Mobile phone apps become the UK's number one way to bank, 14 June [online] https://www.bba.org.uk/news/press-releases/mobile-phone-apps-become-the-uks-number-one-way-to-bank/#.WhIFF7p2vIU [Accessed 17 November 2017]

GDPR (2018) http://gdpr-legislation.co.uk/ [Accessed 4 February 2018]

Hughes, J (2014) Every channel matters when engaging bank customers, Gallup, 28 March [online] http://news.gallup.com/opinion/gallup/173606/every-channel-matters-engaging-bank-customers.aspx [Accessed 29 October 2017]

INSEAD (2017) The 'omni-channel approach': digital banking for Generation Y [online] https://knowledge.insead.edu/node/3753/pdf [Accessed 17 November 2017]

Marous, J (2014) Omnichannel banking: more than a buzzword, *The Financial Brand*, 24 March [online] https://thefinancialbrand.com/37996/bank-channel-usage-research/ [Accessed 29 October 2017]

Parrish, R (2014) Transform customer experience by rethinking your ecosystem, *UX Magazine*, 25 June https://uxmag.com/articles/transform-customer-experience-by-rethinking-your-ecosystem [Accessed 23 July 2018]

08

The role of technology in the evolution of retail banking

INTRODUCTION

Throughout the decades and even centuries, technology has undoubtedly enabled the development of retail banking. This chapter looks at the historical patterns of technology and the main events that have directly affected major changes in the financial sector. In some instances, customers have driven the technological need for banks to change and on other occasions banks have taken the lead to change and evolve their operating models. Implementing technology change comes at a cost and, in some cases, not all technology is received favourably.

LEARNING OBJECTIVES

By the end of this chapter you will be able to:

- evaluate the rise of technology in retail banking;
- evaluate the drivers for technological change;
- analyse who benefits and who loses from technological change;
- review whether all technological change is positive;
- evaluate what banks can learn from other sectors.

The rise of technology in retail banking

Throughout the ages, the catalyst for all major innovations in retail banking has been the industrial revolutions and the underlying technologies that gave rise to them. The financial sector has had to continually adapt and change in response to the external environment. As was the case with the original Industrial Revolution in the late 18th century when the technology innovation of the time was the creation of machine-based manufacturing and the evolution of machine-powered textile looms – consequently merchant banking emerged to support the growth of industry and trade. Similarly, with the second Industrial Revolution in the early 19th century, technological innovation was again at its heart – this time through the development and exploitation of steam-powered transportation, be it by rail or boat. Steam also powered the engines in factories, hence industry was able to upscale and produce goods on mass production. **Taylorism** or Scientific Management became the time-and-motion operations mantra of the day, as factories looked to become increasingly productive. Technology also played a part in communications, with the development of electronic communications via telegraph. All of these components led to an increase in personal wealth and demand for the early stages of personal banking.

Taylorism   Introduced by Frederick W Taylor in the early 20th century, this scientific approach to production management breaks down all work activities into the smallest tasks so that they can be both taught and performance managed. The methodology breaks out actual work from planning and further can demark direct labour from indirect labour. It takes guesswork out and provides precise time and motion measurements, which leads to optimum job performance.

The third Industrial Revolution took place in the second half of the 20th century, yet again with technological innovation as the key. It brought electronics, computers and IT together to automate the manufacturing production process. Increased use of robotics emerged on production lines. The third Industrial Revolution witnessed the advent of mobile telephony and the emergence of the internet, though the supporting ADSL telecoms infrastructure was only in its infancy and was not always reliable. As discussed in Chapter 6, towards the late 1980s, retail banks developed early forms of home and office banking, but the branch was still very much the cornerstone of the retail bank environment. It wasn't yet time for 'clicks to replace bricks'.

The boundaries between the third and fourth industrial revolutions are a little bit obscure, but the underlying technology changes became more rapid and more substantial in nature by the turn of the 21st century. By the early 2000s mobile phones had effectively become handheld computers; by 2012, 2 billion people were using the internet. We are now well and truly immersed in the digital era. As 3D print production businesses today look over their shoulders at the factories of yesteryear with an incredulous shake of the head, the fintechs are eyeing up the traditional banks – they can see the opportunity of the modern day and are primed to seize it. But the traditional banks have adapted and adjusted to meet the changing needs of customers and businesses before. This is no longer the dawning of a new age, we are in the Digital Industrial Revolution; is this the time for fintechs to become the new-generation retail banks or will the traditional retail banks be the dominant force?

Changes in the way that customers access their banking services

Historically, the traditional banks have been perhaps too insular as they endeavour to address and resolve historical technology-based legacy problems of the past and are arguably ill-prepared for the impending competitive storm that lies ahead. Retail banks have to redefine their approach to customers and become more customer-centric in the design of distribution channels, products and services and the part technology plays in self-servicing. A simple example of this has been Barclays, which has enabled and empowered its debit card customers to take control of their own daily limit for cash withdrawals and to switch off/on remote payment option via the mobile banking app. This means customers can control the functionality of their own debit card in alignment with their own perspective of risk management and fraud prevention (Finextra, 2017a).

Regulation has helped lower the technological competitive barriers to entry that have protected the traditional banks for many years. Those barriers are now coming down. As discussed in Chapter 5, Open Banking and the Payment Services Directive 2 (PSD2) will enable customers to authorize other external parties (other than their primary bank) to have access to their personal financial data. The traditional technology barriers, created through years of campaigning and bank propaganda to 'keep your data safe' and 'don't share your PIN with anyone', is about to evaporate. The future is about sharing data and data is a valuable commodity.

Traditional retail banks have to continue to invest in their technology platforms. Lloyds Banking Group signed a 10-year deal with IBM for the provision of dedicated private cloud offerings hosted in both Lloyds and IBM datacentres. HSBC are bucking the trend by creating their own app which will enable all of a customer's bank accounts, from up to 21 providers, to be shown in one place (Shaw and Jones, 2017). Openbank, a Spanish-owned subsidiary of Santander, now offers customers a full range of products and services via its mobile app and website. Openbank is unique in that it uses only a cloud-based IT platform, which means Openbank can provide innovative services, speedy decisions and better security (Finextra, 2017b).

ACTIVITY 8.1

- Reflect on the lowering of the regulatory barriers that relate to technology. How do you think customers will react to Open Banking, allowing third-party access to their financial and transactional data?

- Apply the principles of Open Banking to your bank. If you were acting CEO, what strategy would you adopt to ensure your bank does not suffer from customer defection?

- Customer choice and flexibility are at the heart of the future model of retail banking. Once the technology barriers are down and customers provide open access to their data, what problems do you envisage the industry may encounter? How should the sector prepare for all eventualities?

- Evaluate the pros and cons of Open Banking – when the dust settles, who do you think the winners and losers will be and why?

The drivers of technological change

Customer driven

The financial marketplace is currently experiencing a customer-led revolution. Customers are grasping new technologies to make their lives easier. The rapid development of hardware devices, such as tablets and smartphones underpinned by 4G infrastructure, means that customers expect to be able to interact with banks at any time. This means that customers have roaming access to their information virtually anywhere and virtually instantaneously, without having to find somewhere to connect to Wi-Fi. This in turn has led to the boom of smartphones and the rapid development of apps.

Technology is simply an enabler. Banks need to be careful not to develop technologies just because they can. There needs to be a specific customer need, otherwise organizations can create elaborate technologies that don't really have any significant tangible customer value. Yet sometimes banks can get lucky and customer inertia can take a narrow demographic product and drive it to a mass-market value-add proposition. 'Get Cash' was developed by RBS and NatWest on the back of an emergency cash solution that enabled customers to gain money from an ATM with a four-digit code, without having to present their physical card. This service was initially aimed at a very narrow niche segment of customers, yet Get Cash has now evolved in to a mass-market, core service that a wide range of customers choose to use (in combination with a simple bank app) making it their standard way of transacting at the ATM (Chartered Banker, 2014a).

Bank driven

It is vital that technological innovation be harnessed by banks, as it is transitioning from innovation into social norms and habitual behaviour. Yet traditional banks have struggled to adapt and develop their multiple, legacy, channel-specific operating systems into a dynamic, agile, customer-centric operating platform fit for the omni-channel world in the 21st century.

The new entrants to the retail banking marketplace start from a technological blank slate and can therefore design their new operating platforms without having to worry about the back-book and legacy systems of the past.

Open banking will potentially remove all the technological barriers and enable customers to move seamlessly between traditional banks and new entrants. Yet customer knowledge of Open Banking is limited. Recent research from Equifax found that 9 out of 10 people in Britain had not heard of Open Banking and almost half of the respondents said that they would not be likely to use Open Banking. Two out of three said they would not consent to sharing of their personal data through Open Banking. However, 41 per cent of 25- to 35-year-olds were more accepting of the scheme, stating that they are likely to use Open Banking (Chartered Banker, 2017a) so whilst the headlines may look positive for traditional banks, the reality is that the younger generation is more readily keen to adopt Open Banking.

This may buy the traditional banks some time, but based upon this evidence, Open Banking will become increasingly dominant. The traditional banks cannot simply cross their fingers and hope it will go away. It won't.

ACTIVITY 8.2

- Reflect upon the impact and influence customers have in driving the successful implementation of technology-based products and services. What are the underlying factors that cause this to happen?

- How would you describe your bank's approach to Open Banking? If you were responsible for your bank's customer strategy, what recommendations would you be making to the CEO of your organization?

- What groups of customers do you think will be attracted to the Open Banking proposition? If customers from this segment came to you for advice as to whether or not they should sign up for Open Banking, what would you recommend they do?

Who benefits and who loses from technological change?

What does the future hold?

Whilst historically banks competed against each other over interest rates on loans and savings, the new competitive environment is more likely to be based upon who provides the best app and/or video banking service.

As discussed in Chapter 5, the digital revolution has taken hold; a new digital currency has even emerged for the 21st century – Bitcoin. Blockchain is the technology that sits behind Bitcoin and it has the potential to transform the financial services marketplace. Whilst Blockchain start-up businesses continue to grow rapidly, established financial services are less sure about what Blockchain actually is. PwC reported that 57 per cent don't know how (even if) they'll respond to the development of Blockchain (Chartered Banker, 2016a).

An extension of future technology is the emergence and growth of social media – this is a golden opportunity for the traditional banks to redress public perceptions of them, though many have been slow to grasp the nettle, fearing that social media may provide the ideal platform for customers to immediately vent their frustrations and concerns.

Costs of developing technology

Traditional banks have had to create digital applications that connect to their legacy systems to create the illusion of a digital bank for the modern day, whilst new players start from a blank sheet of paper and can build their service on a more agile technology platform fit for the modern day. The complexity of legacy IT systems is borne out by RBS's abandoning plans to separate out the Williams & Glyn brand bank. It was simply far too complicated, was taking far too long (almost eight years) and it was proving to be extremely costly (£1.8bn to April 2017) to extract a distinct group of customers and 300 branches from the complex web of IT systems in which they were embroiled.

The existing large banks have traditionally invested more financial resources into technological security and resilience than enhancing customer experience: 'In 2014 banks accounted for just 19 per cent of the total $10bn of fintech investment. By contrast, non-banks made up 62 per cent' (Chartered Banker, 2015/2016). If traditional banks want to keep up with the emerging competition, then they will need to invest significantly more in the fintech sector.

How banks can recoup their costs

Developing and implementing new technology represents a major investment for retail banks. Financial organizations need to decide whether they want to invest in the costly development phase (which carries risk, but high reward of being first to market) or whether they want to wait and see, then follow and copy or indeed acquire successful implementers of new technology. Either way, banks then have to consider how to recoup their costs so that they can maximize their return on investment. As discussed in Chapter 4, there are many ways that banks can manage their costs and many ways to maximize income.

Banks need to determine whether the implementation of technology forms part of the marketing mix and is a channel that customers can have access to as part of an omni-channel strategy (as discussed in Chapter 7) and accordingly should be covered from an additional degree of margin which forms part of the net interest margin that is charged, so that investment costs can be recovered, or whether the technology forms part of a distinct and discrete offering that needs to be accommodated within the pricing of a specific product or service for which a fee may be charged.

Is all technological change positive?

Technology is intended to make the lives of people simpler and more efficient. Yet to what degree does new technology achieve this? This section looks at how emerging technologies aim to enhance customers' retail banking experiences and the challenges that face retail banks in achieving the ultimate goal of customer adoption of new technologies.

Key technological changes and how they impact customers

The pace of technological change that has been used to underwrite applications such as Facebook and Google and lets us share information and help customers engage with digital services via smartphones and computers is ready to take the financial service sector by storm. These almost-hidden technologies that underpin the applications were discussed in Chapter 5 and are known as APIs.

Open APIs will enable the sharing of customer information across the financial sector and will help customers identify the best financial provider based upon the open information that has been provided and is available. This leads to the dawning of a truly open banking environment. If (and it is a very big if) customers agree to their information being made available and shared, then they will potentially have access to a vast financial services marketplace including the services provided by specific, niche specialist providers that will be able to promote their services directly to target customer segments. Whilst people already share their information openly via applications such as Facebook, the adoption of sharing sensitive financial information may be another matter entirely. For years customers have been warned about disclosing their PIN and passwords, so naturally they will have concerns about relinquishing their bank account details to the Open Banking environment. Past experiences such as erroneous credit history ratings adversely affecting applications for mortgages or loans still concern customers. The Data Protection Act was designed to safeguard customer information and to ensure that customer financial information was only ever used for the purposes for which it was originally intended, hence extreme caution needs to be taken to ensure appropriate customer authority is received and that both the banks and the third parties recognize and accept their respective responsibilities to ensure open access to customer information is appropriately managed. As part of HM Treasury's Autumn Statement in 2014, a report called 'Data Sharing and Open Data for Banks' was released by the Open Data Institute and Fingleton Associates. The key findings were (HM Treasury, 2014):

- Greater access to data is required to create increased competition in UK banking.

- Additional steps are required to utilize already widely used technologies and standards for data sharing.

- APIs are identified as the industry standard for sharing data and the large data holders will become the platforms for third-party innovation.

- OAuth has become the standard simple and secure mechanism for users to authenticate themselves and to provide their authority and basis upon which their data can be shared. OAuth enables the customer to permit the sharing of personal data, but without providing specific login details.

- Demand for data remains strong; however, the traditional methods of accessing information are both complex to use and costly to deploy. The desire by industry to see banks providing external APIs was universal.

- As part of open data, there is a need for more than specific customer data to be supplied.

- Aggregated data (grouped account data) and reference data (including charges, fees and terms & conditions) should also form part of the open data set.

- Standardization of open APIs would create the ideal platform for re-use of data.

- Third-party access to consumer data is perfectly compatible with both the Data Protection Act and the principles of privacy, provided it is implemented cautiously.

- Upon customer authorization being given, both the bank and the third party become Data Controllers and are bound by the Data Protection Act.

- Upon receipt of a customer's authority to share data with a third party, a bank will not be held liable once the information is shared. Banks must, however, ensure that they only share the specific components that have been approved by the customer for sharing.

- Traditional banks' legacy IT systems may add complexity to the API data-sharing process, but are not believed to be a prohibiting factor.

With a blueprint for the future of APIs and Open Banking in hand, and the phased implementation schedule planned to get underway from 2018 as part of Payment Services Directive 2, we are good to go, right? Well actually no. Customers need to be brought along on the journey too. Whilst the overarching proposition for customers is to allow them to see all of their finances through a single interface, and to take advantage of numerous financial services providers with absolute ease, the customers seem to remain ambivalent. A YouGov poll commissioned by Equifax in 2016 found that 90 per cent had not heard of Open Banking, with a further 45 per cent stating that they would be unlikely to use it. When specifically asked about providing consent to the release of their information via APIs, 60 per cent stated that they would not provide consent for their information to be shared, citing security and third-party contact as being the primary reasons for not wanting to join Open Banking (Equifax, 2016).

Customer financial information which was once the sole property (and arguably a competitive advantage) of the customer's bank, could not be used for marketing purposes, as decreed by the Data Protection Act (1998). With the advent of Open Banking, however, customer data can be easily shared with any new or existing player in the sector. The first tentative steps have already begun. As discussed in Chapter 7, General Data Protection Regulation (GDPR) legislation has replaced the Data Protection Act as of 25th May 2018 and offers greater protection to customers for the modern digital era.

American Express allows its customers to connect their account to their TripAdvisor profiles. Not only do customers do this willingly on a voluntary basis, but they are incentivized to do so, receiving bespoke offers and rewards. The key to successfully removing the cyber-security barrier will be incremental steps for adopting APIs, small steps which will gradually take the customer towards the guarantee of data security and protection from unsolicited and unregulated approaches so that customers always feel as though they retain control of their information. Open APIs will be designed in such a way as to give the customer total control over what data is shared and with whom. However, once authority has been provided by the customer and their information has been shared with other parties, it cannot be taken back. Customers therefore need to be really sure that they want to authorize this to happen before giving their permission.

The traditional banks remain in 'slow adoption' mode for Open Banking – preferring to closely watch the marketplace and keep an eye on the evolving competition. Whilst not ignoring Open Banking entirely, the traditional banks have other priorities. Primarily they are dealing with legacy litigation issues of the past financial crises, organizational restructuring and retrenchment of operations as the once global banks endeavour to become more localized UK-based banks. They have the additional regulatory requirement to ring-fence their retail banking operations as separate legal entities from the perceived riskier corporate businesses.

Technology is an enabler for some of the most vulnerable people in society. Simple app-based solutions such as US-based fintech Dave analyses customers' spend information from their bank accounts and promotes better money management, without the need for using overdraft facilities (Chaparro, 2017.) The Dave app also offers 0 per cent interest pay-day loan-style advances, without credit checks, to be repaid whenever they can, though customers who do not pay back will be precluded from using the app's service in the future. Whilst the Dave app charges a nominal $0.99 monthly charge, customers can voluntarily donate a tip, should they be pleased with the service they have received.

Key technological changes and how they impact internal operations

Technology improvements are not always aimed directly at customers. Instead the focus may be upon simplifying operations and reducing internal costs of the business to seek out better ways of delivering retail banking services in the future. Retail banks such as Barclays are keen to stay close to the technological innovation. In May 2017, Barclays created an innovation centre in Shoreditch called Rise London. This environment brings together Barclays' own internal technology and banking teams with 40 fintech start-up enterprises. The innovation centre will also host in excess of 200 hours of workshops, learning and networking. Collaboration in the emerging technologies market space is key to Barclays' strategic vision for the future (Barclays, 2017).

Santander is investing heavily in the fintech market too. Santander's InnoVentures venture capital investment fund of $200m (with $100m coming from parent Santander Group) has been used extensively to take minority stake investments in fintech start-ups such as Personetics Technologies, Gridspace and iZettle (Lemmon, 2016).

HSBC is investing $2.1bn in the digital transformation of retail banking, wealth management and commercial banking between 2015 and 2020 (HSBC, 2017). Part of the programme included the use of digital services such as e-signatures and document upload services, thus simplifying the customer experience and enabling straight-through processing.

Nationwide has established a five-year contract with CapGemini until 2020 to supply it with IT infrastructure services covering service integration, service desk and end-user services. Further investment has been made with partner BT to upgrade Nationwide's retail operations network to drive its digital transformation strategy and to realize efficiencies and introduce customer-facing and back-office technologies (Scroxton, 2016).

TSB has rolled out iris-scanning technology, thus enabling customers that use Samsung Galaxy 8 smartphones to register their irises and to log in to their TSB banking app by simply looking at their phone (Cellan-Jones, 2017).

What banking can learn from other sectors

There are many ideas that retailers have introduced that could be readily adopted by retail banks. This section will cover a few of those ideas and concepts.

Retail branch/store design

McDonald's convenience restaurants are designed around the customer – large, open, creatively decorated areas, some with children's play areas, some areas with bar stools, some with lounge chairs, some with drive-through facilities and some with self-service facilities. All manner of customer segmentation has been considered. However, McDonalds' store design is not all about the customer; store design is aligned to leveraging optimum operational logistics. Consider the delivery of the product to the store. The delivery lorry reverses and docks on to the rear of the store. From here, the shutter door of the lorry opens and the products are transported straight into the refrigerators of the store. Next to the refrigerators and storage area are the preparation and kitchen zones that then feed directly through to the servery area, which in turn interfaces to the front-of-house area where the store staff meet and engage with customers. Slick and efficient. Store design follows the path of the product. How does this compare to retail banking? Consider the delivery of cash to and from a branch. How does the cash make its way in and out of a branch? What happens next? How well does current branch design a) meet the needs of the modern-day customer, and b) align to optimizing the operational logistics of managing a 21st-century retail bank?

Ease of purchase

Digital retailers such as Amazon have built their application in an intuitive fashion that enables customers to browse a huge marketplace of products, select an item and execute payment with a swipe and a mere depression of their fingerprint on their smartphone. Consider this in comparison to the process that customers need to go through to purchase products from traditional banks. Forms need completing, signatures are required, validation is needed, ordering then takes place. Bureaucracy, red tape, call it what you like, it all adds up to customers perceiving retail banks as having a highly inefficient process that fails to meet the needs of customers in the 21st century. If we take this to the next stage, Amazon will add value to the customer experience by promoting complementary products at the point of purchase.

Knowing your customer

The luxury hotel chain, Ritz-Carlton, is known for its exemplary customer service. It appears to have an uncanny knack for knowing precisely what its customers need and want. But this is no fluke or quirk of fate. Luck plays no part, rather it is an investment in a relentless programme of attention to customer detail that means every customer and returning customer will experience a service that few can compare with. All employees of Ritz-Carlton are empowered to deliver service excellence and to share their feedback with other Ritz-Carlton employees. The room attendants, bar staff, waiters and reception all have a part to play in delivering the ultimate customer experience and recording the things that matter most to their customers. The 12 Service Standards demonstrate the individual commitment that each and every employee agrees to uphold when they work for Ritz-Carlton:

1 I build strong relationships and create Ritz-Carlton guests for life.

2 I am always responsive to the expressed and unexpressed wishes and needs of our guests.

3 I am empowered to create unique, memorable and personal experiences for our guests.

4 I understand my role in achieving the Key Success Factors, embracing Community Footprints and creating The Ritz-Carlton Mystique.

5 I continuously seek opportunities to innovate and improve The Ritz-Carlton experience.

6 I own and immediately resolve guest problems.

7 I create a work environment of teamwork and lateral service so that the needs of our guests and each other are met.

8 I have the opportunity to continuously learn and grow.

9 I am involved in the planning of the work that affects me.

10 I am proud of my professional appearance, language and behaviour.

11 I protect the privacy and security of our guests, my fellow employees and the company's confidential information and assets.

12 I am responsible for uncompromising levels of cleanliness and creating a safe and accident-free environment.

The credo encapsulates what Ritz-Carlton stands for:

> The Ritz-Carlton Hotel is a place where the genuine care and comfort of our guests is our highest mission. We pledge to provide the finest personal service and facilities for our guests who will always enjoy a warm, relaxed, yet refined ambience. The Ritz-Carlton experience enlivens the senses, instils well-being, and fulfils even the unexpressed wishes and needs of our guests (Ritz-Carlton, 2018).

This forms part of Ritz-Carlton's DNA. Consider by comparison the approach retail banks adopt in gathering customer information, truly understanding individual customer preferences and empowerment to deliver service excellence. Are banks operating at the same level?

How other industries have shaped banking

Organizations such as PayPal and Apple developed their own payment applications to simplify and speed up the process of making and receiving payment for goods and services.

Launched initially as Project Innovate in 2014 (Chartered Banker, 2017b) and formally in November 2015, FCA Sandbox enables all financial institutions the opportunity to innovate new technologies, for them to be tested in a safe and secure environment, without having to go to the open market. In phase 1, the FCA received 69 applications, and 24 requests were accepted for testing in the Sandbox (Finextra, 2016). In the most recent phase, the FCA received 77 submissions with 31 organizations progressing to have their innovative ideas tested in the Sandbox.

Other external environmental factors

Technology is not the only external environmental factor that banks need to consider either. The last part of the chapter will look at the external market further. Life has been tough for UK retail banks in recent years, with competition never fiercer than it is today, and many external factors other than technology influencing the marketplace. Financial regulation, changes in the political landscape and social pressures have all increased and added to the competitive nature of the financial sector environment. When all of these external factors happen at once, then the marketplace encounters even more disruption.

Regulation

Following the financial services crisis in 2008, there has been an increase in the extent of regulation placed upon banks. Many changes such as the separation of the riskier wholesale businesses from the less-risky retail operations may lead to a reduction in the competitive power of the large banks – this is due to the inability of the previously larger organization to effectively purchase market share by funding its purchase via loss-leading products elsewhere in the organization.

Some regulations will remove barriers to entry – in 2013 the Bank of England simplified the process for new entrants to acquire a bank licence and also lowered the capital requirements. Since 2010, 19 new retail and commercial banking licences have been granted, with many more applications allegedly in the pipeline for approval, though client confidentiality means no information is available about the specific parties.(PwC, 2017).

Whilst the capital barriers to entry have been reduced and the PRA proffer a fast-track application process, new entrants such as Hampden & Co still face a challenging and rigorous application process to secure a cherished banking licence (Dakers, 2015).

Other regulatory changes have helped level the playing field – PSD2 and Open Banking will lead to the opening up of the much-valued, if not under-utilized rich customer data resource that has traditionally been solely owned by the traditional banks. Traditional banks will lose their data-based competitive advantage.

Yet, there is still an undercurrent of uncertainty as to the actual impact that the regulatory changes will have within the financial sector. Mobile-first bank Atom, which received its bank licence in June 2015 and went live operationally in April 2016, has delayed the launch of its current account, citing that it wants to see the impact of new payments regulation, Open Banking and data protection prior to introducing its new account (Boyce, 2017). This is one of the first clear public statements which throws into doubt that even with new regulations coming into effect intended to encourage competition, there is no guarantee that customers will choose to actually give consent for their data to be shared. Even with the enabling regulations in place, if customers do not want to sanction the sharing of their data, then the desired outcome of increasing competition may fail to materialize. This is further endorsed by the pre-PSD2 research completed by Accenture, which found that two-thirds of UK customers said they would not share their personal financial data with third-party providers (Ismail, 2017).

Political

The most significant political event in many years took place in the UK on Thursday 23 June 2016, when citizens were invited by the UK government to participate in a referendum to decide whether the UK should leave or stay within the European Union. Leave won by 51.9 per cent to 48.1 per cent. Accordingly, the UK is now scheduled to depart the European Union at 11 pm GMT on Friday 29 March 2019.

Brexit is an extremely complex matter, the precise details of which will take time to flesh out. The first stage was to determine the headline principles and the cost of departure from the EU – this was achieved in December 2017, with many political commentators suggesting that now the real work begins. Fundamentally the extent of the nature of Brexit remains unclear (Chartered Banker, 2016b). There are two derivatives:

1 Hard Brexit – cessation of being part of the single market and reduced ability to move freely within Europe.

2 Soft Brexit – freedom of movement will continue and from a banking perspective banks could continue to sell their services to the EU.

Until the exact nature of Brexit is known, then the marketplace is in a state of flux and if there is anything that causes turmoil in the financial sector, it is uncertainty.

The unrest of Brexit has led to many banks reconsidering where they should base their European operations. Lloyds Banking Group has identified Germany as its post-Brexit base and applied for a banking licence in early 2018 (Davies, 2017). In a similar vein, Barclays Bank has identified Dublin as its European headquarters location post-Brexit (Martin, 2017).

The UK government is also keen to support new entrants financially – UK digital-only bank Atom received a £30m investment from the Chancellor. It is envisaged that Atom will now increase its presence in the small business lending sector (Williams-Grut, 2017).

Social

Consumer trust with UK retail banks is at an all-time low. Notwithstanding the financial crisis in 2008, there has been a litany of mis-selling including life assurance, loan insurance and packaged accounts, and more accusations followed, citing collusion and rigging of interest rates and LIBOR between the big banks. Technology failures have also caused additional trust-related concerns that customers have about the traditional banks. Further, bankers' bonuses have fuelled the public perception of a corrupt and self-centred industry. With the reputations of the retail banks so low, it means that they are vulnerable to attack from new, fresh, unaffected brand entrants.

In October 2011, the Chartered Banker Institute embarked on a journey to develop and implement professional standards for bankers (Chartered Banker, 2014b). The Chartered Banker Professional Standards Board (CB:PSB) aims to instil public confidence in individual bankers through the achievement of professional standards. Since it was introduced in 2012, almost 250,000 individuals have met the Foundation Standard for Professional Bankers and some banks are also working towards the Leadership Standard for Professional Bankers. CB:PSB's purpose is defined on their website as:

> To enhance customer confidence in every banker in every bank in the UK,
> by setting out the professional values, attitudes and behaviour expected of
> bankers in the Chartered Banker Code of Professional Conduct. Developing and
> implementing professional standards for bankers and providing pathways for
> bankers to meet and maintain relevant professional qualifications (Chartered
> Banker Institute, 2018).

CB:PSB comprises several distinct components:

- board of senior industry leaders dedicated to driving professionalism in the banking industry;
- a Professional Standards Committee (PSC) to help develop professional standards;
- an Independent Monitoring Panel (IMP) to focus on the monitoring of CB:PSB professional standards;

- a Stakeholder Forum (which has superseded the Advisory Panel) to engage with a broad range of 'end users';

- a dedicated Professional Standards Team within the Chartered Banker Institute.

Whilst organizations such as the Chartered Banker Institute have made positive steps to redress the shortcomings of the past, it will take a long time to restore customers' confidence in the traditional banking sector. The creation of the Banking Standards Board (BSB) was originally proposed by Bank of England Governor Mark Carney in May 2014. Whilst the BSB is funded by the banks, it is entirely independent of them. One of the primary objectives of BSB is to return professionalism to banking and to help support increased numbers of bankers to attain Chartered Banker status and attain membership and accreditation of professional bodies including the Institute (Chartered Banker, 2015).

Examples of banks working to restore customer confidence can be seen in initiatives introduced by Lloyds Bank and NatWest. Lloyds Bank has set itself the goal of being 'the best bank for customers' and aims to do so through a plan of Helping Britain to Prosper. This means being there when customers need their bank most. Lloyds, in conjunction with Macmillan Cancer Support, has created Lloyds' Cancer Support team. At a time when customers are most vulnerable and need help, Lloyds bank aims to be there to support them (Chartered Banker, 2017c).

NatWest introduced a concept called 'Ideas Bank', which was intended to be a repository for customer suggestions for improvements and ideas to resolve problems. The very fact that NatWest is asking customers for feedback and indeed enabling customers to offer solutions to develop products and services, helps close some of the trust deficit (Chartered Banker, 2014c).

Chapter summary

- Fintechs are the new kids on the block. Built on app- and cloud-based technology, these low-cost disrupters are looking to capitalize on the opportunity of PSD2 and Open Banking. Customers have yet to vote with their feet and move to the new players; time will tell if the fintechs are the winners or, when all the dust settles, the big banks remain standing to fight another day.

- The great unknown factor lies in the organizations that are substitutes to banks. Google, Amazon, Apple – do they want to play in the financial sector? If so they may well be the dark horses in the race to financial sector supremacy. With their ability to develop intuitive applications, combined with complex algorithms to present tailored customer offers, the substitutes present perhaps the most potent threat of all to the retail banking industry.

- Technology creates new opportunities in the marketplace. Open Banking will create both a threat and an opportunity for the current and new participants within the UK financial sector. Investment in technology is essential to keep pace with the change in demand from UK customers.

- The political landscape in the UK is still uncertain. Brexit has thrown a shadow of doubt over the UK financial sector, with some organizations making contingency plans to relocate their head offices away from London.

- Since the financial crisis of 2008, UK regulators have lowered the barriers of entry to encourage new banks to evolve and compete in the UK financial sector.

Objective check

1 How has technology come to prominence in retail banking?

2 What have been the main drivers for technological change?

3 Who benefits and who loses from technological change?

4 Is all technological change positive?

5 What can banks learn from other sectors?

6 How have external factors other than technology influenced retail banking?

References

Barclays (2017) Barclays launches Rise London, the new 'Home of Fintech', 5 May [online] https://www.home.barclays/news/2017/05/barclays-launches-new-home-of-fintech.html [Accessed 1 December 2017]

Boyce, L (2017) Digital-only Atom bank delays current account launch with boss blaming threat of new regulation, *This is Money*, 8 June [online] http://www.thisismoney.co.uk/money/saving/article-4584938/

Digital-Atom-Bank-delay-current-account-launch.html [Accessed 6 December 2017]

Cellan-Jones, R (2017) TSB to roll out iris scanning tech, *BBC News*, 20 July [online] http://www.bbc.co.uk/news/technology-40663365 [Accessed 5 December 2017]

Chaparro, F (2017) Mark Cuban is backing an app that's trying to help people avoid overdraft fees, *Business Insider*, 25 April [online] http://uk.businessinsider.com/mark-cuban-backed-fintech-dave-raised-3-million-2017-4 [Accessed 21 November 2017]

Chartered Banker (2014a) Home-Grown Visionaries, February/March, pp28–29

Chartered Banker (2014b) A leadership standard for professional bankers, February/March, p24

Chartered Banker (2014c) To the heart of the business, April/May, pp22–23

Chartered Banker (2015) Committed to professionalising banking, June/July, pp40–41

Chartered Banker (2015/2016) Striking a balance, December/January, pp17–18

Chartered Banker (2016a) PwC Blockchain and to support the financial sectors engagement with FinTech firms – closing the gap, April/May, p38

Chartered Banker (2016b) Voice of reassurance, October/November, pp24–25

Chartered Banker (2017a) Customers unaware of Open Banking, April/May

Chartered Banker (2017b) Passport to the future, August/September, p31

Chartered Banker (2017c) Show, don't tell, October/November, pp32–33

Chartered Banker Institute (2018) Professional Standards Board [online] https://www.charteredbanker.com/employers/chartered-banker-professional-standards-board.html [Accessed 25 June 2018]

Dakers, M (2015) How to set up a new bank: 'It'll take you longer than you think and cost more than you think', *The Telegraph*, 18 Jan [online] https://www.telegraph.co.uk/finance/newsbysector/banksandfinance/11351625/How-to-set-up-a-new-bank-Itll-take-you-longer-than-you-think-and-cost-more-than-you-think.html [Accessed 23 July 2018]

Davies, A (2017) Brexit: Lloyds Bank close to choosing Berlin as European base to secure EU access, *The Independent*, 14 February [online] http://www.independent.co.uk/news/business/news/brexit-latest-news-lloyds-bank-berlin-choose-european-hq-base-eu-access-a7578886.html [Accessed 6 December 2017]

Equifax (2016) Use of personal data [online] http://www.equifax.com/assets/unitedkingdom/yougov_survey_use_of_personal_data.pdf [Accessed 19 August 2017]

Finextra (2016) FCA to kickstart Sandbox with 24 applicants, 22 September [online] https://www.finextra.com/newsarticle/29480/fca-to-kickstart-sandbox-with-24-applicants [Accessed 30 November 2017]

Finextra (2017a) Barclays campaigns to take on fraudsters, 8 May [online] https://www.finextra.com/newsarticle/30529/barclays-campaigns-to-take-on-fraudsters [Accessed 9 November 2017]

Finextra (2017b) Santander's Openbank relaunched as 100% digital bank, 16 June [online] https://www.finextra.com/newsarticle/30697/santanders-openbank-relaunched-as-100-digital-bank [Accessed 9 November 2017]

HM Treasury (2014) Data sharing and open data for banks – a report for HM Treasury and Cabinet Office, 3 December [online] https://www.gov.uk/government/publications/data-sharing-and-open-data-for-banks [Accessed 19 August 2017]

HSBC (2017) Strategic Report: Group Chief Executive's review, HSBC Holdings plc Annual Report and Accounts 2016, 21 February, p8

Ismail, N (2017) Open banking: Lack of trust in third-party providers creating major opportunity for banks, *Information Age*, 2 October [online] http://www.information-age.com/lack-trust-third-party-providers-creating-opportunity-banks-123468818/ [Accessed 6 December 2017]

Lemmon, C (2016) Santander InnoVentures doubles FinTech fund, *Fstech*, 19 July [online] http://www.fstech.co.uk/fst/Santander_InnoVentures_Doubles_FinTech_Fund.php [Accessed 2 December 2017]

Martin, B (2017) Barclays prepares to expand Dublin office after Brexit, *The Telegraph*, 26 January [online] http://www.telegraph.co.uk/business/2017/01/26/barclays-prepares-expand-dublin-office-brexit/ [Accessed 6 December 2017]

PwC (2017) Who are you calling a 'challenger bank'? [online] https://www.pwc.co.uk/industries/banking-capital-markets/insights/challenger-banks.html [Accessed 6 December 2017]

Ritz-Carlton (2018) Gold standards [online] http://www.ritzcarlton.com/en/about/gold-standards [Accessed 4 May 2018]

Scroxton, A (2016) Nationwide renews BT network contract to support digital transformation, *Computer Weekly*, 6 January [online] http://www.computerweekly.com/news/4500270032/Nationwide-renews-BT-network-contract-to-support-digital-transformation [Accessed 5 December 2017]

Shaw, V and Jones, R (2017) HSBC app will show all your bank accounts in one place, *The Guardian*, 1 October [online] https://www.theguardian.com/money/2017/oct/01/hsbc-app-all-bank-accounts-one-place [Accessed 8 November 2017]

Williams-Grut, O (2017) Atom Bank gets £30 million from the government as Philip Hammond pledges investment boost, *Business Insider*, 21 June [online] http://uk.businessinsider.com/atom-bank-british-business-bank-tier-2-investment-2017-6?r=US&IR=T [Accessed 7 December 2017]

09

The impact of legislation and regulation on retail banking operations

INTRODUCTION

Legislation and regulation are intrinsically intertwined, with regulation inevitably being a direct by-product of a change in domestic or international legislation or law. Far from being merely a necessary evil or a set of bureaucratic policies, legislation and regulation are designed for very good reasons, primarily to address the issues of the past, but increasingly to proactively meet the needs of future political, economic and social demands. Legislation and regulation need to continually adapt and evolve to reflect the ever-changing environment of the marketplace. No other marketplace has undergone as much change, either due to financial crises or through rapid change caused by various industrial revolutions; the need for legislation and regulation will continue to shape the foundations of the banking industry both locally and globally.

LEARNING OBJECTIVES

By the end of this chapter you will be able to:

- explain the difference between legislation and regulation;
- analyse the development of regulation and legislation for banking;
- evaluate the costs and benefits to banks and customers of legislation and regulation;
- evaluate the Combined Code's effect on UK banking;
- analyse the drivers for changes in legislation, regulation and governance.

The difference between legislation and regulation

Legislation is law passed by a legislative body such as a government, whilst **regulation** is a set of rules or guidelines issued by a regulatory body such as a government agency in compliance with the law. When laws are created that require changes to the function of financial institutions, it is the responsibility of the regulatory body to enforce the law through its own regulation of its members. Whilst legislation aims to provide resolutions to protect, to restrict, or to change the working environment of the marketplace, it is through regulation that the desired legal outcome is achieved.

Legislation The process of creating laws that govern an industry or country. The initial step of creating law is the drafting and proposing of a Bill, so that the legislation can be fully discussed and considered in Parliament, before a vote to pass the Bill happens and makes it a law.

Regulation Once the law has been passed by Parliament, it then becomes the responsibility of the appropriate regulatory body to implement the law. This is achieved by creating a framework of rules and principles that align with the law. The rules and principles are the specific regulations that all impacted organizations must abide by. It is the regulator's responsibility to ensure that the rules are followed and therefore the laws of the land are adhered to.

Without structure and rules there would be social anarchy. Society needs a framework of known parameters to work within, to maintain standards and consistency within an industry or country. Rules help businesses and people to organize themselves, to determine right from wrong and to abide by the laws. If not, consequences will follow.

Costs of regulation and legislation

Costs of regulation and legislation cover a wide range of activities including annual fees, development payments, one-off fines and opportunity costs. Not all costs are measured in purely monetary terms – some changes in regulation, such as Brexit, can lead to a human cost, resulting in the loss of jobs in the domestic UK market, with equivalent roles moving abroad.

Fees payable to regulatory authorities

Retail banks and other financial institutions in the UK have to pay annual fees to regulatory organizations. In 2015, the annual fee payable to the Prudential Regulatory Authority rose 4 per cent from £246.8m for the financial year 2014–2015, to £257.8m for 2015–2016. In addition, the Financial Conduct Authority is also paid for by the businesses that it regulates. Its annual funding requirement was £446m, which is spread across 70,000 companies (Bingham, 2015).

Implementation of laws and policies

In addition to the annual fees that all UK retail banks pay the UK regulators, they also have to pay separately to fund a variety of additional regulator-led projects, such as the Prudential Regulatory Authority's work on ring-fencing (of retail bank deposits from wholesale divisions). This is calculated on an hourly rate for PRA personnel, which can be as much as £170, according to a consultation paper published by the Bank of England (Bingham, 2015). Ring-fencing is covered extensively in Chapter 3.

Payments imposed by regulators

From a regulatory perspective, during the 15-year period between 2000 and 2015, banks and building societies collectively had to pay out approximately

£50bn, primarily due to adopting an aggressive sales culture within their business. Chapter 4 covers Payment Protection Insurance in greater detail; however, mis-selling of PPI accounted for around £40bn, followed by interest rate hedging mis-selling, which cost the industry a further £5bn (Treanor, 2016).

Capital reserves

As regulators respond to capital inadequacies of the past and increase the degree of capital that banks need to hold in reserve, there is an opportunity cost of doing so. Increasing the amount of money banks have to hold means that banks cannot use the money for other business purposes, hence there is a cost associated to holding capital versus the loss of return on investment opportunity.

In addition, other regulatory costs related to cybersecurity and changes to the political landscape need to be provided for, albeit the precise impact may not yet be known. At the time of writing, the full impact of Brexit on UK retail banks has not yet been fully clarified; however, what is certain is that there will be inevitable changes in regulation, hence more costs to the UK retail banks. HSBC was the first UK retail bank to put a price tag on Brexit, estimating that the immediate disruption would cost in the region of $200m–$300m. Stuart Gulliver, chief executive of HSBC, said that $1bn of revenue in its global banking and markets unit would be put 'at risk' from Brexit and that HSBC planned to protect this revenue by moving up to 1,000 of its 6,000 UK investment banking jobs to France (Arnold, 2017). Sam Woods, chief executive of the Bank of England's Prudential Regulatory Authority believes that about 10,000 UK-based jobs are probably at risk on 'day one' of Brexit, with potentially as many as 75,000 job losses in banking and insurance being 'plausible' if the UK leaves the European Union without a trade deal (Glover, 2017).

It has been estimated that UK retail banks' regulatory costs could more than double over the next five years. Banks typically spend 4 per cent of their total revenue on compliance, but that could rise to 10 per cent by 2022 (McNulty, 2017).

ACTIVITY 9.1

- Costs associated with customers reclaiming mis-sold Payment Protection Insurance will end in 2019. What lessons should be learnt from the PPI scandal and how should banks adjust their behaviour so that they do not have to encounter such costs ever again?

- The costs associated with regulation and legislation show no sign of abating; what should banks do to best prepare themselves for the next wave of regulatory change and associated costs?

- Not all costs of regulation are financial; what are the human costs of regulation and how do they impact upon wider society?

REGULATION

For updates on Regulatory Fees, check here: https://www.fca.org.uk/firms/fees

Benefits of regulation and legislation

There are many reasons why regulation is needed and why it benefits the financial service sector. Three main reasons are noted below:

1 To control the power of the few and to ensure there is sufficient room for healthy competition. In the financial market, particularly post-financial crisis, the number of banks has reduced due to several bank mergers and acquisitions and hence further regulation has been needed to engender greater competition within the financial services marketplace.

2 To regulate and to protect customers. Customers' deposits in UK financial institutions are generally protected by deposit insurance; however, further regulations are in place to ensure that banks hold minimum levels of capital to protect themselves against any future crisis. In addition, banks have to implement a more prudent and stringent approach to consumer lending – to ensure that customers can comfortably afford to repay their loans and obligations.

3 To protect the financial sector from unanticipated systemic shocks. Regulation is required to protect individual banks against the spread of potential systemic contagion caused by other banks. Regulation can help prevent further bank failures.

From a public perspective the government has a social responsibility to ensure that the banking system meets the needs of the public. Governments and their regulatory bodies therefore need to ensure the stability and resilience of the banking system and that the banks in society act in a fair and reasonable manner.

ACTIVITY 9.2

- Does all regulation within the UK financial sector benefit customers and communities?

- Regulation controls the number of banks and their influence upon society. What benefit does regulation and legislation bring to a) existing banks, b) new entrants to the financial market?

- Regulation and legislation help resolve the ills of the past, but fail to be forward-thinking and dynamic enough to meet the rapidly evolving needs of the 21st century digital age. Would you agree with this statement? Elaborate on your views.

The development of regulation and legislation for banking

Banking laws and regulations have developed and adapted over time to reflect the financial conditions of society. The following themed approaches have emerged over the last four decades.

1980s

Introduction of the modern-day regulatory system, including self-regulation among asset managers and oversight of banks and insurers. The introduction of the Financial Services Act 1986 (FSA, 1986) leads to a significant change in the way UK investment businesses are regulated. Five main self-regulating groups are formed to establish rules for ensuring investor protection, internal monitoring of conformance and enforcement of policy within their respective arms of the industry. The self-regulating group covers five different areas of financial services: 1) futures and broking via the Association of Futures Brokers and Dealers (AFBD), 2) financial intermediation via the Financial Intermediaries, Managers and Brokers Regulatory Association (FIMBRA), 3) investment management via the Investment Management Regulatory Organisation (IMRO), 4) life assurance brokering via the Life Assurance and Unit Trust Regulatory Organisation (LAUTRO), and 5) securities broking via The Securities Association (TSA) – all self-regulating organizations are overseen by the Securities and Investment Board (SIB) which holds statutory powers.

1990s

After a variety of regulatory failures, including the Maxwell pension funds scandal in 1991, self-regulation begins to be challenged due to inconsistency, lack of clarity, and the regulators potentially acting in self-interest. The Andrew Large Report of 1993 recommends more leadership be provided by the SIB; whilst not stopping self-regulation entirely, the move towards the creation of an overarching single-tier regulator begins.

A new three-tier structure of standards is imposed on firms by the SIB:

- Top tier – 10 Principles to provide a universal set of expected standards for the conduct of investment business and the financial standing of all authorized persons.
- Second tier – Core Rules that are legally binding on self-regulating organizations, covering financial resources, the way to do business and the management of customer funds.
- Third tier – specific self-regulating business rules.

The failure of Barings Bank in 1995 and a change in government in 1997 lead to independent monetary policy becoming the responsibility of the Bank of England. The SIB is renamed as the Financial Services Authority (FSA), effectively ending the era of self-regulation.

2000s

The new millennium witnesses further changes within the banking regulatory structure with the creation of a more principles-based approach to regulation. The impact of being part of the European Union leads to further banking legislation coming from Europe, whilst supervision still remains the responsibility of local nations.

The single largest change in domestic legislation comes through the introduction of the Financial Services and Markets Act 2000, which regulates banking, insurance and investment business in the UK.

2010s

Respective European countries' supervisory organizations adapt to enable increased harmonization at a pan-EU level. In response to the financial crisis of 2008, the single regulatory structure is reformed.

The role of government and the Bank of England

In 2012, the UK government announces plans to break up the Financial Services Authority in 2012 to create three new sub-divisions:

- Prudential supervision of banks and insurers is transferred from the FSA to a new Bank of England subsidiary, the Prudential Regulatory Authority (PRA).

- The creation of a new Bank of England committee, designed to ensure financial stability within the new regulatory system, forms the Financial Policy Committee (FPC).

- The FSA was rebranded to become the Financial Conduct Authority (FCA). The primary objective of the FCA is to drive more intrusive supervision of the banks – to challenge financial institutions harder and to kick the tyres more than ever before.

The drivers and recent changes in regulation and legislation

In keeping with the approach taken in this chapter thus far, the following section looks at some recent examples of legislation and regulation that have impacted the UK banking sector. For each, the legislation is named along with the associated regulatory body (at the time of conception) that is accountable for the policy. The respective reviews outline the original objectives of the legislation and how the regulation was intended to be enforced. Each section concludes with any shortcomings identified as a result of the implemented legislation and consequential regulations that may have emerged subsequently.

1 Legislation: Bank of England Act 1998

Regulator: Monetary Policy Committee (MPC).

Traditionally, the setting of interest rates in the UK was the responsibility of the UK government's Treasury department. This led to potential conflict of interest for the UK government. How could the government manage both the political agenda for the country whilst simultaneously being responsible for independently controlling monetary policy? The potential to interfere with monetary policy as a mechanism to realize other political opportunities meant that the government could be accused of not being truly independent.

On 6 May 1997, the government took the unprecedented step of transferring the responsibility for setting interest rates from the government, HM Treasury, to the Bank of England, to ensure a truly independent perspective could be taken on the setting of interest rates for the UK financial sector.

The Bank of England Act 1998 included the guidelines for the formation of a new Monetary Policy Committee with the specific remit to:

- set interest rates to achieve the government's inflation target of 2 per cent per annum;
- meet monthly to review prevailing and projected economic information to determine if interest rates need to be adjusted;
- membership to include the Governor, two Deputy Governors, two of the Bank's Executive Directors and four independent members appointed from outside the bank by the Chancellor;
- publish minutes of all meetings within six weeks.

The Act gave the government responsibility for specifying its price stability target and growth and employment objectives at least annually.

REGULATION

For updates on Bank of England Act 1998, check here: http://www.legislation.gov.uk/ukpga/1998/11/contents

---

2 Legislation: Financial Services and Markets Act 2000

Regulator: Financial Services Authority (FSA).

The Financial Services and Markets Act 2000 was created through an Act of the Parliament in the UK that established the Financial Services

Authority (FSA) as a regulator for insurance, investment business and banking, and the Financial Ombudsman Service to resolve disputes as an independent, low-cost alternative to resolution via law courts.

The Act has subsequently been amended by the Financial Services Act 2012 and the Bank of England and Financial Services Act 2016.

The FSA now has four primary objectives:

- to maintain market confidence in the UK financial system;
- promotion and education of public understanding of the UK financial system;
- maintaining protection of consumers;
- to reduce the impact of financial crime.

The FSA principles-based approach to regulation created a set of rules contained within the FSA Handbook which also contained principles as to how financial institutions should 'Treat Customers Fairly' (National Archives, 2009).

REGULATION

For updates on the Financial Services and Markets Act 2000, check here: http://www.legislation.gov.uk/ukpga/2000/8/contents

---

3 Legislation: Financial Services Act 2012

Regulator: FCA, PRA and FPC.

The Financial Services Act 2012 was an Act of Parliament in the UK that built upon the Financial Services and Markets Act 2000 – it introduced a revised regulatory framework for the financial system and financial services in the UK. Out went the previous all-encompassing, single regulator (Financial Services Authority); it was replaced by two new regulatory bodies, the Financial Conduct Authority (FCA) and the Prudential Regulation Authority (PRA), and further created the Bank of England-based Financial Policy Committee (FPC). This new framework came into effect on 1 April 2013.

Financial Conduct Authority (FCA)

The FSA was abolished and replaced with the FCA, which has the strategic objective of ensuring that the financial markets are functioning properly.

The FCA has three primary objectives:

- to provide protection for consumers;
- to protect and enhance the integrity of the UK financial system;
- to promote effective competition in the interests of consumers in the markets for regulated financial services.

Prudential Regulation Authority (PRA)

The PRA was established as a new part of the Bank of England. It has **micro-prudential** regulatory authority to regulate deposit takers, insurers and a small number of significant investment firms. The primary objective of the PRA is to ensure the safety and soundness of UK financial institutions. The PRA will be proactive in its assessment of the way firms conduct their respective business and to ensure financial stability of individual organizations under their oversight.

Financial Policy Committee (FPC)

The third facet of the 2012 Act introduced the FPC which will be responsible for **macro-prudential** regulation. The FPC is responsible for monitoring the stability and resilience of the UK financial system in its entirety. The FPC is a committee of the Bank of England, with responsibility for implementing the UK government's economic policies and for removing or reducing potential systemic risks from the financial sector.

Micro-prudential bank regulation This approach relies on the regulatory supervision to assess the stability and safety of individual banks. The process of micro-prudential regulation requires that supervisory checks are made against specific metrics, but it does not take a wider view of external risks such as to consider the implications of systemic and contagion influences.

Macro-prudential bank regulation The broader view takes into account the wider financial sector and considers the implications of interconnected risk between individual financial institutions. The overarching objective is to ensure the stability of financial services within the economy. Under Basel III, macro-prudential regulation encourages additional 'counter-cyclical' capital buffers to be retained during boom times and relaxed during downturns. Further, the capital that has been built up in the buffers can be used to fend off any potential shocks that may arise.

REGULATION

For updates on Financial Services Act 2012, check here:
http://www.legislation.gov.uk/ukpga/2012/21/contents

4 Legislation: The Combined Code/UK Corporate Governance Code 2016

Regulator: Financial Reporting Council.

The UK Corporate Governance Code is enshrined in UK company law, underpinned by a set of principles for good corporate governance aimed at companies listed on the London Stock Exchange. The first version of the UK Corporate Governance Code was produced in 1992 by the Cadbury Committee. The Code has gone through several iterations since its original conception, to ensure it remains relevant and pertinent to organizations as economic and social conditions change over time.

The UK Corporate Governance Code 2016 adopts a principles-based approach by providing general guidelines of best practice rather than a stringent rules-based approach which rigidly defines the exact protocols that should be conformed to.

The UK Corporate Governance Code 2016 sets standards of good practice in relation to:

- Leadership – how the board is constructed, clear roles and responsibilities and demarcation of what the board does versus what the business does.

- Effectiveness – the board should have the appropriate skills, experience and knowledge to perform their respective duties. The board should review their own individual and collective performance on an annual basis.

- Accountability – the board should provide a balanced view of the financial institution's current position and future potential. The board should set the risk appetite that they are willing for the organization to take in order to achieve its strategic ambitions. The board have to ensure they comply with corporate and financial reporting and maintain a relationship with the organization's auditor.

- Remuneration – board directors are entitled to be paid an attractive level of remuneration commensurate with the role, but organizations should not pay more than is necessary. Individual performance should be an element of the overall remuneration package, but all such bonuses and benefits should be sensitively considered before being finalized and included within directors' remuneration packages. Directors should not participate in setting their own remuneration packages.

- Relations with shareholders – the board are responsible for regular communication (including an annual general meeting) with shareholders to ensure there is clear understanding of the organization's business objectives.

As part of UK listed companies' annual report and accounts, firms are required to report on how they have applied the principles of the Code. Whilst they don't have to provide specific measures, firms need to state whether they have complied or not and where they have not, an explanation should be provided.

REGULATION

For updates on the Combined Code/UK Corporate Governance Code 2016, check here: https://www.frc.org.uk/directors/corporate-governance-and-stewardship/uk-corporate-governance-code

ACTIVITY 9.3

- The Combined Code sets the parameters for good corporate governance in the UK. How does the Combined Code apply to retail banks? Specifically consider senior and executive bankers' pay and bonus payments and the social opinions of the UK general public.

- Many retired professionals take up directorship positions on a variety of company boards. What are the pros and cons of this approach? According to the Combined Code, what criteria should be used when considering the appointment of directors?

- If the board of directors appoint the chief operating officer, what potential conflict of interest might this cause the board? How does the Combined Code help manage this situation?

5 Basel Accords

Founded in 1975 by the central bank governors of the Group of 10 (G-10) countries, the Basel Committee of Banking Supervision (BCBS) aims to provide guidelines for banking regulations. Three formal policies or 'accords' have been introduced to maintain banking credibility and supervision globally, namely Basel I, Basel II and Basel III. Each of the accords will be elaborated on in greater detail below. Basel I sets a minimum ratio of capital to risk-weighted assets for banks, Basel II introduced supervisory responsibilities and enhanced the minimum capital requirement, and Basel III promotes the need for additional liquidity buffers.

Basel I – 1988

With the impending Latin American debt crisis looming in the early 1980s, the Basel Committee on Banking Supervision (BCBS) created the first set of minimum capital requirements to help resolve concerns relating to the diminishing capital adequacy position of global banks. The main thrust of Basel I was to focus on addressing credit risk exposure. This was achieved by reviewing and grouping all of a bank's assets subject to their perceived degree of credit risk. The following risk-weighting percentages were applied to various groups of assets. Examples of each risk-weighted asset (RWA) group are given below:

- 0 per cent – including cash and government debt;
- 20 per cent – including claims on banks incorporated in the OECD;
- 50 per cent – including residential mortgages;
- 100 per cent – including premises, plant, private sector and corporate debt.

Banks with an international presence were required to hold capital equal to 8 per cent of their risk-weighted assets (RWA). The original Basel plan was to have the capital adequacy plan implemented within the G-10 countries (via their respective central banks) by the end of 1992.

Basel II – 2006

Whilst Basel I focused narrowly upon credit risk, Basel II built on and developed the minimum capital adequacy requirements of Basel I and introduced two further dimensions: introduction of a supervisory review process and market discipline of banks' capital adequacy, and assessment of internal performance metrics. This became known as the 'three pillars' concept

(Bank for International Settlements, 2006). Basel II was an improved framework for managing capital requirements and took account of the changing environment to better anticipate risks and to address the rapid innovation that had happened in the preceding years.

CASE STUDY
Northern Rock – opportunity and demise due to change between Basel I and Basel II and regulatory failures

Based upon House of Commons Treasury Committee Report, 'The run on the Rock', Fifth Report of Session 2007–08, 26 January 2008.

Whilst Northern Rock is notorious for being the first to fall during the 2008 banking crisis, this case study looks at the role of the regulators and specifically the part Basel II played in Northern Rock's ultimate demise.

Playing the game

At its core, Basel II allows banks to self-determine their management of credit risk. In an exercise akin to marking your own homework, banks provide an internal ratings-based approach to determine their Basel II requirements for capital adequacy. Banks can follow the 'foundation approach' or the 'advanced approach'; either way they provide their own estimation of the probability of default, with supervisory estimates being provided for other components. This approach allows banks to effectively determine their own level of capital adequacy. The Financial Services Authority confirmed to Northern Rock that its application for an advance approach waiver was approved on 29 June 2007.

Within a month, on 25 July, Northern Rock announced that it would increase its interim dividend to 30.3 per cent. This was primarily due to Northern Rock anticipating that it would now be able to generate a regulatory capital surplus over the next three to four years due to the waiver that had been approved only a matter of weeks earlier. Northern Rock espoused a positive image, promoting that they had come through a rigorous period of supervision and stress testing and that now they were in a very healthy position, so much so that they could pay an increased dividend to shareholders.

Having attained Basel II approval, the risk weighting of certain assets in Northern Rock's balance sheet could change. In Northern Rock's case, the perceived quality of the loan was such that the risk weighting for residential mortgages came down from 50 per cent to 15 per cent.

Accordingly, this required Northern Rock to hold significantly less capital, hence why Northern Rock was able to increase the dividend to shareholders.

Undoubtedly the Northern Rock crisis was built on the lack of availability of liquidity and funding rather than insolvency itself, but Basel II had a part to play. The waiver was established on the capital position of Northern Rock, as was the payment of the dividend to shareholders: the planets aligned at exactly the wrong time:

> Whilst we accept that Basel II is a capital accord and the problems at Northern Rock that soon became all too evident were ones of liquidity, it was wrong of the FSA to allow Northern Rock to weaken its balance sheet at a time when the FSA was itself concerned about problems of liquidity that could affect the financial sector' (House of Commons Treasury Committee Report, 26 January 2008, p45, Point 25).

Growth alarm bells

In the House of Commons Treasury Committee Report, 26 January 2008 (p22), Professor Woods expressed his surprise that the FSA had missed this signal from the rapid growth of Northern Rock: 'The FSA... was asleep on the job; that is manifestly right. A very clear signal of a bank running a big risk is rapid expansion. Northern Rock was giving that signal quite clearly; it really is remarkable that [the FSA] missed it.'

Yet in times of economic upturn, regulators are loath to meddle or overly regulate for fear of stifling the market and being accused of putting the brakes on growth. Regulators are typically more inclined to be involved in reacting and responding to problems and challenges, rather than proactively investigating organizations that appear to be making good profits from their business operations. If an organization is performing significantly better than the rest of the sector, then alarm bells should be ringing somewhere.

Northern Rock's predicament was not one of insolvency, rather it was a mismatch between availability of short-term liquidity to repay customer deposits and the over-reliance of funding generated through the mortgage-backed securitization process that underpinned 50 per cent of Northern Rock's business model.

The FSA classified Northern Rock as a 'high-impact bank, which was under close and continuous supervision', yet a gap of three years was planned between its last assessment in January 2006 and its next review at the beginning of 2009. Though further conversations would happen in between the formal reviews, the length of time between the formal assessments was too long to identify the problems that emerged in late 2007/early 2008.

> The FSA has acknowledged that there were clear warning signals about the risks associated with Northern Rock's business model, both from its rapid growth as a company and from the falls in its share price from February 2007 onwards. However, insofar as the FSA undertook greater 'regulatory engagement' with Northern Rock, this failed to tackle the fundamental weakness in its funding model and did nothing to prevent the problems that came to the fore from August 2007 onwards. We regard this as a substantial failure of regulation' (House of Commons Treasury Committee Report, 26 January 2008, p24, Point 42).

Questions

1 Based upon what happened with Northern Rock, what improvements could be made to Basel II?

2 Explain how the liquidity problem arose in Northern Rock – how did the mismatch happen and what triggered the ultimate collapse?

3 What lessons can be learnt from the Northern Rock case study when considering future regulation of financial institutions?

4 Consider the UK Corporate Governance Code 2016: what role and responsibilities should be apportioned to the Board of Northern Rock?

5 Find out how your organization performs in relation to the capital adequacy thresholds. Are they close to, bang on or over and above the required levels? What would you recommend that they do?

Basel III – 2010

As you will remember from Chapter 3, following the financial crisis of 2008, there was a need to refresh Basel II and to respond to the learnings taken from the financial crisis, in particular to prevent banks from becoming too highly leveraged and to ensure higher levels of capital are retained and that additional capital buffers be introduced during periods of rapid growth to help protect banks against subsequent downturns. Further, Basel III aims to address shortcomings in risk management and corporate governance. It is intended that Basel III will be fully implemented by 2019.

In September 2010, global banking regulators agreed to increase the amount of capital that the world's banks should hold through a variety of requirements. The detail of Basel III is covered in Chapter 3, but as a reminder, the initial requirements of Basel III are noted below:

- Tier 1 capital (equity and retained profits): 4.5 per cent of risk-weighted assets.

- Additional tier 1 capital (supplementary capital): 1.5 per cent of risk-weighted assets.

- Conservation buffer: 2.5 per cent of risk-weighted assets. This is an additional requirement under Basel III – if the buffer is not achieved, then the payment of dividends and discretionary bonuses will not be permitted.

- Countercyclical buffer (common equity) 0–2.5 per cent of risk-weighted assets. This is a discretionary buffer that can be implemented in national circumstances as part of macro-prudential regulation to be enforced during periods of excessive growth and withdrawn during times of economic pressure.

Beyond increasing the capital ratios, Basel III also called for banks to ensure that they hold sufficient cash and readily liquid assets to survive a 30-day crisis. As well as the obvious concern about banks having to hold substantially more capital than previously, the risk-weighting values used to calculate the degree of risk-weighted assets that should be held are outdated and remain the same as those of Basel II.

Basel Accords summary

All three Basel Accords were introduced to address the challenges that existed in the business environment at the time. Initially, Basel I considered credit risk only, and Basel II took a wider view of risk including operational, strategic and reputational risk. Basel III built on Basel II and added a focus on liquidity risk.

Whilst each Basel Accord is an improvement on the last, Basel III will not prevent a future financial crisis from happening. The additional levels of capital required under Basel III will be insufficient to prevent a financial crisis, because the calculations to establish the new capital requirements to protect banks excluded the extent of government intervention that was required to save the banking sector. Another shortcoming is the historic and backward-looking use of risk-weighted assets as a basis for calculating the extent of capital required. The risk weightings used are dated and relate to a perception of underlying risk at a past moment in time. If the underlying risk relating to a group of assets should change, then the risk weighting should be adapted to reflect the change of the underlying risk. The key is agility, to be able to move swiftly and to ensure the risk-weighted assets are prudently adjusted on a regular basis. Failure to react quickly to changes in the risk environment may lead to inadequate levels of capital being held by banks.

Finally, as was shown in the Northern Rock case study, the Basel Accords have traditionally focused on banks' assets rather than liquidity. It seems bizarre now to think that Northern Rock was well within the thresholds of Basel II regulation, yet soon after returning excess capital to its shareholders, the bank ran out of money. Whilst Basel III introduced measures to address banks' liabilities and liquidity risk, this alone will not prevent future bank failures and undoubtedly there will be a need for Basel IV and beyond in the future.

REGULATION

For updates on Basel Accords, check here: https://www.bis.org/bcbs/basel3.htm

---

6 Legislation: Payment Services Directive (PSD) – 2009

Regulator: Payment Services Regulation via FCA.

We touched briefly on the Payment Services Directive in Chapter 8. Here we will provide more detail about this key piece of payments-related legislation in Europe. The original aims of PSD were to:

- create a Single Euro Payments Area (SEPA);
- set common standards for payments;
- regulate the existing financial payment institutions and to encourage non-banks to enter the market;
- protect customers and provide greater transparency;
- set benchmark processing times and standards for payments in euro and other EU currencies.

PSD was the first European law to affect sterling payments and was implemented in the UK through the Payment Services Regulations 2009. It creates a standard set of rules for payments across the whole European Economic Area (European Union plus Iceland, Norway and Liechtenstein), and enables customers to make cross-border payments easily, consistently and safely.

PSD covers all types of electronic and non-cash payments, including:

- card payments;
- credit transfers and standing orders;
- direct debits;
- mobile and online payments.

In an effort to increase customer choice and stimulate competition in the payments market, PSD incorporates payment services offered by organizations other than banks and stipulates that providers should:

- provide adequate information to consumers;
- ensure fast and efficient service;
- compensate the consumer if services are not provided correctly.

The PSD framework created the foundations of the single euro payments area (SEPA), which enables customers to make payments under the same conditions across the euro area.

Payment Services Regulations 2009 (PSR)

In the UK, The Payment Services Regulations 2009 (PSR) came into being on 1 November 2009, under the guidance and stewardship of the FCA.

PSR scope and definitions (FSC, 2015)

The primary regulated payment services activities are:

- cash deposits and withdrawals;
- payment transactions:
  - credit transfers, including standing orders;
  - all direct debits;
  - payment card transactions;
- issuing payment instruments such as debit cards or acquiring payment transactions;
- money remittance – payments sent through the intermediary of a telecom, IT system or network operator.

PSR also list some of the activities that are out of the scope of the PSD legislation:

- cash-only transactions (cash transactions to or from a payment account are included);

- cheques and paper instruments;

- transporting cash (eg cash deliveries by commercial security companies);

- payment transactions related to securities asset servicing;

- technical services including independent ATM providers.

7 Legislation: Payment Services Directive 2 (PSD2) – 2016

Regulator: European Banking Authority (EBA) has European oversight. FCA regulates UK (FSC, 2015).

The aim of PSD2 is to improve the existing PSD framework and to expand it to incorporate the emerging digital payment services into scope. PSD2 is a further piece of payments-related legislation in Europe, which came in to force in January 2016 with all participating EU countries to implement the rules as national law by 13 January 2018. The geographic scope of PSD2 covers the making and receiving of payments within the European Economic Area (EEA) – which comprises the 28 European Union Member States plus Norway, Iceland and Liechtenstein. PSD2 will radically change the payments industry, through enabling of greater competition, expanding the nature of payments services and improving protection of customers.

PSD2 aims to make the EU's single market fit for the digital age; you will remember that we discussed this in Chapter 5 when exploring the market conditions for new fintech entrants. The new regulations will ensure that all payment services providers within the EU market are subject to the same degree of supervision and that they conform to a standard set of rules and practices. The impact of PSD2 is likely to change the face of transactional banking as we know it today. The emergence of fintechs as new dynamic payment service providers will provide customers with even more choice than ever before.

A fundamental aspect of PSD2 is the recognition that customers have 'a right to use what are termed Payment Initiation Service Providers (PISPs) and Account Information Service Providers (AISPs) where the payment account is accessible online and where they have given their explicit consent' (FSC, 2015). This ruling, combined with the impending revolution of Open Banking, gives customers access to far more choice of payment service provider and gives the opportunity for emerging new players, including fintech businesses, to enter the payments marketplace.

PSD2 aims to:

- protect customers from fraud and protect customers' rights;

- make internet payment services more secure and easier for customers to use;

- enable innovative mobile and internet payment services;

- empower the European Banking Authority (EBA) to have supervisory authority over EU members.

REGULATION

For updates on PSD2, check here: https://www.fca.org.uk/firms/revised-payment-services-directive-psd2

---

8 Legislation: ring-fencing – Financial Services (Banking Reform) Act 2013

Regulator: PRA and FCA.

From 1 January 2019, the largest UK banks have to separate or 'ring-fence' their core retail banking business from the perceived riskier investment banking divisions of their organizations. Banks required to implement ring-fencing are those that hold core deposits in excess of £25bn.

In September 2011, ring-fencing was the primary recommendation of the Independent Commission on Banking chaired by Sir John Vickers. Subsequently, legislation was created through the Financial Services (Banking Reform) Act 2013, with further amendments made in 2014, 2015 and 2016.

Within the ring-fence will be the recognizable high street retail banking businesses and banks will need to create a separate legal subsidiary for the newly created business. The ring-fenced bank will have its own board of directors and will be required to produce and publish accounts as though it were an independent organization. In addition, the ring-fenced businesses need to create their own legal, HR, risk and operational support services. The specific details of what should reside in the ring-fence allow a degree of flexibility. John Vickers clearly stated that deposits and overdrafts of retail customers and small businesses should be inside while wholesale and investment banking operations, such as derivatives and trading activities, should be outside. There is, however, room for ambiguity, as the respective banks will be able to decide whether to put their large, non-financial, corporate clients inside the ring-fence; as some lending to these customers could be inside the ring-fence and some outside.

The changes are designed to protect the ring-fenced businesses from shocks that originate in the broader banking group or the wider financial system. The framework should prevent disruption and maintain continuity of core banking services to personal and small business customers.

Ring-fencing should make the day-to-day retail banking operations safer and it is highly unlikely that the general public will ever be impacted by a financial failure again. If the investment banking side of a large bank should fail, then the regulators and the Bank of England can keep the domestic side of retail banking operations running and may allow the troubled investment part of the business to fail.

There are high costs involved with the creation of ring-fencing retail banking organizations. For the largest UK banks, it will cost an estimated £200m each to implement the reforms and thereafter £120m per year for the additional staff in support areas such as IT, HR and risk (Wallace, 2017).

A further pressure on ring-fenced banks will be that they need to set aside billions of pounds into capital buffers to protect the stand-alone entity.

REGULATION

For updates on ring-fencing – Financial Services (Banking Reform) Act 2013, check here: https://services.parliament.uk/bills/2013-14/financialservicesbankingreform.html

---

Impact of regulation on retail banks

Capital requirements

Governments can regulate the amount of capital that banks hold in order to protect the banks from the risks that they take. When capital requirements are low, it means that when banks take risks, they have low, insufficient reserves to be able to absorb unanticipated losses. Low levels of capital make banks vulnerable, so much so that even small shocks causing asset values to fall by just a couple of percentage points could lead to insolvency. By regulating for higher levels of capital, the banks become more self-sufficient and are more prepared to protect themselves against tremors such as insolvency suspicions and systemic reactions. Conversely, the regulatory imposed levels of capital can create a barrier to entry for new-to-market banks.

Supervision

The supervisory authorities create the framework, principles and rules within which all financial institutions in the UK should operate. In doing so, all participating organizations understand the parameters and conditions that they should conform to in order to achieve compliance. Failure to meet the criteria may lead to non-compliance with legislation and regulation, which may ultimately lead to the supervisory body serving fines on the non-compliant organization. Activities provided by the supervisory bodies include the provision of bank licences, stress testing, key performance metric assessment and fining banks for non-compliance. Should the regulators have any concerns, they can use their powers to protect the public interest and safety and the robustness of the banking system.

Supervision should not become a self-fulfilling prophecy – it needs to do a job and to do it well. It should not become overly bureaucratic or try to run the banks, nor should the gathering of fines be seen as a way of governments to fund other policy decisions.

Stress testing

As covered in Chapter 3, the Financial Policy Committee recommended that regular stress testing of the UK banking system should be developed to assess the system's capital adequacy.

The most recently completed stress test in 2017 built upon the 2016 combined scenario of both a domestic and global recession, with simulated impacts on financial market prices, interest rates and an independent stress test of misconduct costs.

The test enhanced was purposely intended to be more severe than the previous tests of 2014, 2015 and 2016. The test also assessed the respective systemic banks against its higher standard, reflecting the phasing-in of capital buffers under Basel III for global systemically important banks. For this first time since stress testing began in 2014, all banks were deemed to have been able to respond favourably to the increasing, spiralling simulated pressures and were deemed to have sufficient capital in place to respectfully protect themselves from the scenario. The 2017 stress test simulated conditions that were far worse than that of the financial crisis of 2008.

The 2016 results identified some capital inadequacies in three of the UK banks (The Royal Bank of Scotland Group, Barclays and Standard Chartered). In a step to increase the robustness of the stress testing of UK banks, the 2017 stress test included two different scenarios. The first was to rerun the annual economic shock scenario test, creating a situation where there is a global recession, with UK GDP falling to 4.7 per cent, domestic interest rates rising to 4 per cent and house values falling by a third – this test assesses how well the respective UK banks are able to respond to the impending crisis. The second of the scenarios was a long-term situation – where there is weak domestic growth and falling international trade, interest rates stay low for a protracted period of time and competition is increasing. The test assessed how well the respective UK banks are able to deal with slow, sustained challenge. The 2017 results confirmed that, 'For the first time since the Bank of England launched its stress tests in 2014, no bank needs to strengthen its capital position as a result of the stress test. The 2017 stress test shows the UK banking system is resilient to deep simultaneous recessions in the UK and global economies, large falls in asset prices and a separate stress of misconduct costs' (Bank of England, 2017).

Restrictions on bank activities

Regulators aim to control the activities that banks participate in. Regulators protect the public from banks taking unduly high degrees of risk that could threaten an individual bank's very existence or, worse, lead to a wider financial crisis. In addition, regulators monitor the largest of banks to ensure they are not becoming too powerful to control and that their presence is not stifling competition. Regulators also assess banks to ensure they remain focused on their core activities and that they do not divest themselves into multi-faceted businesses that make them difficult to assess.

Yet there are occasions when banks should be encouraged to widen their scope of activities. Opportunities should be sought by banks to maximize operational economies of scale and diversify their activities to take advantage of complementary sources of revenue, thus negating dependency on traditional sources of income such as interest rate margin.

Chapter summary

Throughout time, regulation has been introduced to keep banks in check. Usually as the by-product of a financial crisis, regulation is designed to mitigate the 'sins of the past', to ensure historic issues do not happen again:

- Regulators have considerable powers and discretion and need to be held accountable to discharge their duties appropriately.
- The regulatory bodies have themselves to adapt and change to address the needs of the financial sector and the member organizations.
- Legislation and regulation adapts over time to address the challenges of the day, and ensure standards and consistency of operation are maintained within the financial sector.

- The panacea remains one of being able to appropriately legislate and regulate for the future, to anticipate changes in the external environment and specifically how such changes will impact the financial marketplace, and to ensure the best protection possible for the financial ecosystem and for customers.

- Without structure and rules there would be no consistent framework for retail banks to conform to.

- UK banks have to conform to legislation within the domestic market, including Basel capital adequacy requirements.

Objective check

1 What is the difference between legislation and regulation?

2 How have regulation and legislation developed within the financial services industry?

3 Legislation and regulation can be costly to implement; what are the benefits of doing so?

4 What has been the effect of the Combined Code upon UK banking?

5 Legislation, regulation and governance have changed over time – what are the reasons for this?

Further reading

BIS (1988) Basel Committee on Banking Supervision International Convergence Of Capital Measurement and Capital Standards (Basel I) [online] http://www.bis.org/publ/bcbs04a.pdf [Accessed 23 October 2017]

BIS (2010) Basel III: A global regulatory framework for more resilient banks and banking systems [online] https://www.bis.org/publ/bcbs189.pdf [Accessed 23 October 2017]

BIS (2016) History of the Basel Committee [online] https://www.bis.org/bcbs/history.htm#basel_i [Accessed 11 October 2017]

Chartered Banker (2014a) A different philosophy to regulation, April/May, pp24–25

Chartered Banker (2014b) Under supervision, August/September pp14–17)

Chartered Banker (2015) Bigger buffers end 'too big to fail', February/March, p19

Financial Reporting Council (2016) The UK Corporate Governance Code [online] https://frc.org.uk/getattachment/ca7e94c4-b9a9-49e2-a824-ad76a322873c/UK-Corporate-Governance-Code-April-2016.pdf [Accessed 3 October 2017]

Parliament UK (2008) Select Committee on Treasury: The Regulation of Northern Rock 26 January [online] https://publications.parliament.uk/pa/cm200708/cmselect/cmtreasy/56/5606.htm [Accessed 11 October 2017]

References

Arnold, M (2017) Brexit set to raise UK banks' costs 4% and capital needs 30%, *Financial Times*, 1 August [online] https://www.ft.com/content/9fdf35a4-7610-11e7-a3e8-60495fe6ca71 [Accessed 11 October 2017]

Bank for International Settlements (2006) Basel II: International convergence of capital measurement and capital standards: a revised framework – comprehensive version [online] https://www.bis.org/publ/bcbs128.htm [Accessed 23 October 2017]

Bank of England (2017) Stress testing the UK banking system: Key elements of the 2017 stress test [online] http://www.bankofengland.co.uk/publications/Pages/news/2017/270317.aspx [Accessed 25 October 2017]

Bingham, C (2015) Cost of UK regulation rises for banks and insurers, *Financial Times*, 19 March [online] https://www.ft.com/content/b79b75de-ce30-11e4-9712-00144feab7de [Accessed 11 October 2017]

FA (1986) IMA Survey 2012 [online] https://www.theinvestmentassociation.org/assets/components/ima_filesecurity/secure.php?f=research/figure9.pdf [Accessed 24 August 2018]

Financial Services (Banking Reform) Act 2013 [online] http://www.legislation.gov.uk/ukpga/2013/33/contents; http://www.legislation.gov.uk/ukpga/2013/33/pdfs/ukpga_20130033_en.pdf [Accessed 25 October 2017]

Financial Services and Markets Act (2000) 15 June [online] http://www.legislation.gov.uk/ukpga/2000/8/pdfs/ukpga_20000008_en.pdf [Accessed 11 October 2017]

FSC (2015) Revised Payment Services Directive (PSD2) [online] https://www.fca.org.uk/firms/revised-payment-services-directive-psd2 [Accessed 23 October 2017]

Glover, J (2017) Brexit may cost 75,000 UK finance jobs, top regulator says, *Bloomberg*, 1 November [online] https://www.bloomberg.com/news/articles/2017-11-01/top-u-k-bank-regulator-says-brexit-may-cost-75-000-finance-jobs [Accessed 2 April 2018]

House of Commons Treasury Committee (2008) 'The run on the Rock', Fifth Report of Session 2007–08, Volume 1, 26 January [online] https://publications.parliament.uk/pa/cm200708/cmselect/cmtreasy/56/56i.pdf [Accessed 23 October 2017]

McNulty, L (2017) Compliance costs to more than double by 2022, *Financial News*, 27 April [online] https://www.fnlondon.com/articles/compliance-costs-to-more-than-double-by-2022-survey-finds-20170427 [Accessed 11 October 2017]

National Archives (2009) FSA 2009/6 Listing Rules Sourcebook (Rights Issue Subscription Period) Instrument 2009, 10 February [online] http://webarchive. nationalarchives.gov.uk/20090210110354/http://fsahandbook.info/FSA/html/ handbook [Accessed 23 October 2017]

Payment Services (PSD1) (nd) Directive 2007/64/EC [online] https://ec.europa.eu/ info/law/payment-services-psd-1-directive-2007-64-ec_en [Accessed 23 October 2017]

Payment Services (PSD2) (nd) Directive (EU) 2015/2366 [online] https://ec.europa. eu/info/law/payment-services-psd-2-directive-eu-2015-2366_en [Accessed 23 October 2017]

Treanor, J (2016) Misconduct 'has cost UK's banks £53bn over 15 years', *The Guardian*, 11 April [online] https://www.theguardian.com/money/2016/ apr/11/misconduct-has-cost-uks-banks-53bn-over-15-years-ppi [Accessed 11 October 2017]

Wallace, T (2017) Q&A: What is bank ring-fencing? *The Telegraph*, 22 October [online] http://www.telegraph.co.uk/finance/bank-of-england/11934139/QandA- What-is-bank-ring-fencing.html [Accessed 25 October 2017]

GLOSSARY

Additional Tier 1 (AT1)   A supplementary component of Tier 1 capital. AT1 comprises capital instruments that are continuous, in that there is no fixed maturity and include items such as preference shares.

Application Programming Interfaces (APIs)   A set of protocols for building software applications. An API specifies how software components should interact. APIs are the foundation blocks that make Open Banking possible.

Bank licence   A legal requirement for any financial institution that wants to conduct a banking business. The Prudential Regulation Authority and Financial Conduct Authority are keen to assist applicants to help reliable new banks enter the market.

Barter   The agreed exchange of one commodity or service for another commodity or service.

Bill of Exchange   A written, unconditional order signed by one party addressed to another, to pay a certain sum, either immediately or on a fixed date for payment of goods and/or services received.

Bitcoin   A specific type of crypto-currency that uses encryption techniques to create and regulate the units of currency and validate the transfer of funds.

Blockchain   The digital ledger or accountancy book within which all transactions made in bitcoin or another crypto-currency are recorded chronologically and publicly.

Brokerage   Providing a service or introduction that generates fee income.

Building society   The modern-day term relates to a member-owned, mutual-oriented financial institution that provides a broad range of services similar to those of retail banks, but without having accountability to shareholders as it is not a public company.

Clearing bank   Refers to a group of banks that had an organized arrangement to clear customer cheques and settle claims between them. All clearing banks were large financial institutions and they all provided a broad range of services to various customer segments.

Cloud   Resources that are retrieved from the internet through web-based tools. There is no physical or direct connection to computer servers.

Common Equity Tier 1 (CET1)   The primary, high-quality component of Tier 1 capital that has the best potential loss-absorbing qualities and includes common share holdings held by a bank or other financial institution. CET1 is a capital metric that was introduced in 2014. It is anticipated that all banks should meet the minimum required CET1 ratio of 4.50 per cent by 2019.

Cost-to-income ratio 'The cost-to-income ratio is a key financial measure, particularly important in valuing banks. It shows a company's costs in relation to its income. To get the ratio, divide the operating costs (administrative and fixed costs, such as salaries and property expenses, but not bad debts that have been written off) by operating income' (Money Week, 28 May 2013, see Chapter 4).

Credit risk When credit card balances, loans, overdrafts and mortgages fail to be repaid and may need to be written off as bad debts.

Credit union A group of people with a common bond, who save together and lend to each other at a reasonable rate of interest.

Crypto-currency A digital currency that uses cryptography for security, which makes it difficult to counterfeit. Crypto-currencies are not owned or controlled by any central authority, which means they are immune from government and central bank control.

Deregulation The reduction or removal of government powers, usually intended to stimulate competition within the marketplace of the industry.

Divestment The action of selling off or disowning subsidiary business interests.

Fintech An abridged expression, related to technology used behind the scenes to support and underpin financial institutions. Now in the 21st century, the term has grown to mean any technological innovation in the financial sector and relates to a new genre of innovative financial service providers that have begun to disrupt the traditional financial services marketplace through direct provision of their services to customers.

Illiquid Owned assets or possessions that are not easily converted in to cash.

Insolvency Occurs when a person or company is unable to meet their financial obligations when they are due.

Interest rate risk Occurs when a bank has to pay more money out on its deposits than it receives on its loans.

Legislation The process of creating laws that govern an industry or country. The initial step of creating law is the drafting and proposing of a Bill, so that the legislation can be fully discussed and considered in Parliament, before a vote to pass the Bill happens and makes it a law.

Lender of last resort Protects and ensures the stability of a specific bank or the banking and financial system at large, usually via central bank intervention (eg Bank of England) to ensure the affected bank(s) have sufficient liquidity to meet their day-to-day obligations. The lender of last resort will also guarantee/protect customer deposits, thus preventing 'run-on-the-bank' deposits.

Liquidity The ability of an individual or a business to meet their immediate and/or short-term obligations, through the holding of sufficient cash and/or assets that can be quickly converted to cover their indebtedness. Current (short-term) assets should equal to or exceed current (short-term) liabilities.

Liquidity risk   Where the need for a bank to pay short-term debt obligations cannot be met due to lack of readily available cash or short-term liquidity that can be converted to cash.

Macro-prudential bank regulation   The broader view takes into account the wider financial sector and considers the implications of inter-connected risk between individual financial institutions. The overarching objective is to ensure the stability of financial services within the economy. Under Basel III, macro-prudential regulation encourages additional 'counter-cyclical' capital buffers to be retained during boom times and relaxed during downturns. Further, the capital that has been built up in the buffers can be used to fend off any potential shocks that may arise.

Medium of exchange   The physical commodity that has a perceived value.

Merchant banks   Historically merchant banks were created to support the trade of commodities. The first merchant banks were established in Italy in the Middle Ages. Today merchant banks provide a wide range of complex financial services to organizations and companies (rather than personal individuals and distinct from retail banking). Services include the provision of business loans, supporting foreign trade and underwriting.

Micro-prudential bank regulation   This approach relies on the regulatory supervision to assess the stability and safety of individual banks. The process of micro-prudential regulation requires that supervisory checks are made against specific metrics, but it does not take a wider view to external risks such as considering the implications of systemic and contagion influences.

Moral hazard   Encouraged to take additional risk through the perception of a safety net being in place.

Multi-channel   The provision of more than one way or channel for customers to conduct their financial business. Typically, this will be a combination of branch, ATMs, call centre, internet banking and, increasingly, mobile. Retail banks may choose to offer some or all of the channels as part of their retail banking distribution strategy.

Net interest margin   The difference between the interest income made by banks (usually on loans and advances) and the amount of interest paid out (to their depositors and lenders).

Non-core   Not part of the centre or foundations of a business.

Omni-channel   A seamless approach to customer experience that integrates different methods of interaction (eg branch, call centre, online and mobile).

Open Banking   Enables customers to securely share their financial data with other financial organizations, making it easier to transfer money between different accounts and simpler for customers to shop around and buy the best product offerings. Open Banking will lead to bespoke banking experiences, specific to customer needs.

Payment Services Directive (PSD)   Originally published in 2007, PSD was the first European law to affect sterling payments. PSD2 came in to force on 13 January 2018. It is legislation that helps member states move towards a single, digital market in Europe.

Promissory note   Written, signed unconditional, and unsecured promise by one party to another that commits the maker to pay a specified sum on demand, or on a fixed or determinable date.

Quantitative easing   The process when central banks introduce new money into the monetary supply of an economy.

Rate of exchange   The ratio of one product or service against another product or service.

Regulation   Once the law has been passed by Parliament, it then becomes the responsibility of the appropriate regulatory body to implement the law. This is achieved by creating a framework of rules and principles that align with the law. The rules and principles are the specific regulations that all impacted organizations must abide by. It is the regulator's responsibility to ensure that the rules are followed and therefore the laws of the land are adhered to.

Ring-fencing   Refers to the process of separation of retail banking operations from the perceived riskier investment bank activities.

Risk-weighted assets   Where a bank's assets are adjusted or weighted in accordance with a risk profile aligned to the capital requirement or capital adequacy ratio for a financial institution.

Run on the bank   Usually predicated by concerns or rumours about a bank or financial institution's solvency, bank runs happen when large numbers of customers hurriedly withdraw their deposits. Scenes of mobbed banking halls and queues around the block are probably confined to the pages of history books now, as the digital and mobile age means customers can move their money far more easily and more quickly without the need to visit their branch to take physical cash out. Irrespective of the era, a run can and will undoubtedly happen. Arguably, a modern-day run would be even more devastating due to the ease with which customers can gain access to their money and the speed with which they can transfer it elsewhere – unless of course the affected bank's mobile and digital banking applications don't crash under the strain. Inevitably bank runs cause widespread consumer panic and confusion and could lead to other financial institutions suffering a similar fate.

Sale and leaseback   The sale of an asset or group of assets that the seller then immediately rents back from the buyer, thereby raising cash and enabling an allowable tax deduction.

Savings bank   Non-publicly owned financial institutions that do not have shareholders and whose members do not have voting rights or the power to influence the organization's directors or trustees.

Securitization   The process of packaging together a group of loans or mortgages of a similar nature, with the intention of selling them on as marketable commodity to raise finance from investors.

Sub-prime   Infers the provision of loans and credit facilities to customers who are unlikely to have sufficient means to meet their obligations should they come under any additional pressures. Some customers may already have a poor credit rating and/or history.

Systemic   Refers to the knock-on effects of an event that impact upon the inter-connected parts of the financial system and beyond into other aspects of society.

Systematically important financial institution   A financial organization that would pose a major risk to an economy should it fail or collapse; accordingly, SIFIs are subject to increased regulation and control to ensure their safety and security.

Taylorism   Introduced by Frederick W Taylor in the early 20th century, this scientific approach to production management breaks down all work activities into the smallest tasks so that they can be both taught and performance managed. The methodology breaks out actual work from planning and further can demark direct labour from indirect labour. It takes guesswork out and provides precise time and motion measurements, which leads to optimum job performance.

Teller cash recycling machine (TCR)   Provides a safe and secure repository for cash in an open branch environment. The TCR counts and verifies all bank notes received and issued, thus saving teller cashier time and eradicating any potential human errors in cash management.

Tier 1 leverage ratio rate   The relationship between a bank's Tier 1 capital (CE1 + AT1) and its total assets, though central banks will look at the specific relationship of CE1: Total Assets, before considering the extended use of AT1 to bolster the Tier 1 position. The Tier 1 leverage ratio is used by central monetary authorities to ensure the capital adequacy of banks.

INDEX

NB: page numbers in *italic* indicate figures or tables.